Ilya Kabakov / **Илья Кабаков** Album de ma mère My Mother's Album Album meiner Mutter **Альбом моей матери**

Ilya Kabakov / Илья Кабаков

L'Album de ma mère / My Mother's Album
Album meiner Mutter / Альбом моей матери

Flies France
Paris

Sommaire Abstract Inhalt Содержание

Préface 6	Introduction 6
La vie humiliée 12	Life as an insult 12
Album photos 233	Photo album 233
Installations 249	Installations 249
Biographie 262	Biography 262
Vorwort 6	Предисловие 6
Leben als Erniedrigung 12	Жизнь как оскорбление 12
Album der Fotografien 233	Фотоальбом 233
Installationen 249	Инсталляции 249
Biographie 262	Биография 262

Préface Introduction Vorwort Предисловие

L'Album de ma mère comprend les mémoires de la mère de l'artiste, Beïlia Solodoukhina, rédigées à l'époque où elle avait 83 ans. C'est un récit détaillé évoquant son enfance dans la Russie prérévolutionnaire, les années difficiles d'un pays en pleine recomposition, la vie au temps de la « grande époque stalinienne » et plus tard. Ce récit, à la fois pénible et touchant, raconte des souffrances infinies, des espoirs qui surgissent et disparaissent.

Mais parallèlement l'*Album* se développe sur un autre plan. En haut de chaque feuille de l'*Album* on voit des photos en couleurs : coupures de magazines officiels des années 1950, époque du « socialisme épanoui ». Ces « images du bonheur » sous-titrées de légendes repré-

Préface Introduction Vorwort Предисловие

sentent le rêve de l'humanité réalisé — la construction aboutie du « pays de beauté et de justice ».
Ces deux plans — « les Fêtes du Travail et des Victoires » et les tourments infinis de l'homme réel — s'entrecroisent pour créer un portrait véridique de la vie en Russie au début et milieu de notre siècle.
The series *My Mother's Album* consists of autobiographical notes of an artist's mother, Bailey Solodukhina, written by her when she was 83 years old. It is a detailed story about childhood in prerevolutionary Russia, about the difficult years in a country undergoing post-revolutionary reform, about life during the "Great Stalinist Era" and afterwards. It is a touching and agonizing story about a life full of endless suffering,

Préface Introduction Vorwort Предисловие

of appearing and disappearing hopes.
But the *album* has another, parallel level. There are color photographs on the top part of each page — cut-outs from original magazines from the 1950's, the era of "flourishing socialism". All of these "pictures of happiness" and the inscriptions beneath them recount humanity's dream-come-true — the building, finally, of a "just and beautiful country".

Two of these series, "Holidays of Labor and Victories" intersecting with the incessant torment of a real person, create a realistic portrait of life in Russia during the beginning and middle of our century.

Die Serie *Album meiner Mutter* besteht aus den autobiographischen Aufzeichnungen der Mutter des

Künstlers, Bejla Soloduchina, die sie im Alter von 83 Jahren geschrieben hat. Das ist eine genaue Beschreibung der Kindheit in der Zeit vor der Revolution, der schweren Umwälzungen im Land nach der Revolution, des Lebens in der »Großen Epoche Stalins« und danach. Es ist die ergreifende und quälende Beschreibung eines Lebens, voll von endlosen Leiden, von aufkeimenden und verlöschenden Hoffnungen.

Aber das *Album* hat auch eine zweite, parallele Reihe. Am oberen Teil jedes Blattes sind Farbfotos angebracht: Ausschnitte aus offiziellen Zeitschriften der 50iger Jahre — der Epoche des »blühenden Sozialismus«. Alle diese »Bilder des Glücks« und die dazugehörigen Bildunterschriften berichten von einem Mensch-

Préface Introduction Vorwort Предисловие

heitstraum, der in Erfüllung gegangen ist — vom Aufbau eines »gerechten und wunderbaren Landes«... Diese zwei Reihen — der »Feiertag der Arbeit und der Siege« und die endlosen Leiden des realen Menschen — ergeben, sich überschneidend, ein reales Porträt des Lebens in Rußland zu Beginn und in der Mitte unseres Jahrhunderts.

Серия «Альбом моей матери» составлена из автобиографических записок матери художника, Бейли Солодухиной, написанных ею, когда ей было 83 года. Это подробный рассказ о детстве в дореволюционной России, о тяжелых годах в перестраивающейся после революции стране, о жизни в «Великую Сталинскую эпоху» и после нее.

Это и трогательный и мучительный рассказ о жизни, полной бесконечных страданий, приходящих и исчезающих надежд.

Но у «Альбома» есть и другой, параллельный ряд. В верхней части каждого листа помещены цветные фотографии: вырезки из официальных журналов 50-х годов — эпохи «цветущего социализма». Все эти «картины счастья» и подписи под ними повествуют о сбывшейся мечте человечества — о построенной наконец «справедливой и прекрасной стране»...

Два этих ряда — «Праздник Труда и Побед» и беспрерывные мучения реального человека — пересекаясь, создают реальный портрет жизни в России начала и середины нашего века.

La Vie humiliée
Life as an insult
Leben als Erniedrigung

Жизнь как оскорбление

Au camarade L. I. Brejnev,
Secrétaire général du
Comité Central du PCUS,
Kremlin, Moscou.

Cher Léonid Ilitch!

Je m'adresse à vous en désespoir de cause pour améliorer ma difficile situation car personne, à part vous, ne peut résoudre mon problème.
J'ai 79 ans, je vis seule à Berdiansk, région de Zaporojié, 7, rue des Partisans Rouges. J'habite dans une vieille maison un logement de 20 m² sans aucun confort. Aujourd'hui, vieille et malade, je ne suis plus capable de faire le chemin pour rapporter de l'eau et du bois, ni d'allumer le poêle, à mon âge, tout cela est au-dessus de mes forces.
Depuis deux ans, je supplie les autorités du comité exécutif de Berdiansk d'améliorer mes conditions de logement, mais tout reste comme avant. J'ai depuis peu la possibilité d'échanger mon appartement (20 m²) contre un appartement municipal (15 m²) avec tout le confort. Mais je me heurte à un nouveau refus du camarade V. P. Verjikovski, président du Comité exécutif de Berdiansk, qui n'autorise pas l'échange en se référant à l'arrêté interdisant l'échange d'un logement individuel contre un logement municipal. Je suis au courant de cet arrêté, mais, cher Léonid Ilitch, est-il si impossible, dites-moi, d'accéder à la demande d'une personne âgée comme moi, à qui il reste si peu de temps à vivre? Est-il vraiment impossible d'examiner chaque cas avec attention, comme se doit de le faire un cadre compétent et proche des gens? J'ai à mon actif 40 ans de travail continu. Dans les premières et éprouvantes années de guerre, après avoir perdu mes parents, j'ai élevé toute seule quatre petits frères et sœurs, dont deux ont péri au Front.
A la retraite depuis déjà 20 ans, j'assume un important travail social: j'avais organisé une chorale de retraités qui a reçu de la ville et de la région un grand nombre de prix, je collabore avec les bibliothèques, je fais des conférences. Mon travail social est bien connu à Berdiansk: la presse locale m'a consacré des articles et ledit comité exécutif de Berdiansk m'a décerné des prix et des diplômes. Croyez-moi, cher Léonid Ilitch, je n'écris pas tout ça pour me vanter, mais je le fais avec douleur et amertume. J'ai toujours cherché à me rendre utile aux gens et à l'Etat, et voilà que sur mes vieux jours, je me heurte à tant d'insensibilité et de vexations. Pourtant je ne demande pas un logement, juste une autorisation d'échange! Et c'est le comité exécutif de Berdiansk qui me refuse ce rien, bien que le comité exécutif de la région de Zaporojié — je l'ai appris à la suite de mes nombreuses demandes — y soit favorable (mais il a remis la décision à « la discrétion des autorités locales »).
Cher Léonid Ilitch! Je me rends bien compte que vous êtes très occupé, j'ai eu du mal à me décider à vous déranger au sujet de cette affaire personnelle, mais je suis tellement désespérée que j'ai quand même pris cette décision, veuillez m'en excuser.
Je vous prie de m'aider à obtenir l'autorisation d'échanger mes 20 m² sans confort (propriété privée) contre 15 m² tout confort (propriété d'Etat).

Bien respectueusement
B. Y. Solodoukhina, retraitée.

Moscow, The Kremlin,
To the General Secretary
of the CC CPSU
Comrade BREZHNEV, L.I.

Dear Leonid Ilich!

I am appealing to You, as my last hope to improve my calamitous situation, since no one, except for You, can solve my problem.
I am 79 years old, I live alone in the city of Berdyansk in the Zaporozhsky region on Red Partisans Street, house 7. I live in an old building (20 sq.m. area), without utilities. Now, when I am already an old and sick person, I no longer have the strength to carry water long distances, to drag firewood, to heat the apartment — at this age it is all beyond my strength.
I have been pleading with the authorities of the Berdyansk Executive Committee for two years to improve my living conditions, but everything remains unchanged. The opportunity has now arisen to exchange my apartment (20 sq.

Москва, Кремль, Генеральному Секретарю
ЦК КПСС товарищу БРЕЖНЕВУ Л.И.

Дорогой Леонид Ильич!
Обращаюсь к Вам, как к последней надежде улучшить мое бедственное положение, т.к. никто, кроме Вас не может решить мой вопрос.
Мне 79 лет, живу я одна в г.Бердянске Запорожской области, по ул. Красных Партизан, д. 7. Живу я в старом доме (площадь - 20 кв.м.), лишенном всех удобств. Сейчас, когда я уже старый и больной человек, я уже не в силах издалека носить воду, носить дрова, отапливать квартиру - в этом возрасте все это не по силам.
Два года я умоляю руководство Бердянского исполкома улучшить мои жилусловия, но все остается без изменений. Сейчас появилась возможность обменять мою квартиру (20 кв.м.) на государственную квартиру (15 кв.м.) с удобствами. Но я получаю снова отказ председателя Бердянского Исполкома тов.Вержиковского В.П., который не разрешает этот обмен, ссылаясь на постановление о запрещении обмена частной жилплощади на государственную. Я знаю об этом постановлении, но, дорогой Леонид Ильич, скажите, неужели же нельзя пойти навстречу такому старому человеку, как я, которому жить осталось так немного? Разве нельзя чутко подойти к каждому конкретному случаю, как и полагается хорошему руководителю, работающему с людьми? У меня за плечами 40 лет беспрерывного трудового стажа. В первые тяжелые годы войны я, потеряв своих родителей, одна воспитала четырех младших братьев и сестер - двое из них погибли на фронте.

m.) for a state apartment (15 sq. m.) with utilities. But once again I have been turned down by the Chairman of the Berdyansk Executive Committee, comrade Verzhikovsky, V.P., who will not permit this exchange, citing the resolution forbidding the exchange of private living space for state-owned space. I am aware of this resolution, but, dear Leonid Ilich, tell me, is it really impossible to meet such an old person as myself half-way, someone who has but a short time to live? Is it really impossible for a good manager who works with people to approach each specific case sympathetically, as he should? I have 40 years of uninterrupted employment. During the first difficult years of the war, having lost my parents, I raised four younger brothers and sisters alone — two of them perished at the front.

For the past 20 years since I retired, I have been very active in community service. I organized a pensioners' chorus which has received numerous awards in the city and the region, I work in libraries, I give lectures. My social service is well-known in Berdyansk: articles have been written about me in the local press, I have received many awards and commendations from that very same Executive Committee of the city of Berdyansk. Believe me, dear Leonid Ilich, I am not writing this for the sake of praise, but with pain and bitterness. I have always tried to do everything within my power for people and the state, and yet in my old age I encounter such callousness and insult. After all, I am not requesting any living space — only permission for an exchange! And it is precisely in the Berdyansk Executive Committee that I am being turned down, even though I know as a result of my many appeals, that the Zaporozhsky Regional Executive Committee looks favorably on my case (but passed it on for "review by local authorities").

Dear Leonid Ilich! I understand that You are such a busy person, and it was difficult for me to decide to bother You with my personal problem, but I have now reached such a state of desperation that I nevertheless decided to write to You — forgive me.

Please, help me receive permission for this exchange — my 20 meters without utilities (private property) for 15 meters with utilities (state property).

With the greatest respect for You,
Solodukhina, B. Yu., pensioner.

An den
Generalsekretär des ZK der KPdSU
Genosse L.I. Breschnew

Sehr geehrter Leonid Iljitsch!

Mit letzter Hoffnung auf eine Verbesserung meiner ärmlichen Lage wende ich mich an Sie, da niemand außer Ihnen meine Frage entscheiden kann.

Ich bin 79 Jahre alt und lebe allein in Berdjansk, Saporoschjer Gebiet, Straße der Roten Partisanen 7. Ich wohne in einem alten Haus (Wohnfläche 20 m²) ohne Wasser und Heizung. Als alter und kranker Mensch bin ich nicht mehr imstande, von weither Wasser zu holen und Holz zu tragen, um meine Wohnung zu heizen — ich habe nicht mehr die Kraft dazu.

Seit zwei Jahren flehe ich die Leitung des Exekutivkomitees von Berdjansk an, meine Wohnsituation zu verbessern, aber nichts ändert sich. Jetzt ergab sich die Möglichkeit, meine Wohnung (20 m²) in eine staatliche Wohnung (15 m²) mit Komfort umzutauschen. Aber wieder erhielt ich vom Vorsitzenden des Berdjansker Exekutivkomitees, Genosse V.P.Verschikovskij, eine Absage — er gestattet diesen Tausch nicht, wobei er sich auf die Bestimmung beruft, die es verbietet, privaten Wohnraum in staatlichen zu tauschen. Diese Bestimmung ist mir bekannt, aber ich frage Sie, sehr geehrter Leonid Iljitsch, ist es wirklich unmöglich, einem so alten Menschen wie mir, der nicht mehr lange zu leben hat, entgegenzukommen? Könnte man nicht etwas einfühlsamer an einen konkreten Fall herangehen, wie es sich für einen guten Leiter, der mit Menschen arbeitet, gebührt? Ich habe 40 Jahre ununterbrochenen Arbeitslebens hinter mir. In den ersten schweren Kriegsjahren habe ich, nach dem Verlust meiner Eltern, vier jüngere Brüder und Schwestern versorgt — zwei von ihnen fielen im Krieg.

Seit meiner Pensionierung bin ich nun schon seit 20 Jahren vielseitig ehrenamtlich tätig — ich habe einen Pensionistenchor

После выхода на пенсию я вот уже 20 лет веду большую общественную работу - мною организован хор пенсионеров, который получил множество наград в городе и области, я работаю в библиотеках, читаю лекции. Моя общественная работа хорошо известна в Бердянске: обо мне написаны статьи в местной печати, меня неоднократно награждали премиями и грамотами того же исполкома г.Бердянска. Поверьте, дорогой Леонид Ильич, что пишу я это не ради похвальбы, а с болью и горечью. Я всегда старалась сделать все мне посильное для людей и государства, а в старости встречаю такую черствость и обиду. Ведь я же не прошу никакой площади - а только разрешение на обмен! И в этой малости мне отказывают именно в Бердянском исполкоме, хотя, как я знаю по своим неоднократным обращениям, Запорожский облисполком относится к моему делу положительно (но предоставил его на "усмотрение местных властей").

Дорогой Леонид Ильич! Я понимаю, какой Вы занятый человек, и мне трудно было решиться побеспокоить Вас по своему личному делу, но я дошла сейчас до такого отчаяния, что все-таки решилась написать - простите меня. Пожалуйста, помогите мне получить разрешение на этот обмен - моих 20 метров без удобств (частная собственность) на 15 метров с удобствами (государственная).

С глубоким уважением к Вам

(Солодухина Б.Ю., пенсионерка)

organisiert, der viele Auszeichnungen hier
in der Stadt und im Gebiet erhielt, ich arbeite in
Bibliotheken, halte Vorträge. Meine ehrenamtliche Tätigkeit ist
in Berdjansk gut bekannt: über mich wurden Zeitungsartikel
in der Lokalpresse veröffentlicht, mehrmals wurde ich mit
Prämien und Urkunden des schon erwähnten
Exekutivkomitees von Berdjansk ausgezeichnet. Glauben Sie
mir, sehr geehrter Leonid Iljitsch, ich schreibe das nicht aus
Selbstlob, sondern mit Schmerz und Bitterkeit. Ich habe mich
immer bemüht, alles in meiner Kraft stehende für die
Menschen und den Staat zu tun — und im Alter treffe ich
auf so viel Hartherzigkeit und Kränkung. Ich bitte ja nicht
um Wohnraum — nur um eine Tauschgenehmigung! Und
diese Kleinigkeit wird mir vom Berdjansker Exekutivkomitee
abgelehnt, obwohl sich das Saporoschjer Gebietskomitee, wie
mir auf meine mehrmaligen Ansuchen mitgeteilt wurde, in
dieser Angelegenheit durchaus wohlwollend verhielt (die
Entscheidung aber den lokalen Behörden überließ).
Sehr geehrter Leonid Iljitsch! Ich verstehe, daß Sie ein sehr
beschäftigter Mensch sind, und es fällt mir schwer, Sie mit
meinen persönlichen Angelegenheit zu belästigen, aber ich bin
so verzweifelt, daß ich mich trotzdem entschlossen habe, zu
schreiben — verzeihen Sie mir.
Bitte helfen Sie mir, diese Tauschgenehmigung zu erhalten —
meiner 20 m² ohne Wasser und Heizung (Privateigentum) in
15 m² mit Komfort (Staatseigentum).

Mit vorzüglicher Hochachtung
Ihre
Soloduchina B.J., Pensionistin.

La Vie humiliée
Life as an insult
Leben als Erniedrigung

Жизнь как оскорбление

La Vie humiliée Life as an insult Leben als Erniedrigung Жизнь как оскорбление

Une excavatrice est arrivée sur le chantier du canal. C'est une nouveauté de l'industrie soviétique. Son rendement est de 1800 mètres cubes de terre à l'heure. La machine est munie d'un convoyeur à bande qui évacue la terre extraite.

A land-digging plough — an innovation of Soviet technology — arrived at the construction site of the canal. Its capacity is 1800 cubic meters per hour. The machine is equipped with a 45-meter transport-conveyor which tosses the extracted soil to the side.

Am Kanalbau ist eine Baggerbarke eingetroffen — eine Neuheit der sowjetischen Technik. Ihre Produktivität liegt bei 1.800 Kubikmeter Erde pro Stunde. Die Maschine ist mit einer 45 m langen Förderband-Brücke ausgerüstet, welche zum Abladen der Erde an den Seiten dient.

Mon cher fils!
Tu m'avais demandé d'écrire l'histoire de ma vie. Je me suis décidée à satisfaire ta demande. Je commence le 22.1.1982. J'ai 80 ans. Avant de parler de moi-même, il faut que je parle de mes parents. Pendant longtemps, j'ai gardé l'acte de naissance de mon père, qui disait qu'il était originaire du bourg de Trab, district d'Otopian, gouvernement de Vilno, bourgeois. Je ne me souviens pas des papiers de ma mère. Mes parents étaient

Dear son!
You asked me to write down the story of my life. I have decided to grant your request. I am beginning on 22.I.1982. I am 80 years old. Before I talk about myself I must first talk about my family. I kept my father's certificates and papers for a long time, where it is noted that he is a native of the small town of Trab of the Otopyan region of the Vilno province, he was a petty bourgeois. I don't remember any documents about my mother. My parents were

Lieber Sohn!
Du hast mich gebeten, meine Lebensgeschichte zu schreiben. Ich habe beschlossen, deine Bitte zu erfüllen. Ich beginne am 22.1.1982. Ich bin 80 Jahre alt. Bevor ich über mich spreche, muß ich über meine Eltern sprechen. Lange habe ich den Geburtsschein meines Vaters aufbewahrt, wo angegeben war, daß er aus dem Dorf Trab, Otopjansker Gebiet, Gouvernement Vilna, gebürtig ist, Stand Kleinbürger. Von der Mutter sind mir keinerlei Dokumente erinnerlich. Meine Eltern waren

На строительство канала прибыл землеройный струг — новинка советской техники. Его производительность — 1800 кубических метров земли в час. Машина снабжена 45-метровым мсстом-транспортером, по которому отбрасывается в сторону вынутый грунт.

Дорогой сынок!
Ты просил написать историю моей жизни. Решила исполнить твою просьбу. Начинаю 22.I-1982 г. Мне 80 лет.
Прежде чем говорить о себе, нужно говорить о моих родных. Долго у меня хранились метрические отца, где значилось, что он уроженец местечка Траб, Отопянского уезда, Виленской губ., мещанин. О матери никаких документов я не помнила. Родные мои

Nouveau magasin du village de Vassilievka.

A new store in the settlement of Vasilievka.

Das neue Geschäft im Dorf Vasiljewka.

orphelins, lorsqu'ils ont été adoptés par un couple âgé, sans enfants. J'ai gardé longtemps une photo des deux vieux, c'était leur famille adoptive. Quand mes parents deviennent grands, on les place : ma mère comme femme de ménage, mon père comme apprenti tailleur. Devenus majeurs, ils se marient. Ils ont des caractères très différents. Mon père, replié sur lui-même, silencieux, ne connaît que son travail et la synagogue. Il ne maîtrise pas le russe. Il peut juste signer.

orphans when they were taken in by a childless old couple. I also kept photographs of these old folks for a long time — they were foster relatives. When my father and mother grew up, my mother was given away as a servant, my father as a tailor's apprentice. When they reached legal age, they married. They were totally different from one another. My father was closed, not talkative, he knew his work and the synagogue. He hadn't been taught Russian. He could only sign his name in it.

Waisen, die von einem kinderlosen alten Ehepaar aufgenommen wurden. Lange habe ich die Fotografie dieser beiden Alten aufbewahrt — das waren die Pflegeeltern. Als der Vater und die Mutter heranwuchsen, gab man sie fort, die Mutter wurde Dienstmädchen, der Vater lernte Schneider. Als sie volljährig wurden, heirateten sie. Charakterlich waren sie sehr verschieden voneinander. Der Vater war verschlossen und wortkarg, er kannte nur seine Arbeit und die Synagoge. Russisch konnte er nicht. Er konnte nur unterschreiben.

Новый магазин в поселке Васильевке

были сиротами, когда их взяли на воспитание бездетные старики. Долго тоже хранилась у меня фотография двух старичков – это и были приемные родные. Когда отец с матерью подросли, их отдали, мать в домработницы, отца учеником портного. Достигнув совершеннолетия, они поженились. Характерами они были совсем не похожи друг на друга. Отец замкнутый, неразговорчивый, знал свою работу и синагогу. По русски не был обучен. Мог только расписаться

En congé de maladie, l'ouvrière du textile Véra Gouskova touche une allocation de la sécurité sociale équivalente à son salaire. Profitant de l'assistance médicale gratuite, elle suit un traitement de radiothérapie.

Having fallen ill, the textile worker Vera Guskova began to receive assistance equivalent to her usual salary from the resources of social insurance. Utilizing free medical care, she is undergoing an x-ray therapy procedure.

Als die Textilarbeiterin Vera Guskowa erkrankte, erhielt sie einen Zuschuß aus der Sozialversicherung, der ihrem üblichen Gehalt entsprach. Sie unterzieht sich einer Röntgentherapie, die der staatliche Gesundheitsdienst gratis anbietet.

Ma mère, ne sachant lire qu'en yiddish, dévore des romans. Je me souviens d'elle, penchée sur son livre, l'air rêveur; elle adore s'habiller avec élégance. Elle porte le cache-peigne, à la mode de l'époque. Des escarpins à hauts talons. Tout en elle me ravit, je m'efforce de la copier. Je me rappelle qu'elle m'a toujours habillée en rouge. C'est sa couleur préférée. Mon père se promène avec moi plus souvent qu'elle. Mais il me parle peu, on se balade en silence, car il aime répéter :

My mother was only literate in Yiddish, she loved reading novels. I remember her bent over a book, dreaming, she loved to dress nicely. She wore high heels. She wore her hair in a fashionable bun-style. I admired everything about her, and tried to be like her. I remember how she would dress me all in red. That was her favorite color. I went out more often with my father. But he didn't talk much to me, we would walk around in silence, he would say :

Die Mutter beherrschte jiddisch in Wort und Schrift und las viele Romane. Ich erinnere mich an sie, wie sie sich über ein Buch beugt, verträumt, sie zog sich gerne schön an. Sie ließ sich die Haare ondulieren, das war damals Mode. Hohe Absätze. Alles an ihr begeisterte mich, ich wollte so sein wie sie. Ich erinnere mich, wie sie mir rote Kleider anzog. Das war ihre Lieblingsfarbe. Spazieren ging ich mehr mit dem Vater. Aber er sprach wenig mit mir, meistens gingen wir schweigend, er sagte :

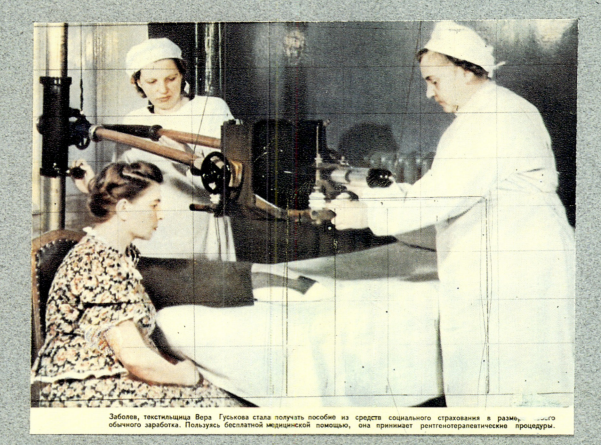

Заболев, текстильщица Вера Гуськова стала получать пособие из средств социального страхования в размере ___ его обычного заработка. Пользуясь бесплатной медицинской помощью, она принимает рентгенотерапевтические процедуры.

Мать, грамотная только по еврейски, зачитывалась романами. Я ее помню склоненной над книгой, мечтательной, любила красиво одеваться. Носила прическу валиком, это было тогда модно. Туфли на высоком каблуке. Все что в ней было, восхищало меня, я старалась быть похожей на нее. Помню как она одевала меня во все красное. Это был ее любимый цвет. Гуляла я больше с отцом Но он мало говорил со мной, больше мы гуляли молча, он говорил

La Vie humiliée Life as an insult Leben als Erniedrigung Жизнь как оскорбление

La tisseuse Youlia Zoueva va se reposer au sanatorium des ouvriers du textile, son séjour est pris en charge par la caisse maladie.

The weaver Julia Zueva is going to the sanatorium for textile workers in Sochi on a trip paid for from the resources of social insurance.

Die Weberin Julia Sujewa fährt ins Sanatorium der Textilarbeiter in Sotchi zu einer Kur, welche von der Sozialversicherung bezahlt wird.

« La parole est d'argent, mais le silence est d'or ». Je me promène aussi avec ma mère quand elle se libère de ses travaux ménagers. Elle est très attachée à moi. Car avant moi, ils ont eu un fils handicapé qui est mort peu après la naissance, je suis leur deuxième enfant, le fils né après moi est mort en bas âge, lui aussi. Mes parents vivent paisiblement, sans se disputer, mais je sens qu'il n'y a pas d'intimité entre eux. Ma mère reporte toute son affection sur moi. Elle m'habille comme une princesse, même

"The spoken word is silver — the unspoken is gold". I would also take walks with my mother when she wasn't busy with housework. She was very attached to me. The thing is, that before me she had a deformed boy who didn't live very long and died. I was the second child, and after me another son died in infancy. My parents lived peacefully, they didn't argue, but I felt that there really wasn't a closeness between them. My mother devoted all of her affection to me. She dressed me like a picture, even

» Reden ist Silber, Schweigen ist Gold «. Manchmal ging ich auch mit der Mutter aus, wenn sie mit der Hausarbeit fertig war. Sie hing sehr an mir. Es war nämlich so, daß sie vor mir einen Sohn hatten, der mißgebildet war und bald darauf starb, ich war die zweite in der Reihe, nach mir starb auch ein Sohn im Säuglingsalter. Die Eltern lebten ruhig, sie stritten nicht, aber ich spürte, daß sie einander nicht nahestanden. Ihre ganzen Gefühle hatte die Mutter auf mich gerichtet. Sie kleidete mich wunderhübsch, eigentlich

Ткачиха Юлия Зуева едет в санаторий текстильщиков в Сочи по путевке, оплаченной из средств социального страхования.

"сказанное слово серебро, а не сказанное золото". Гуляла я и с матерью, когда она была свободна от домашних дел. Она очень была привязана ко мне. Дело в том, что до меня родился сын урод и не долго пожив умер, я была вторая по счету, после меня тоже умер сын в младенческом возрасте. Жили родные спокойно, не ссорились, но я чувствовала, что близости между ними не было. Всю свою привязанность мать посвятила мне. Одевала как картинку, даже не по

La Vie humiliée Life as an insult Leben als Erniedrigung Жизнь как оскорбление

V. Tchoulovitch. Né en 1922. LE SOIR AUX ENVIRONS DE MOSCOU. 1980. Exposition d'artistes moscovites.

V. Chulovich. Born 1922. EVENING NEAR MOSCOW. 1980. An exhibit of works by Moscow artists.

V. Tschulowitsch. Geb. 1922. ABENDSTIMMUNG BEI MOSKAU. 1980. Ausstellung von Werken Moskauer Künstler.

au-dessus de ses moyens. Mon père est maladif. Il souffre de l'estomac et ma mère prépare pour lui des repas à part. Souvent il a des nausées après le repas. Il n'a jamais été voir un médecin. Ma mère le préserve d'une nourriture grossière autant qu'elle le peut. Je me revois à Donetsk (ancienne Youzovka), où mes parents ont déménagé ; j'ai 3 ans. Pendant le pogrom de 1905, ils se trouvent là, mais logés chez le chef de la police locale, ils échappent au massacre. Je me rappelle Youzovka, couverte de poussière de charbon ; une robe blanche

beyond her means. My father was a sickly man. He had a bad stomach, and mother cooked for him separately. He often vomited after eating. He never went to the doctor. Mother protected him from bad food when she could. When I was three I remember myself in the city of Donetsk (formerly Yuzovka), where my parents moved. They were in Yuzovka during the pogrom of 1905, but since they were living in the house of the police chief, they escaped the beatings. I remember Yuzovka all covered with soot, you could wear a white dress

über ihre Verhältnisse. Der Vater war kränklich. Er litt an Magenschmerzen, die Mutter kochte getrennt für ihn. Nach dem Essen mußte er oft erbrechen. Zum Arzt ging er nie. Die Mutter bereitete ihm leichte Speisen zu, soweit das möglich war. Im Alter von drei Jahren erinnere ich mich an die Stadt Donezk (früher Jusowka), wohin die Eltern gezogen waren. Während des Pogroms im Jahr 1905 waren sie in Jusowka, aber da sie im Palais des Polizeihauptmanns wohnten, entgingen sie der Gewalt. Jusowka ist in meiner Erinnerung ganz mit Ruß bedeckt, ein weißes Kleid

В. Чулович. Род. 1922. ВЕЧЕР ПОД МОСКВОЙ. 1980. Выставка произведений московских художников.

средствам. Отец был болезненный человек. Страдал желудком, мать ему готовила отдельно. У него часто после еды были рвоты. К врачу он никогда не ходил. Мать оберегала его от грубой пищи, пока была возможность. Когда мне было года 3, я помню себя в г. Донецке (раньше Юзовка) куда родные выехали. Когда был погром 1905 года они были в Юзовке, но т.к. жили во дворе полицмейстера избегли избиения. Юзовку я помню всю покрытую копотью, белое

Au rayon confiserie.

In the confectionery department.

In der Konditoreiabteilung.

ne peut être portée qu'une fois, elle noircit aussitôt. Mon père trouve une place dans une boutique de confection; nous vivons modestement. Mon père n'est pas un grand tailleur, il travaille sur patrons et parfois il rapporte des commandes à la maison. Il ramène aussi des vêtements à retoucher. Il est toujours très consciencieux dans son travail. Mais très lent. J'hérite ce trait de lui. Ma mère et lui me répètent toujours: il ne faut pas se presser, l'essentiel c'est de bien faire son travail. Malheureusement,

only once and it was covered with coal soot. Father got a job in a dress store, and we lived modestly. Father wasn't a first-class tailor, he worked from patterns, he would bring his work home. He would bring home alterations, he was conscientious about his work. But very slow. I got this trait from father. Both my mother and father taught me — there is no need to hurry, the main thing is to do your work conscientiously. Unfortunately,

konnte man nur einmal anziehen, gleich war es voll Kohlenstaub. Der Vater arbeitete in einem Geschäft für Konfektionskleidung, und wir lebten bescheiden. Der Vater war kein erstklassiger Schneider, er nähte nach Schnitten, brachte auch Änderungen mit nach Hause. Er war sehr gewissenhaft bei der Arbeit, aber auch sehr langsam. Diesen Zug habe ich vom Vater übernommen. Beide, Vater und Mutter, lehrten mich — Eile tut nicht gut, Hauptsache, man ist gewissenhaft bei der Arbeit. Leider

В кондитерском отделе.

платье можно было одеть только раз, оно покрывалось угольной копотью. Отец устроился при магазине готового платья и жили мы скромно. Отец был не первоклассный портной, работал по стандарту, брал и домой работу. Приносил домой переделки, отец был добросовестный в работе. Но очень медлительный. Я эту черту переняла от отца. Меня учила и отец и мать, - спешить не нужно, главное выполнять работу добросовестно. К сожалению это мне не

Tossia Nazarova et Vassili Korolev ont passé 1 h 1/2 à la patinoire. Ils décident de se retrouver au concert du club des étudiants.

Tosya Nazarova and Vasily Korolev spent an hour and a half at the skating rink. Now they are making arrangements to go to a concert in the student club.

Tosja Nasarowa und Vasilij Koroljow waren eineinhalb Stunden auf dem Eislaufplatz. Jetzt verarbreden sie ein Treffen zum Konzert im Studentenklub.

cette leçon ne m'a jamais servi dans la vie. J'ai toujours dû me hâter. Surtout quand j'ai commencé à travailler, mais j'en parlerai plus tard. Les médecins conseillent à mon père de quitter Donetsk à cause du climat et nous déménageons à Jdanov (à l'époque, c'était Marioupol). Là, nous changeons plusieurs fois d'appartement, mais je me souviens surtout de l'un d'entre eux, rue Nikolaevskaïa. Comme nous habitons près du théâtre, nous louons une pièce à des artistes. Quels gens merveilleux, ces artistes : comme ils savent bien décorer leur pièce

this didn't serve me in life. It was always necessary to hurry. Especially when I started to work, but I'll talk about that later. The doctors advised father to leave Donetsk because of the climate, and we moved to the city of Zhdanov (formerly called Mariupol). Here we lived in various apartments, but I especially remember one apartment on Nikolaevskaya Street. We rented one room to actors since we lived close to the theatre. What wonderful people the actors were : how they decorated the room

konnte ich mich nicht daran halten in meinem Leben. Immer mußte ich hetzen. Besonders, als ich zu arbeiten begann, aber darüber später. Die Ärzte rieten meinem Vater, aus Donezk wegzuziehen wegen des Klimas, und wir übersiedelten nach Schdanow (früher hieß es Mariupol). Wir lebten dort in verschiedenen Wohnungen, besonders erinnerlich ist mir eine Wohnung in der Nikolajewskaja Straße. Ein Zimmer vermieteten wir an Schauspieler, da wir nicht weit vom Theater wohnten. Was für wunderbare Leute diese Schauspieler waren : wie sie das Zimmer schmückten

Тося Назарова и Василий Королев полтора часа провели на катке. Теперь они условливаются с встрече на концерте в студенческом клубе.

пригодилось в жизни. Нужно было спешить всегда. Особенно когда я стала работать, но об этом позже. Врачи посоветовали отцу выехать из Донецка из-за климата и мы переехали в г. Жданов (раньше назывался Мариуполь). Здесь мы жили на разных квартирах, но особенно запомнилась мне одна квартира на улице Николаевской. Одну комнату мы сдавали артистом, т.к. жили недалеко от театра. Какие прекрасные люди были артисты, как они украшали комнату

La Vie humiliée Life as an insult Leben als Erniedrigung Жизнь как оскорбление

V. S. Panine est un grand amateur de peinture. Sa collection comporte des œuvres de grands artistes russes. Sur la photo — Vassili Sémionovitch et sa petite-fille Nadia examinent leur nouvelle acquisition — le croquis de I. Lévitan *Automne*.

V. S. Panin — a great fan of painting. Works by leading Russian artists can be seen in his private collection. On the photo: Vasily Semionovich and his granddaughter Nadya are looking at the sketch "Fall" by I. Levitan that was acquired by Panin.

V. S. Panin ist ein großer Kunstliebhaber. In seiner Privatsammlung sind Werke bedeutender russischer Maler zu sehen. Auf dem Bild — Vasilij Semjonovitsch mit seiner Enkelin Nadja beim Betrachten der von ihm erworbenen Studie I. Lewitans » Herbst «.

avec des bibelots! Ils ne restent pas longtemps en tournée, et d'autres les remplacent. Ils m'aiment tous et me donnent des souvenirs. Mais voilà qu'à mon grand regret l'époque des artistes s'achève: la pièce est reprise par un célibataire, pas très jeune, un vieux garçon. Arpenteur de métier. Il est très attentif à maman et à moi. Chaque jour, en rentrant, il ne manque pas de m'apporter du chocolat. Sur chaque papier d'emballage il y a un militaire des différents

with different knick-knacks. They didn't stay long on tour and were replaced by others. They all loved me, and would leave me souvenirs to remember them by. But then the period of actors stopped, I was very sorry about this, and a lonely man, not young, an old bachelor, moved into the room. He was very attentive to my mother and to me. He brought me chocolate from work every day without fail. All of them had wrappers with a military man from different

mit verschiedenen Kleinigkeiten. Ihre Engagements dauerten nicht lange, es kamen wieder andere. Sie liebten mich alle sehr und schenkten mir Souvenirs zur Erinnerung. Dann aber ging die Periode der Schauspieler zu Ende, was mir sehr leid tat und das Zimmer bezog ein alleinstehender, nicht mehr ganz junger Mann, ein alter Junggeselle. Von Beruf war er Landvermesser. Er war sehr aufmerksam zu meiner Mutter und zu mir. Von der Arbeit brachte er mir jeden Tag regelmäßig Schokolade mit. Das Einwickelpapier war immer mit irgendeiner Waffengattung

В. С. Пан-н — большой любитель живописи. В его личном собрании можно увидеть произведения выдающихся русских художников На снимке — Василий Семёнович с внучкой Надей рассматривают приобретённый им этюд И. Левитана «Осень».

разными безделушками. Они долго не задерживались на гастролях и их сменяли другие. Меня все они любили, оставляли на память сувениры. Но вот период актеров прекратился, о чем я очень жалела и в комнате поселился одинокий человек, не первой молодости, старый холостяк. По профессии он был землемер. Он очень был внимателен к моей маме и ко мне. С работы он непременно каждый день приносил мне шоколад. Все они имели обертку военного из родных

La Vie humiliée Life as an insult Leben als Erniedrigung Жизнь как оскорбление

Zoïa Bélova reçoit son amie Tamara Griaznova.

Tamara Gryaznova has come to visit her friend Zoya Belova.

Soja Belowa hat Besuch von ihrer Freundin Tamara Grjasnowa.

corps d'armée. Je collectionne ces papiers et je réunis une armée entière avec laquelle j'aime jouer. Le locataire nous invite souvent, ma mère et moi, au cinéma. A cette époque, Matveï est né. Il est handicapé de naissance. Les pieds retournés, il ne peut pas se tenir debout. Commencent d'innombrables visites chez des médecins et voyages à travers le pays et à la capitale. Pas d'amélioration. Seul un vieux professeur nous conseille de laisser agir la nature

troops. I collected these wrappers and I had an entire troop that I liked to play with. This tenant often invited mama and me to go to the movies with him. By that time a son was born, Matthew. He was born with a birth defect. Both of his feet were turned out and he couldn't stand. Thus began our constant trips to doctors, local and those in the capital. Nothing helped. Only one elderly professor recommended leaving everything to nature,

der Armee bedruckt. Ich sammelte diese Etiketten und bald hatte ich ein ganzes Heer, mit welchem ich sehr gern spielte. Der Untermieter lud Мама und mich oft ins Kino ein. Zu jener Zeit wurde uns ein Sohn Matwej geboren. Er war von Geburt an behindert. Seine Fußsohlen waren nach außen gekehrt und er konnte nicht stehen. Es folgten unzählige Arztbesuche am Ort und in der Hauptstadt. Nichts half. Einzig ein uralter Professor riet, der Natur ihren Lauf zu lassen,

К Зое Беловой пришла ее подруга Тамара Грязнова.

войск. Я собирала эти этикетки и у меня образовалось целое войско, с которым я любила играть. Квартирант часто приглашал маму со мной в кино. К этому времени у нас родился сын Матвей. Он родился не полноценным. У него были вывернуты обе ступни и не мог становиться на ноги. Начались бесконечные поездки к врачам местным и столичным. Ничего не помогало. Только один престарелый профессор посоветовал предоставить все природе

« Cette marque est bien meilleure ! »

"And this kind is even better!"

» Und diese Sorte ist noch besser! «

et, en effet, au fur et à mesure les pieds se redressent et il se met à marcher normalement. Il déforme ses talons de chaussures, c'est vrai, mais cela n'a pas d'importance. Le locataire achète des jouets pour lui aussi. Le temps est venu de commencer mes études. On décide d'inviter un répétiteur-lycéen pour me préparer à l'examen d'entrée. Il y a deux gymnases dans la ville. L'un, qui porte le nom de Maria Fiodorovna, est public, l'autre, le gymnase V. I. Ostoslavskaïa, privé. Ma mère insiste pour que je sois inscrite au gymnase privé où

and in fact his legs gradually began to straighten out, and he began to walk normally. It's true, he did wear down the outside of his heels, but that didn't matter. Our tenant bought him various toys, too. The time approached for me to start studying. It was decided to hire a tutor to prepare me for school. There were two gymnasia in town. One was state owned and named after Maria Fedorovna, the other was private and named for V. I. Ostoslavskaya. My mother insisted on enrolling me only in the private gymnasium where

und wirklich wurden die Füße mit der Zeit gerade, und er begann normal zu gehen. Zwar kehrte er die Absätze immer noch etwas schräg nach außen, aber das war nicht mehr wichtig. Der Untermieter kaufte auch ihm verschiedene Spielsachen. Die Zeit kam, mich auf die Schule vorzubereiten, ein Gymnasiast wurde für mich als Hauslehrer bestellt. Es gab bei uns zwei Gymnasien, ein staatliches, das Maria Fjodorovna-Gymnasium, und ein privates, das V. I. Ostoslavskaja-Gymnasium. Mutter bestand darauf, mich nur ins private Gymnasium zu geben, wo

— А этот сорт еще лучше!..

и действительно постепенно ноги выравнялись и он стал ходить нормально. Правда кривил каблуки наружу, но это было уже не важно. Квартирант покупал и ему разные игрушки. Подходило время мне начать учиться. Решили взять репетитора гимназиста, чтобы подготовить меня в школу. У нас были две гимназии. Одна казенная имени Марии Федоровны и другая частная им. В.И.Остославской. Мать настаивала отдать меня только в частную гимназию, где я

Le nouveau transistor « Biélarusse » obtient actuellement un grand succès.

The new radio receiver "Belarus" has been enjoying particular success recently.

Besonderen Erfolg hat in der letzten Zeit der Radioempfänger » Belarus «.

je pourrai recevoir une meilleure éducation. Même le fait de devoir payer des frais de scolarité ne la rebute pas. Ainsi, j'apprends l'alphabet, bien que ce ne soit pas obligatoire, vu que je vais entrer au cours préparatoire 1 et qu'il y aura encore un cours préparatoire 2 suivi de huit classes de base. Il y a deux huitièmes : l'une, générale, qui permet d'enseigner à l'école primaire, à condition de passer le concours auprès du gymnase de garçons ; l'autre spécialisée, où l'on apprend le latin, et qui permet

I would receive a better education. You had to pay for the right to study, but that didn't bother mother. And so, I learned my ABC's, even though this wasn't necessary since I was entering the first preparatory grade, there was still one more preparatory grade and then eight elementary grades. There were two different eighth grades, a general education one, which gave one the right to teach the elementary grades, but one had to pass the exam given at the men's gymnasium ; and a special one where Latin was studied and thus gave one the right

ich eine bessere Ausbildung erhalten sollte. Man mußte Schulgeld bezahlen, aber das störte Mutter nicht. Also lernte ich Zuhause das Alphabet, obwohl das nicht erforderlich war, da ich in die erste Vorbereitungsklasse eintrat, darauf folgte noch eine zweite Vorbereitungsklasse und dann die acht Hauptklassen. Es gab zwei Lehrgänge — einen allgemeinbildenden, der dazu berechtigte, in den unteren Klassen zu unterrichten, allerdings war ein Examen am Knabengymnasium abzulegen, und einen speziellen, bei dem Latein unterrichtet wurde, d.h. man konnte

Особым успехом пользуется в последнее время новый приемник «Беларусь».

получу лучшее образование. Нужно было платить за право учения, но мать это не смущало. Итак, узнав первые азы, хотя это было не обязательно, т.к. поступала я в младший подготовительный класс был еще дальше старший приготовительный класс и 8 классов основных. Восьмых было 2 - Общеобразовательный, который давал право преподавать в младших классах, но нужно было держать экзамен при мужской гимназии, и специальный, где проходили латынь, т.к. давал пр

La Vie humiliée Life as an insult Leben als Erniedrigung Жизнь как оскорбление

La population indigène de Kabarda dispose maintenant de ses propres cadres dans plusieurs domaines scientifiques et techniques, littéraires et artistiques. Sur la photo — la famille du Kabarde Blenaov. Un des fils, Inal, est devenu fondeur émérite, un autre, Léon, responsable des éditions kabardes, une fille, Bitza, est chef de chœur de l'ensemble de chants et danses de la République de Kabarda, la seconde, Raïa, suit des cours à l'Institut pédagogique.

The native population of Kabarda has produced a cadre of specialists in various fields of science and technology, literature and the arts. On the photo: the family of the Kabarda Blenaov. His son Inal became a distinguished founder, Leon became the editor of the Kabarda publishing house, his daughter Bitsa became choir master of the State Song and Dance Ensemble of Kabarda ASSR, Raya studies at the pedagogical institute.

Die Kabardiner sind ein Volksstamm, der viele Spezialisten auf den Gebieten der Wissenschaft und Technik, der Literatur und Kunst hervorgebracht hat. Auf dem Bild — die Familie des Kabardiners Blenaov. Sein Sohn Inal wurde ein bekannter Gießer, Leon ist Redakteur des Kabardiner Verlages, seine Tochter Biza ist Chorleiterin des Sing- und Tanzensembles der Kabardinischen Autonomen Sowjetrepublik, Raja studiert am pädagogischen Institut.

d'entrer à l'école de médecine. Je rêve de devenir médecin, et je m'inscris dans la classe spécialisée. J'en parlerai plus tard. Mes résultats sont médiocres. Je ne suis pas très douée. Parfois j'ai des « passables », mais toujours des « très bien » pour la conduite. Le locataire m'a préparée à l'école. Il m'a acheté les livres, il s'intéresse à mes études. C'est un véritable ami de la maison. Mon père se montre plein de prévenances pour lui. Il apprécie l'attention qu'il témoigne à notre famille. Mais je n'arrive pas à comprendre

to enter the medical institute. I dreamed of becoming a doctor and therefore I entered the special eighth grade. But more about that later. I didn't have any special aptitude. I got some "C"'s, but I always got excellent marks in behavior. Our tenant prepared me for school. He bought all the textbooks, and was interested in my studies. He was a good friend of the family. My father cared a great deal for him. He appreciated the fact that he paid so much attenton to our family. And then I didn't understand at all

anschließend Medizin studieren. Ich träumte davon, Ärztin zu werden und trug mich deshalb in den Spezialkurs ein. Aber davon später. Ich war eine mittelmäßige Schülerin. Besondere Begabungen besaß ich nicht. Auch Genügend kamen vor, aber das Betragen war ausgezeichnet. Der Untermieter half mir bei den Hausaufgaben. Er kaufte mir alle Schulbücher und interessierte sich für den Lehrstoff. Er war ein wahrer Freund der Familie. Vater war sehr aufmerksam ihm gegenüber. Er wußte es zu schätzen, daß dieser unserer Familie soviel Aufmerksamkeit schenkte. Dann aber passierte etwas mir völlig Unverständliches,

Из среды коренного населения Кабарды выросли кадры специалистов в различных областях науки и техники, литературы и искусства. На снимке — семья кабардинца Бленаова. Его сын Инал стал знатным литейщиком, Леон — редактором Кабардинского издательства, дочь Бица — хормейстером Государственного ансамбля песни и пляски Кабардинской АССР, Рая учится в Педагогическом институте.

во поступать в медицинский институт. Я мечтала быть врачом и потому поступила на специальный. Но об этом позже. Училась я средне. Особенно способностей у меня не было. Были и тройки, но поведение было отличное. Квартирант подготовил меня к школе. Купил все учебники, интересовался учебой. Был настоящим другом дома. Отец относился к нему внимательно. Ценил, что он так много уделяет нашей семье внимание. Но вот совершенно не понятно мне что

La Vie humiliée Life as an insult Leben als Erniedrigung Жизнь как оскорбление

En mémoire du grand Staline le personnel de l'usine de machines-outils « Prolétaire Rouge » s'est engagé à redoubler d'efforts. Sur la photo — l'ajusteur S. M. Bakélov qui a dépassé deux fois le plan.

In memory of great Stalin, the collective farm from the machine-building factory "Red Proletarian" takes an oath to work with double energy. On the photo: metal worker S. M. Bakelov, who has over-fulfilled the production goal twofold.

Das Kollektiv der Moskauer Werkzeugmaschinenfabrik » Roter Proletarier « legte zum Gedenken an den großen Stalin den Schwur ab, mit verdoppelter Energie zu arbeiten. Auf dem Bild der Schlosser S. M. Bakelov, der die Produktionsvorgaben zweifach übererfüllt hat.

ce qui se passe : à un moment donné, maman lui dit de partir et peu de temps après, il déménage. Plus tard, ma mère me racontera que les voisins avaient commencé à insinuer des choses au sujet du locataire et elle s'est vue obligée de lui donner congé pour mettre fin aux bavardages. Je m'ennuie terriblement sans lui. Je ne comprends pas la raison de son départ. Je me suis attachée à lui, il m'expliquait bien des choses, il m'apportait et m'offrait des livres. Je me passionne pour la lecture, mais certaines choses m'échappent et je n'ai plus personne à qui poser des questions. Je garde un très mauvais souvenir de l'école.

what happened, because mama forbid him from living with us, and he quickly moved out. Later mother told me that the neighbors started to hint to her about the tenant, and she threw him out to stop the rumors. I missed him terribly. I didn't understand the reason for his leaving. I had gotten used to him, he could explain a lot to me, he used to bring me books as presents. I had acquired a passion for reading, but there was a lot that I didn't understand and there was no one to ask. I remember school with a heavy feeling.

nämlich meine Mutter kündigte ihm und er zog bald aus. Später erzählte mir Mutter, sie sei wegen ihm bei den Nachbarn ins Gerede gekommen, deshalb habe er ausziehen müssen. Ich vermißte ihn schrecklich. Ich verstand ja den Grund seines Auszugs nicht. Ich hatte mich an ihn gewöhnt, er konnte mir viel erklären, er hatte mir Bücher gebracht und mir auch viele geschenkt. Ich las leidenschaftlich gern, verstand aber vieles nicht und fragen konnte ich niemand. An die Schule habe ich bedrückende Erinnerungen.

Коллектив московского станкостроительного завода «Красный пролетарий» в память великого Сталина дал клятву работать с удвоенной энергией. На снимке — слесарь-наладчик С. М. Баколов, вдвое перевыполняющий производственные задания.

произошло, т.к. мама отказала ему жить у нас и он вскоре выбрался. Позже мать рассказывала мне, что соседи стали намекать ей о квартиранте и она, чтобы прекратить разговоры, отказала ему. Я ужасно скучала за ним. Не понимая, что была за причина его ухода. Я привыкла к нему, он многое мне мог объяснять, приносил и дарил мне книги. Я пристратилась к чтению, но многое не понимала, а спросить было не у кого. Школу я вспоминаю с тяжелым чувством

La Vie humiliée Life as an insult Leben als Erniedrigung Жизнь как оскорбление

A la place des anciens marais. La kolkhozienne biélorusse Anna Roussakova admire le seigle que le kolkhoze Souvorov cultive dans les marais asséchés.

This used to be swampland. The Belorussian collective farm worker Anna Rusakova admires the rye which the Suvorov collective farm grew on the drained earth.

Dort, wo Sümpfe waren. Die weißrussische Kolchosbäuerin Anna Rusakowa erfreut sich am Anblick des Roggens, welchen der Suworow-Kolchos auf trockengelegten Böden pflanzt.

La guerre de 1914 commence — la première guerre Patriotique. Mon père perd sa place, son travail stable, et doit se contenter de retouches. La vie devient plus difficile. Payer l'école est au-dessus de nos moyens. Une autre fille est née, Riva. Tous les élèves du gymnase sont issus de familles aisées, de commerçants etc, je suis la plus pauvre. Les filles me traitent de haut. A vrai dire, nous sommes cinq filles qui faisons bande à part, mais je sens

The war started, 1914 — the First Patriotic War. Father lost his permanent job, and began to do odd jobs. It got harder to live. It was beyond our means to pay for school. Another girl, Riva, was born. All of the students in my gymnasium belonged to privileged families who owned stores, etc., and I was the poorest of all. The other girls looked down at me. True, there were five of us girls and we stuck together, but I felt that

Der Krieg kam, das Jahr 1914 — der erste Vaterländische Krieg. Vater verlor seine Arbeit, er war nicht mehr angestellt und übernahm kleine Aufträge. Das Leben wurde schwieriger. Wir konnten das Schulgeld nicht mehr bezahlen. Uns wurde noch ein Mädchen geboren, Riva. Alle Schülerinnen in meinem Gymnasium hatten wohlhabende Eltern, die Geschäfte besaßen oder so, ich war die Ärmste. Die Mädchen schauten auf mich herab. Es stimmt zwar, daß wir 5 Mädchen waren und wir hielten zusammen, aber ich spürte,

Там, где были болота. Белорусская колхозница Анна Русакова любуется рожью, которую колхоз имени Суворова вырастил на осушенных землях.

Настала война, 1914 г. первая Отечественная. Отцу отказали в работе, где он имел постоянную работу и стал перебиваться мелкими починками. Жить стало труднее. Платить за обучение стало не по средствам. Родилась у нас еще девочка, Рива. Все учащиеся в моей гимназии были зажиточных родных, имели магазины или др., самая неимущая была я. Девочки смотрели на меня свысока. Правда нас было 5 девочек, и мы держались вместе, но я чувствовала.

La Vie humiliée Life as an insult Leben als Erniedrigung Жизнь как оскорбление

Ci-dessous — la brigade des jeunes communistes de l'atelier du tissage de poil de la soierie
A. S. Chtcherbakov décide de remplir des engagements socialistes plus élevés.

On the lower photo: the Komsomol youth brigade of the weaving section of the Moscow Silk-weaving factory named after A. S. Shcherbakov pledges increased socialist obligations.

Auf dem unteren Bild — die Komsomol-Jugendbrigade der Web- und Kardier-Zeche des
A. S. Schtscherbakov Kombinats für Seidenweberei, die erhöhte sozialistische Verpflichtungen auf sich genommen hat.

qu'elles ont pitié de moi parce que je suis pauvre et c'est très pénible et humiliant à supporter. La question est la suivante: soit je quitte le gymnase, soit je demande l'exonération du paiement. On est forcé de prendre cette décision (à savoir demander l'exonération) et ça me fait très mal d'entendre annoncer devant tout le monde que je suis exemptée de paiement pour manque de ressources. Nous vivotons. On est déjà cinq dans la famille. Au moment de la première guerre Patriotique, j'ai 12 ans.

they pitied me as a poor girl, and this was very difficult and degrading. The question became: either to quit studying at the gymnasium or to ask that I be exempted from having to pay. I had to do this (ie. ask to be exempt) — it was painful to hear the announcement in front of everybody that I was exempt from payment for school because I didn't have the means. We lived poorly. There were already five of us in the family. I was 12 years old during the First Patriotic War.

daß sie mich bemitleideten, weil ich arm war, und das war schwer zu ertragen und erniedrigend. Es erhob sich die Frage: sollte ich das Gymnasium aufgeben oder um Schulgeldbefreiung ansuchen. Wir mußten diesen Weg gehen, also um Schulgeldbefreiung ansuchen, es war sehr schmerzhaft für mich anzuhören, als vor allen verkündet wurde, ich sei wegen Mittellosigkeit vom Schulgeld befreit. Wir lebten sehr ärmlich. Wir waren zu fünft in unserer Familie. Als der Krieg begann, war ich zwölf Jahre alt.

На нижнем снимке — комсомольско-молодежная бригада ткацко-ворсового цеха Московского шелкоткацкого комбината имени А. С. Щербакова принимает на себя повышенные социалистические обязательства.

что они меня жалеют, как бедную, и это было тяжело переносить и унизительно. Стоял вопрос или бросить учебу в гимназии или просить об освобождении от платы. Пришлось на это пойти (т.е. просить об освобождении – было очень больно слышать, когда при всех объявили, что я освобождена от платы за учение, как не имеющая средств для уплаты. Жили мы уже скудно. Нас было уже 5 человек в семье. Когда была война I-я отечественная, мне было 12 лет.

La Vie humiliée Life as an insult Leben als Erniedrigung Жизнь как оскорбление 52

Afin de résoudre les problèmes que pose la transmission de l'énergie sur très longue distance en provenance des grands chantiers du communisme, les scientifiques soviétiques effectuent des expérimentations et introduisent dans la production les résultats de leurs recherches. Une place importante dans ces recherches revient au laboratoire de décharge du gaz de haut voltage de l'Institut de l'énergie G. M. Krjijanovski (Académie des Sciences d'URSS). Sur la photo — le générateur d'impulsion dont la tension atteint 3 000 000 volts dans un laboratoire de l'Institut.

Resolving the problems of super-long distance transmission of electric energy from the great construction sites of Communism, Soviet scientists conduct the most complicated experiments and put the results of their research into practice. The laboratory of high-voltage gas discharge of the Energy Institute named after G. M. Krzhizhanovsky of the USSR Academy of Sciences plays a significant role in this work. On the photo: an impulse generator with a voltage of 3,000,000 volts in the laboratory of the institute.

Um Probleme elektrischer Fernleitungen von kommunistischen Großbauten zu lösen, stellen sowjetische Gelehrte komplizierteste Versuche an und setzen die Resultate ihrer Forschungen in den Praxis um. Einen wichtigen Platz in dieser Arbeit nimmt das G. M. Krschischanovskij-Laboratorium für Hochspannungsgasentladung an der Akademie der Wissenschaften der USSR ein. Auf dem Bild: der Impulsgenerator mit 3.000.000 Volt Spannung im Laboratorium des Instituts.

Dans notre cour habite une fille de 5 ans mon aînée. Une vraie tête brûlée. Elle me fait rencontrer des garçons. Elle en amène un chez elle et se met en ménage avec lui dans l'ancienne remise. Un jour, elle essaie de me persuader de partir au Front et de m'inscrire au bataillon féminin de la Mort. Elle me dépeint sous un jour exaltant les décorations que nous allons obtenir. Comme je viens de lire *La Vie familiale* de Tcharskaïa, je vois tout en rose et je dis oui. Le jour

A girl that was five years older than me lived on our block. She started to introduce me to the boys. She once brought a guy and they moved into an old shed in the courtyard. And then she started to convince me to go to war, to enlist in the women's death battalion. She described in rainbow colors what kind of medals we would receive. I had just recently read Charskaya's *Family Life*. Everything appeared to me in such extraordinary colors that I agreed. The day of

In unserem Hof wohnte ein Mädchen, die 5 Jahre älter war als ich. Sie war eine Draufgängerin. Sie begann, mich mit Burschen bekanntzumachen. Sie brachte einen Burschen mit und hauste mit ihm in einem alten Schuppen im Hof. Und dann begann sie mich zu überreden, in den Krieg zu ziehen, in das weiblichen Todesbattaillon einzutreten. Sie malte mir in herrlichen Farben aus, was für Auszeichnungen wir bekämen. Ich hatte damals gerade *Familienleben* von Tscharskaja gelesen. Alles erschien mir ungeheuer reizvoll und ich stimmte zu. Ein Abreisetag

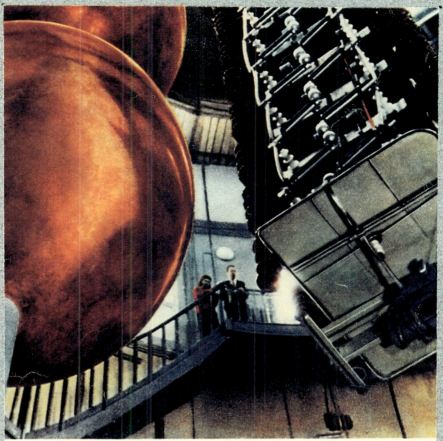

Решая проблемы сверхдальних передач электроэнергии с великих строек коммунизма, советские ученые производят сложнейшие опыты и внедряют в практику результаты своих исследований. Большое место в этой работе принадлежит лаборатории высоковольтного газового разряда Энергетического института имени Г. М. Кржижановского Академии наук СССР. На снимке — импульсный генератор напряжением в 3 000 000 вольт в лаборатории института.

У нас во дворе жила девочка старше меня на 5 лет. Она была сорви-голова. Она стала знакомить меня с ребятами. Она привела парня и поселилась с ним во дворе в бывшем сарае. Но вот она стала уговаривать меня отправиться на войну, записаться в батальон смерти женский. Рисовала в радужных красках, какие мы получим награды. Я только недавно прочла Чарской "Семейная жизнь". Все рисовалось передо мной в каких-то небывалых красках и я согласилась. Был назначен

La Vie humiliée Life as an insult Leben als Erniedrigung Жизнь как оскорбление

Rayon de tissus naturels dans un grand magasin de Minsk.

The department of natural fabrics in the Minsk department store.

Die Abteilung für Naturfaserstoffe im Minsker Kaufhaus.

du départ est fixé et je me prépare à fuir la maison. Mais je ne me réveille pas à temps, tandis qu'elle part pour de vrai. Elle n'est pas très longtemps absente ; revenue à la maison, elle racontera tout ce qu'elle a subi. Elle a eu bien du mal à rentrer. Elle change souvent de garçon. Sa conduite devient très relâchée.
1917. Une vie bruyante et passionnante. Je me mêle aux adultes mais je n'arrive pas à comprendre pour quel parti voter,

departure was set, and she and I got ready to run away from home. But I slept through the agreed upon time, and she really did leave. She didn't stay away particularly long, and upon her return she told of how much she had endured. She barely made it home. She changed men often. She began to lead a promiscuous life. The year 1917 came. A noisy, interesting life. I hung around adults and couldn't understand at all what party they were voting for

wurde festgesetzt, und ich bereitete mich vor, mit ihr auszureißen. Aber ich verschlief die ausgemachte Zeit, und sie fuhr tatsächlich ab. Sie blieb nicht besonders lange weg, als sie zurückkam, erzählte sie, was sie alles durchgemacht hatte. Nur mit Mühe hatte sie es nach Hause geschafft. Ihre Freunde wechselten oft. Sie begann, ein leichtes Leben zu führen.
Das Jahr 1917 begann. Ein geräuschvolles, interessantes Leben. Ich trieb mich unter Erwachsenen herum und konnte nicht verstehen, wer für welche Partei stimmte

Отдел натуральных шелковых тканей в минском универсальном магазине

день отъезда и я приготовилась с ней бежать из дома. Но я проспала назначенное время, а она действительно уехала. Особенно долго она не отсутствовала, возвратившись рассказывала как много она перенесла. Едва вернулась домой, парни у нее часто менялись. Она стала вести легкий образ жизни.

Настал 1917 год. Шумная, интересная жизнь. Я толкалась среди взрослых и никак не могла понять за какую партию голосуют и

Rayon de chaussures pour femmes, faites sur commande du grand magasin.

In the department of women's shoes, produced by special order of the store.

In der Abteilung für Damenschuhe, die auf Bestellung angefertigt werden.

ni en quoi l'un vaut mieux que l'autre. Mes parents n'adhèrent à aucun parti, bien que j'entende leurs discussions sur les monistes et les bundistes. La vie est devenue difficile et je suis obligée de donner des leçons de rattrapage. Heureusement, je vais chez trois frères-bouchers, qui ont des enfants et qui me donnent à manger. Après les classes, je cours à mes leçons, et en rentrant, je m'endors tout de suite pour me lever à 4-5 heures du matin et faire mes devoirs. C'est dur, je ne dors pas assez, mais les repas me réconfortent. Ainsi prennent fin mes études au gymnase :

and why one party was better than another. My parents didn't lean toward any party, though I heard their conversations about the party of monists and bund. It became very hard to live and I got work as a tutor. To my delight there were three brothers with children, butchers, and they would feed me lunch. I would go to tutor after I myself finished school, then I would go home and fall asleep, I would get up at 4-5:00 in the morning to do my own lessons. It was difficult, I didn't get enough sleep, but the lunches kept me going. So ended my studies at the gymnasium,

und warum sie besser sei als die andere. Meine Eltern gehörten zu keiner Partei, obwohl ich sie reden hörte über die Monisten und die Bundisten... Das Leben wurde schwierig, ich begann, Nachhilfe zu erteilen. Zum meinem Glück waren es drei Brüder mit Kindern, alle Fleischhauer, und sie gaben mir Mittagessen. So ging ich nach der Schule zur Nachhilfe, kam nach Hause und schlief sofort ein, dann stand ich um 4 oder 5 Uhr in der Früh auf und machte meine Aufgaben. Es war schwer, ich konnte nie ausschlafen, aber das Mittagessen hielt mich aufrecht. So ging mein Gymnasialbesuch zu Ende,

В отделе женской обуви, изготовляемой по особому заказу универмага.

чем одна лучше другой. Родные мои не примыкали ни к какой партии хотя я слышала их разговор о партии монистов и бундовцев..
Стало трудно жить и я нашла уроки репетитора. На мое счастье были 3 брата с детьми, мясники и они давали мне обед. Сама я после школы ходила на репетиторство, приходила домой и засыпала, а вставала 4-5 часов утра и делала свои уроки. Трудно было, я не высыпалась нообеды меня поддерживали. Так закончилась моя учеба в гимназии,

Le grand magasin de Minsk propose à ses clients une large gamme de radios.

Radio receivers of the most diverse brands are offered to customers in the Minsk department store.

Radioempfänger verschiedenster Marken werden den Käufern im Minsker Kaufhaus angeboten.

en fait, il ne s'agit plus d'une école privée, mais d'une « école du travail ». A la fin de la septième, j'ai mon bulletin de notes où il y a quelques « passables », mais après la huitième je ne reçois qu'une simple feuille arrachée à un cahier portant l'attestation, signée par le président et le secrétaire du conseil pédagogique, comme quoi j'ai suivi les cours de l'« école du travail » pendant 8 ans. C'était en 1920. J'y suis entrée en 1910, à l'âge de 8 ans, et j'en suis sortie en 1920 au bout de 10 ans : deux ans de préparatoire et 8 classes. Que vais-je faire ? Evidemment,

or more precisely, it was already not a private, but a vocational school. I got a diploma that I finished 7 classes with grades, there were some "C"'s, and for the eighth grade I got a blank piece of notebook paper on which was written that I had attended eight grades of the vocational school, this was signed by the chairman and secretary of the pedagogical council. That was in 1920. I entered it in 1910 at eight years old, and finished it in 1920, having studied for 10 years, 2 preparatory years and eight grades. The question now was, what to do next. Of course,

eigentlich war es kein Privatgymnasium mehr, sondern eine Arbeiterschule. Für 7 Klassen bekam ich ein Zeugnis mit Noten, auch Genügend waren darunter, und für die 8. Klasse war auf einem einfachen Stück Papier aus einem Heft bestätigt, daß ich 8 Klassen der Arbeiterschule besucht hatte, unterschrieben vom Vorsitzenden und vom Sekretär des Pädagogischen Sowjets. Das war im Jahr 1920. Ich war 1910 im Alter von 8 Jahren in die Schule eingetreten, hatte sie 1920 nach 10 Jahren Unterricht beendet, 2 Vorbereitungsjahre und 8 Klassen. Die Frage war, was weiter.

Радиоприемники самых разнообразных марок предлагаются покупателям в минском универмаге.

а вернее это было уже не частная, а трудовая школа. Я получила за 7 классов аттестат с отметками, в нем были и тройки, а за 8 класс на простом листке из тетради было написано удостоверение, что я прослушала 8 классов трудовой школы. подписали пред. и секретарь педсовета. Это было в 1920 г. Поступила я в 1910 году 8 лет от роду, закончила в 1920 г. проучившись 10 лет, 2 приготовительных и 8 классов. Стал вопрос, как быть дальше. Конечно о

La Vie humiliée Life as an insult Leben als Erniedrigung Жизнь как оскорбление

Le stagiaire I. Bednov et l'agronome G. Konovalov (au centre) devant une échoppe-buffet du campement agricole du kolkhoze. A droite — la buffetière A. Babitchéva.

The student-intern I. Bednov and the agronomist G. Konovalov (center) near the kiosk-buffet in the field camp of the collective farm. On the right, the buffet worker A. Babicheva.

Der Student-Praktikant I. Bednow und der Agronom G. Konowalow (in der Mitte) beim Buffetkiosk im Feldlager des Kolchos. Rechts die Buffetfrau A. Babitschewa.

il n'est pas question de continuer mes études, il faut aider la famille. D'abord, je trouve une place d'éducatrice à la maternelle, mais je dois l'abandonner, ça ne rapporte pas grand-chose financièrement. J'entre à la Rabkrine, l'inspection ouvrière et paysanne, comme copiste. J'ai une belle écriture, et cela suffit largement. Ensuite j'ai une promotion: je deviens préposée à l'enregistrement. Le courrier est abondant et je m'en tire mal. On me donne une adjointe pour tenir un autre

there couldn't even be talk of further education, I had to help my family. At first I got a job as a teacher in a nursery school, but soon gave that up as it wasn't financially rewarding. I then started to work as a copier at the Rabkrin, that is the Workers-Peasants Inspectorate. My handwriting was good, and nothing else was required. Then I got a promotion and they made me a registrar. There was a lot of mail, I couldn't cope with it all. They gave me an assistant to work with another

Von einem Studium konnte nicht die Rede sein, ich mußte den Eltern helfen. Zuerst begann ich als Erzieherin in einem Kindergarten, aber damit hörte ich bald auf, weil es materiell nichts brachte. Ich trat eine Stelle als Kopistin an bei Rabkrin, der Arbeiter- und Baueminspektion. Ich hatte eine schöne Schrift, und mehr wurde nicht verlangt. Dann wurde ich befördert und kam in die Registratur. Es gab viel Post, ich wurde nicht fertig damit, und so bekam ich eine Mitarbeiterin.

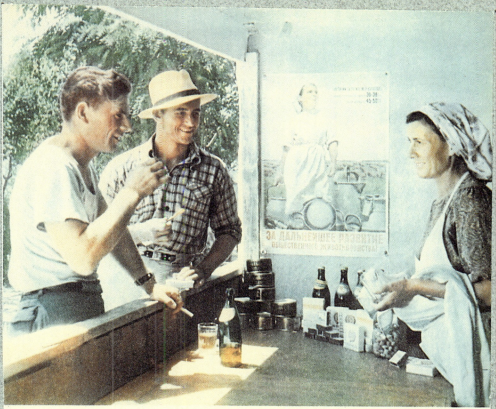

Студент-практикант И. Беднов и агроном Г. Коновалов (в центре) у киоска-буфета в полевом стане колхоза. Справа — буфетчица А. Бабичева.

дальнейшем образовании не могло быть и речи, нужно было помочь родным. Я поступила сначала в детский садик воспитательницей, но вскоре оставила это занятие, оно ничего материально не давало. Поступила на службу в Рабкрин. т.е. рабоче-крестьянскую инспекцию переписчицей Почерк у меня был хороший, а большего и не требовалось. Затем нашла на повышение, назначила регистратором. Почты было много и я не управлялась. Мне дали помощницу, на другой

Le magasin propose toujours un grand choix de tapis industriels et faits main.

There is always a large selection of handmade and machine-made rugs in the store.

Im Kaufhaus ist immer eine große Auswahl an handgewebten und maschinell erzeugten Teppichen.

registre. J'enregistre les entrées, et elle, les sorties. Il se trouve que mon adjointe a été surveillante dans mon gymnase qu'elle a terminé un an avant moi. Nous devenons amies et le resterons plus tard, quand on ne travaillera plus ensemble. Son père est chef de port, elle est bien élevée, sa mère manifeste beaucoup d'attention pour moi et leur amitié me réjouit. Parmi les collègues, il y a une comptable, une certaine K. Une fille très gentille qui habite avec son frère ; ils viennent de Biélorussie,

register. I kept the outgoing register, and she kept the incoming one. It turned out that my assistant was formerly a class supervisor at my gymnasium. She finished school a year before I did. We became friends, and remained so even later when we were no longer working together. Her father was the director of the seaport, she was well brought up, and her mother cared a great deal for me, and their friendship brought me joy. An accountant, K., worked with me. She was a very nice girl, she lived with her brother, they were from Belorussia,

Ich bearbeite das Ausgangsbuch, sie das Eingangsbuch. Es stellte sich heraus, daß meine Mitarbeiterin Klassenaufseherin in meinem Gymnasium gewesen war, sie hatte die Schule ein Jahr vor mir beendet. Wir freundeten uns an und diese Freundschaft dauerte auch an, als wir nicht mehr zusammen arbeiteten. Ihr Vater war Vorsteher des Hafens, sie war sehr gebildet, auch ihre Mutter war zu mir sehr aufmerksam und ihre Freundschaft freute mich. Als Rechnungsführerin arbeitete K. mit mir zusammen, ein sehr liebes Mädchen, die mit ihrem Bruder zusammen wohnte, sie waren aus Weißrußland,

В магазине всегда большой выбор ковров ручной и фабричной работы.

журнал. Я вела исходящий журнал, помощница входящий. Оказалось, что моей помощницей была бывшая бывшая классная надзирательница по моей гимназии, которая закончила ее на год раньше. Мы подружились и после, когда уже вместе не работали. Отец ее был начальником порта, она очень воспитанная и ее мать, ко мне внимательно относилась и их дружба меня радовала. Со мной работала счетоводом К. Очень милая девушка, жила с братом, они были из Белоруссии.

Ci-dessous — au rayon de jouets.

On the lower photo: in the children's toy department.

Auf dem unteren Bild — in der Spielwarenabteilung.

de Moguilev. En partant en vacances, elle me désigne comme remplaçante. Lorsqu'elle rentre, elle nous trouve en pleine restructuration. Connaissant notre amitié, le chef comptable nous laisse trancher : nous devons décider nous-mêmes qui va rester et qui doit partir. Elle dit que j'ai plus besoin de ce travail qu'elle et qu'elle partira. Son frère me propose de l'épouser et ajoute que nous devrons tous partir pour Moguilev. Mais comment laisser mes proches sans soutien ? D'ailleurs, je ne l'aime pas

from Mogilev. She went on vacation and left me to replace her. When she got back from vacation there was a cutback in staffing. Knowing about our friendship, the head accountant gave us a choice as to who should remain and who should be let go. Her brother proposed to me and said that all of us would move to Mogilev. That would have meant leaving my family without support, and I didn't particularly care for him

aus Mogilev. Sie ging in Urlaub und setzte mich als Stellvertreterin ein. Als sie aus dem Urlaub zurückkam, hatten wir Personalkürzungen. Da der Hauptbuchhalter von unserer Freundschaft wußte, überließ er die Entscheidung, wer bleiben und wer entlassen werden sollte, uns. Sie meinte, ich bräuchte die Arbeit dringender, und ging. Ihr Bruder machte mir einen Antrag und schlug vor, wir alle sollten nach Mogilev ziehen. Ich konnte die Eltern nicht ohne Unterstützung lassen und er gefiel mir auch nicht besonders,

На нижнем снимке — в отделе детской игрушки.

из г. Могилева. Она пошла в отпуск и оставила меня заместителем. Когда она вернулась из отпуска, у нас было сокращение штатов. Зная о нашей дружбе, главный бухгалтер поставил перед нами вопрос о сокращении, чтобы мы сами решили кому оставаться, а кому уволиться. Она сказала, что я больше нуждаюсь в работе, а она уволится. Брат ее сделал мне предложение и сказал, что все мы уедем в Могилев Оставить родных без поддержки, да и он мне не особенно нравился

La Vie humiliée   Life as an insult   Leben als Erniedrigung   Жизнь как оскорбление

Episode de fiançailles. Dans le rôle de la Princesse — l'élève de septième Rimma Kouznetzova, dans celui du Roi — l'ouvrier de la filature G. K. Sentiourev, le Frère cadet, alias le Marquis — V. I. Roubtzov, ajusteur de l'usine « Respirateur », le Chat — Raïssa Borodastova.

The wedding scene. The « princess » is seventh-grade student Rimma Kuznetzova; the "king" is a worker from the torsion-spinning factory, G. K. Sentiurev; the "younger brother", the "marquis", is a machine assembler at the factory "Respirator" V. I. Rutsov; and the "cat" is Raisa Borodastova.

Die Verlobungsszene. Als » Prinzessin « Rimma Kusnezowa, Schülerin der 7.Klasse, als » König « G. K. Sentjurew, Arbeiter der Zwirnfabrik, als » jüngerer Bruder « und als » Marquis « V. I. Rubzow, Monteur der Fabrik » Respirator «, und als » Kater « Raisa Borodastowa.

et je refuse. Il est aussi boucher de son état. Peu après, ils partent. On s'écrira pendant un certain temps, et puis, j'apprendrai que mon amie est morte et que son frère s'est marié. En mai 1921, de Jdanov, où nous vivons, les trains recommencent à circuler en direction de Moscou. Je rêve d'entrer à l'école de médecine. Nous sommes cinq : deux garçons, un couple (le mari rêve du Conservatoire, classe de chant) et moi. Mes parents ne sont pas contre. Mon père vend sa veste de sortie, on me fait des galettes de seigle et on me confectionne une jupe

and so I turned him down. He was also a butcher by trade. They left soon after that. We corresponded for a short while, and then I received news that my girlfriend had died and her brother had gotten married. In May of 1921 a train began to run from our town of Zhdanov to Moscow. I dreamed about entering the medical institute, and five of us got together : two young fellows, a husband and wife — he dreamed of entering the conservatory for singing — and I. My parents didn't object. My father sold his dress jacket, made me some darkbread croutons for the road, he sewed me a skirt

so lehnte ich ab. Von Beruf war er auch Fleischhauer. Sie reisten bald ab. Wir schrieben uns eine Zeitlang und kurz darauf wurde mir mitgeteilt, daß meine Freundin gestorben sei und der Bruder geheiratet habe. Im Mai 1921 wurde bei uns in Schdanov ein Zug nach Moskau zusammengestellt. Ich träumte davon, ins Medizinische Institut einzutreten, wir waren zu fünft : 2 Burschen, ein Ehepaar, und ich. Die Eltern hatte nichts dagegen. Der Vater verkaufte seinen Ausgehrock, sie buken mir schwarzen Zwieback, nähten mir einen Rock

Сцена обручения. «Принцесса» — ученица седьмого класса Римма Кузнецова, «король» — рабочий крутильно-ниточной фабрики Г. К. Сентюрев, «младший брат», он же «маркиз», — сборщик аппаратов завода «Респиратор» В. И. Рубцов и «кот» — Раиса Бородастова.

и я ему отказала. По профессии он был тоже мясником. Они вскорости уехали. Была недолго переписка и вскорости сообщили, что моя подруга умерла, а брат женился. В мае 1921 г. у нас в городе Жданове стал отправляться поезд в Москву. Я мечтала поступить в мединститут, собралось нас 5 чел. 2 парня, муж с женой, он мечтал в консерваторию по классу пения и я. Родные не возражали. Отец продал свой выходной пиджак, насушили мне черных сухарей, сшили юбку из

La Vie humiliée   Life as an insult   Leben als Erniedrigung   Жизнь как оскорбление

Episode de l'opéra *Le Chat botté*. Le Chat raconte à son amie (son rôle est tenu par l'étudiante de l'Institut pédagogique d'Orékhovo, Kapitolina Solomatkina) comment il a su tromper le Roi et aider ses amis, les gens du peuple.

A scene from the opera *Puss 'n Boots*. The "cat" is telling his friend (the role of which is being played by a student from the Orekhovo Pedagogical School, Kapitolina Solomatkina) how he tricked the "king" and helped his friends — simple people from the common folk.

Eine Szene aus der Oper *Der gestiefelte Kater*. Der »Kater« erzählt seiner Freundin (deren Rolle die Studentin der Orechovo-Lehranstalt für Pädagogik Kapitolina Solomatkina spielt), wie er den »König« täuschte und seinen Freunden — den einfachen Leuten aus dem Volk — half.

en toile de sac dont je garnis le bas de deux bandes noires. Je suis chaussée de sandales en bois qui m'écorchent les pieds. Et nous voilà partis pour Moscou. Nous nous installons dans un wagon de marchandises : il y a du monde, mais nous restons côte à côte, tous les cinq. A la gare, juste avant le départ, deux jolies filles nous abordent en me demandant de prendre un colis pour leur frère, un peu de farine. J'accepte. Sur le colis l'adresse est marquée. Je m'en souviens encore aujourd'hui : rue Povarskaïa, par la suite

from burlap, and I even decorated it with two black stripes down the sides, I wore wooden sandals on my feet which dug into the bones until they bled. And so, we set off for Moscow. We travelled in the cargo car, there was an enormous number of people, but we stuck close together, that is, the five of us. At the station just before departure two sweet-looking girls came up to me and asked me to take a package to their brother, that is, a little flour. I took it. The address was on the sack. I remember it: Povarskaya Street, it's probably

aus Sackleinen, den ich mit zwei schwarzen Streifen am Saum verzierte, an den Füßen hatte ich Holzsandalen, die fürchterlich drückten. Also fuhren wir nach Moskau. Wir reisten in einem Güterwagen, es waren schrecklich viele Leute, aber wir hielten fest zusammen, wir fünf. Vor der Abreise kamen auf dem Bahnhof zwei liebe Mädchen zu mir und baten mich, ihrem Bruder ein Päckchen mitzunehmen, einen kleinen Sack mit Mehl. Ich nahm es. Auf dem Päckchen war eine Adresse. Ich erinnere mich: Powarskaja Straße, jetzt

Альб — п/н №34

Сцена из оперы «Кот в сапогах». «Кот» рассказывает своей приятельнице (роль которой исполняет студентка Ореховского педагогического училища Капитолина Соломаткина), как он обманул «короля» и помог своим друзьям — простым людям из народа.

мешковы, я даже украсила ее двумя черными полосками по подолу, на ногах деревянные сандалии, которые до крови набивали косточки. Итак мы отправились в Москву. Ехали в товарных вагоне, людей было огромное количество, но мнккрене мы крепко держались вместе т.е нас 5 человек. На станции перед отправкой ко мне подошли 2 миловидные девушки и просили передать брату посылку, т.е. немного муки Я взяла. На мешочке был адрес. Помню ул. Поварская, теперь она,

Dans une parfumerie spécialisée de Moscou. Les clients trouvent dans ces parfumeries une large palette de parfums, d'eau de Cologne, de maquillages, des coffrets-cadeaux de parfums. A droite — échantillons de parfumerie produits par l'industrie soviétique.

In one of the factory-direct perfume shops of Moscow. In such shops customers can purchase the most varied assortment of perfumes, colognes, cosmetics, gift boxes with a selection of perfumes. On the right: various samples of products produced by the Soviet perfume-cosmetic industry.

In einem Spezialgeschäft für Parfümeriewaren in Moskau. In diesen Geschäften wird den Käufern ein äußerst vielseitiges Angebot an Parfums, Eau de Colognes, Kosmetik angeboten, auch ein Überraschungspäckchen mit einer Parfumauswahl. Rechts — einzelne Produktionsmuster, die von der sowjetischen Parfum- und Kosmetikindustrie erzeugt werden.

elle a dû être rebaptisée. Le voyage dure 10 jours, il survient même des aventures. L'un d'entre nous a envie de lire et il allume une petite mèche que la première secousse renverse sur les pieds de quelqu'un (on couche en tas) et tout prend feu. On ouvre la porte et certains, pris de panique, sautent du train. Peu après, tout s'apaise. Pas d'autres incidents. Dans le wagon, on fait la connaissance d'un couple moscovite. Ils sympathisent avec notre petit groupe et, ayant appris que je n'ai personne chez qui aller,

called something else now. And so, we travelled for 10 days, we had all kinds of adventures. One person in the car thought he would read and lit a wick, and at the first jostle it fell on someone's foot, everyone was lying side by side and a fire started. They opened the door and some people jumped out in all the commotion. Soon everything quieted down. There weren't any other big adventures. A husband and wife, Muscovites, were travelling with us in the car. They took an interest in our group, and having learned that I didn't have a single address to go to,

ist sie wahrscheinlich umbenannt. Wir fuhren zehn Tage lang, es passierten auch Abenteuer. Einer der unsrigen wollte etwas lesen und zündete einen Docht an, aber bei der ersten Erschütterung fiel er jemand auf die Beine, alle lagen kreuz und quer, und es begann zu brennen. Die Tür wurde geöffnet und in dem Durcheinander sprang jemand aus dem Zug. Bald beruhigte sich alles. Sonst passierte nichts. Im Waggon mit uns fuhr auch ein Moskauer Ehepaar. Sie interessierten sich für unsere Gruppe und als sie erfuhren, daß ich niemand hatte, an den ich mich wenden konnte,

В одном из фирменных парфюмерных магазинов Москвы. В таких магазинах покупателям предлагается разнообразнейший ассортимент духов, одеколонов, косметики, сюрпризных коробок с набором парфюмерии. Справа — отдельные образцы продукции, выпускаемой советской парфюмерно-косметической промышленностью.

наверное, переименованная. Итак мы ехали 10 суток. случались и приключение. Один из наших в вагоне задумал читать и даже фитилек, , а он при первой тряске опрокинулся кому то на ноги, все лежали вповалку и начался пожар. Открыли дверь и кое-кто в сутолке выпрыгнул из вагона. Вскорости все утихло. Больше приключений не было В вагоне с нами ехали муж и жена москвичи. Они заинтересовались нашей группой и узнав, что у меня не былони одного адреса куда дое-

Les cabinets de beauté où les soins de la peau et du cheveu sont dispensés par des spécialistes et des cosmétologues expérimentés se répandent largement dans le pays des Soviets. Sur la photo de gauche — un cabinet de l'Institut de cosmétologie, rue Gorki à Moscou.

Cosmetics salons, where skin and hair care are conducted under the guidance of specialists and experienced doctor-cosmetologists, have become widespread in the Soviet Union. On the left photo: in one of the salons of the Institute of Medical Cosmetics on Gorky Street in Moscow.

Weite Verbreitung im Sowjetland haben Kosmetiksalons, in denen die Pflege der Gesichtshaut und der Haare mit Hilfe von Spezialisten und erfahrenen Kosmetik-Ärzten durchgeführt wird. Auf dem linken Bild — ein Behandlungsraum im Moskauer Institut für ärztliche Kosmetik auf der Gorkijstraße in Moskau.

ils me laissent leur adresse. A peine arrivés à Moscou, nous nous précipitons au Ministère de l'Education, où nous apprenons qu'il n'y a pas de concours en mai et qu'il faudra revenir en août; entre-temps, ils nous conseillent de rentrer chez nous. Nous décidons de repartir ensemble. Comme j'ai un colis sur les bras, on convient de se retrouver le lendemain. Je me rends à l'adresse indiquée. Un jeune homme sympathique m'accueille. Il travaille pour un organisme militaire, touche une ration et en outre, il fabrique

they gave me theirs. And so, upon arrival in Moscow we set off for the People's Commissariat for Education, where we were told that applications were not accepted in May, and that we should come back in August, and for now we should go back home. We decided to go home together, and to meet the next day. I set off for the address I had on the sack of flour. A very nice young man greeted me. He worked in a military office, he received his rations and made a little extra money moonlighting, that is,

gaben sie mir ihre Adresse. Nach der Ankunft in Moskau begaben wir uns zum Volkskomissariat für Bildung, wo man uns mitteilte, im Mai gebe es keinerlei Aufnahmsprüfungen, wir sollten im August wiederkommen, und derweil fahrt wieder zurück. Wir beschlossen, gemeinsam zurückzufahren. Aber ich hatte das Päckchen, und wir vereinbarten, uns am nächsten Tag zu treffen. Ich ging zur angegeben Adresse. Ein sehr freundlicher junger Mann begrüßte mich. Er arbeitete beim Militär, erhielt eine Lebensmittelration und verdiente auch noch nebenbei,

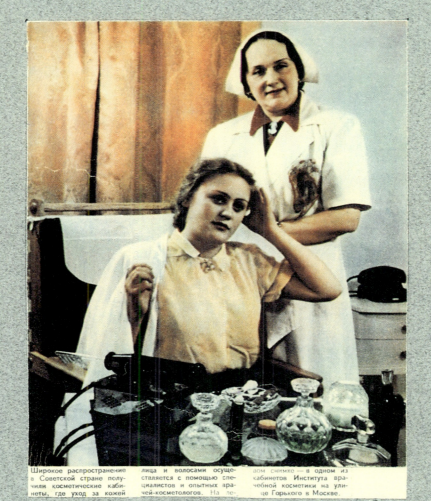

Широкое распространение в Советской стране получили косметические кабинеты, где уход за кожей лица и волосами осуществляется с помощью специалистов и опытных врачей-косметологов. На переднем снимке — в одном из кабинетов Института врачебной косметики на улице Горького в Москве.

хать, дали мне свой адрес. Итак по прибытии в Москву мы отправились в наробраз, а нам ответили, что в мае никакого приема нет, а нужно приехать в августе, а сейчас отправляйтесь пока обратно. Мы решили вместе ехать домой. Но у меня была посылка и мы условились где встретиться на следующий день. Я отправилась по указанному адресу. Меня встретил очень милый молодой человек. Работал он в военном ведомстве, получал паек и еще подрабатывал т.е. делал

La cuisinière du campement agricole Maria Vladova et son aide Varvara Obroutchkova préparent le déjeuner.

A cook from the field camp, Maria Vladova, and her assistant, Varvara Obruchkova, preparing lunch.

Die Köchin des Feldlagers Marija Vladowa und ihre Helferin Warwara Obrutschkowa beim Zubereiten des Mittagessens.

des souricières. La maîtresse de maison, une femme très gentille, elle aussi, me propose de passer la nuit chez eux, car leur locataire est absent. Je me réveille très tôt et je commence à réfléchir à ce que je vais faire. Rester seule à Moscou me fait peur, je n'ai qu'à repartir comme je suis venue, avec mes amis. Sans dire au revoir à ces gens accueillants, j'entrouvre doucement la porte d'entrée et je file. Je gagne la Place Rouge, où l'on s'est donné rendez-vous. Je fais tamponner le laissez-passer de retour et on prend le train. A vrai dire, l'un de nous est resté à Moscou, puisqu'il avait

he made mousetraps. The hostess was also a very nice woman, and she suggested that I spend the night in a spare room since her tenant had left. I woke up very early and thought about what I should do next. It was frightening to stay in Moscow alone, since I came with the group I would leave with them. Not saying good-bye to the hospitable hosts, I quietly closed the door from the outside and left. I arrived at Red Square, where we had agreed to meet. I made arrangements for the return train and we set off for home. One guy, it's true, stayed behind, he had

d.h. er stellte Mausefallen her. Die Frau war auch sehr freundlich, sie schlug mir vor, in ihrem Untermietzimmer zu übernachten, da der Mieter verreist war. Ich wachte sehr früh auf und überlegte, was ich tun sollte. Ich hatte Angst, allein in Moskau zu bleiben, lieber fahre ich mit den Burschen zurück, mit denen ich gekommen bin. Ohne mich von den Gastgebern zu verabschieden, öffnete ich leise die Wohnungstür und ging. Ich ging auf den Roten Platz, wo wir uns treffen wollten. Ich löste die Rückfahrkarte und wir fuhren wieder zurück, nach Hause. Nur einer blieb, er hatte

поварихa полевого стана Мария Владова и ее помощница Варвара Обручкова за приготовлением обеда.

мышеловки. Хозяйка тоже милая женщина, предложила мне переночевать в отдельной комнате, т.к. ее жилец куда то уехал. Я проснулась очень рано и подумала как быть дальше. Оставаться одной в Москве страшно, как приехала, так и уеду с ребятами. Не простившись с гостеприимными людьми, я тихонько открыла дверь наружу и ушла. Пришла на Красную площадь, где договорились встретиться. Оформила пропуск на обратный проезд и покатали обратно, домой. Один правда остался, он имел

La Vie humiliée Life as an insult Leben als Erniedrigung Жизнь как оскорбление

De nouvelles régions pétrolières ont surgi depuis la création de l'Union Soviétique. Il y a de plus en plus d'exploitations pétrolières entre la Volga et l'Oural. Ci-dessous — une des nouvelles exploitations dans les monts Jigouli.

During the years of Soviet power, many new regions of oil-production have appeared. There are more and more oil fields between the Volga and the Urals. On the lower photo: one of the new oil-fields in the Zhiguli Mountains.

In den Jahren der Sowjetmacht sind viele Gebiete für Erdölgewinnung erschloßen worden. Die Erdölindustrie zwischen der Wolga und dem Ural breitet sich immer mehr aus. Auf dem unteren Bild ein Erdölunternehmen auf den Schigulev-Bergen.

l'adresse de quelqu'un de sa famille. J'ai toujours mon sachet avec les galettes de seigle. Je veux les vendre, je m'arrête dans la rue et j'ouvre le sachet. Les passants se jettent sur moi et, en l'espace d'une minute, toutes mes galettes sont volées. Je ne vois pas la couleur de l'argent. Affamés, nous prenons le chemin du retour. Un trajet pénible, dans un wagon à bestiaux, pendant 5 jours. Mon compagnon de voyage souffre de la faim et répète sans cesse qu'il ne tiendra pas le coup, moi, aussi affamée que lui, je dois le consoler et le réconforter.

the address of his relatives. I had a bag of dried biscuits. I decided to sell them and so I stood on the street and opened the bag. People came at me from all directions, and literally in a minute had grabbed all of my biscuits. No one mentioned payment. And so, we set off for home hungry. We had trouble travelling, having packed into a cargo car — 5 days. The fellow to whom I stayed close during the entire trip was really starving and kept saying that he wouldn't make it, and I soothed and kept him going even though I was no less hungry.

Verwandte, bei denen er bleiben konnte. Ich hatte ein Säckchen mit schwarzem Zwieback und wollte ihn auf der Straße verkaufen, aus dem Säckchen. Kaum war es offen, stürzten sich alle auf mich und rissen mir den Zwieback aus der Hand. Von Bezahlung keine Rede. Also hungerten wir auf der Rückfahrt. Es war eine schwierige Fahrt, 5 Tage im Güterwagen. Der Bursch, der mit uns fuhr, litt sehr unter dem Hunger und sagte immer wieder, er halte es nicht aus, und ich war genauso hungrig und tröstete ihn und munterte ihn auf.

Альбом № 38   38

За годы советской власти появилось много новых районов нефтедобычи. Все больше становится нефтяных промыслов между Волгой и Уралом. На нижнем снимке — один из новых нефтепромыслов в Жигулевских горах.

адрес к своим родственникам. Я имела мешочек с черными сухарями. Решила их продать и стала на улице, раскрыв мешочек. Налетели со всех сторон и буквально в минуту растащили мои сухари. Об оплате не было и речи. Итак, голодные покатили обратно. Ехали с трудом, забравшись в теплушку - 5 суток. Парень с которым мы держались вместе всю дорогу, очень страдал от голода и все повторял что он не выдержит, а я не менее его голодная еще его утешала и бодрила

Le médecin A. M. Goubanova (au centre) anime dans l'hôpital un séminaire pratique de radiologie avec deux étudiants de l'Institut de médecine du Kazakhstan, l'étudiant de nationalité ouïgoure, Chaïm Ismaïlov et son camarade russe Youri Outkine.

Doctor A. M. Gubanova (center) is conducting practical radiology class in the polyclinic with students of the Kazakh Medical Institute, an Uigur student, Shaim Ismailov, and his Russian comrade, Yury Utkin.

Der Arzt A. M. Gubanow (im Zentrum) hält in der Poliklinik praktische röntgenologische Übungen mit Studenten vom Kasachischen Medizinischen Institut, dem Uiguren Schaim Ismailow, und seinem russischen Genossen Jurij Utkin ab.

Finalement, on arrive à la maison. A la maison, c'est très difficile, les repas sont maigres. J'entre dans un établissement maritime comme comptable. Je suis la seule femme. Tous ont de la sympathie pour moi. Je calcule la paye des dockers pour les chargements et déchargements, selon les tarifs. Mon salaire est modeste. A cette époque, en 1922, mon père se consume à vue d'œil. Il jaunit et maigrit — plus que la peau et les os. Sous-alimenté, il s'éteint en janvier 1922. Entre-temps,

And so we arrived home. Things were bad at home, we didn't eat very well. I took a job as an accountant in an office at the port. I was the only woman. Everyone liked me. I counted out the tariffs for the dock workers for loading and unloading. My salary wasn't very big. By that time, in 1922, father had begun to waste away before our eyes. He turned yellow, lost weight — he was a bag of bones. He didn't have enough to eat, and in January of 1922 he died. By that time,

So kamen wir nach Hause. Zu Hause ging es schlecht, wir hatten kaum zu essen. Ich trat eine Stelle als Rechnungsführerin im Schiffahrtsamt an. Ich war die einzige Frau. Alle waren gut zu mir. Ich berechnete die Löhne der Dockarbeiter für Verladearbeiten je nach Tarif. Meine Gehalt war niedrig. Damals ging es dem Vater immer schlechter, er wurde von Tag zu Tag weniger. Er wurde gelblich blaß, magerte ab — er bestand nur mehr aus Haut und Knochen. Seine Ernährung war unzureichend, und im Januar 1922 ging er von uns. Damals waren uns noch

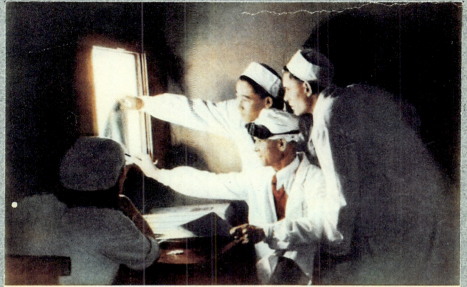

Врач А. М. Губанов (в центре) проводит в поликлинике практические занятия по рентгенологии со студентами Казахского медицинского института уйгуром Шаньсы Исмаиловым и его русским товарищем Юрием Уткиным.

Итак приехали домой. В доме было тяжело, питались мы скудно. Поступила на службу счетоводом в морское учреждение. Я была одна женщина. Все ко мне хорошо относились. Я по тарифу начисляла грузчикам за погрузочно-разгрузочные работы. Оклад был небольшой. К этому времени в 1922 году отец стал таять буквально на глазах. Он пожелтел, похудел -одни кости точали. Питание было для него недостаточным и в январе 1922 г. его не стало. За это время у нас роди-

La Vie humiliée Life as an insult Leben als Erniedrigung Жизнь как оскорбление

Sur la photo de droite — le contremaître-adjoint Amir Nadjapov. Il étudie la pression dans un puits à pétrole. Les habitants de la cité ouvrière de Rochers Pétroliers ont élu A. Nadjapov au Soviet local des députés.

On the right photo: apprentice Amir Nadzhapov. He is monitoring the pressure in the oil well. The residents of the settlement Oil Rocks elected A. Nadzhapov deputy to the local Council of the deputies of laborers.

Auf dem rechten Bild — der Gehilfe des Meisters Amir Nadschapow. Er achtet auf den richtigen Druck im Erdölbohrloch. Die Bewohner der Siedlung Erdölsteine haben A. Nadschapow als Abgeordneten in den Siedlungssowjet der Werktätigen gewählt.

deux filles sont nées — en 1913 et en 1915. Lidotchka et Jénetchka. Après le décès de mon père, je dois chercher un autre emploi. Je suis admise comme préposée aux enregistrements à l'Ukomgolod, Comité ukrainien de lutte contre la famine, devenu plus tard l'Ukomposledgolod, Comité ukrainien des conséquences de la famine. Nous recevons des colis de l'Amérique et organisons des cantines. Ma mère y entre comme distributrice. On sert de la purée de seigle. La nourriture est peu nutritive. On a beau manger à volonté, on a toujours faim. En juin 1922, l'épidémie de choléra asiatique

two more girls had been born, in 1913 and in 1915. Lidochka and Zhenechka. After the death of father, I had to look for a new job. I became a registrar in Ukomgolod (Ukranian Committee for the Fight against Hunger), later Ukomposlegolod (Ukranian Committe for the Fight against the Effects of Hunger). We received packages from America and started to organize cafeterias. Mama worked as a distributor. There was soup with brown flour. There was no nutrition from this food. No matter how much we ate, we remained as hungry as before. In June 1922 we had an outbreak of Asian

zwei Mädchen geboren worden, 1913 und 1915. Lidotschka und Schenetschka. Nach dem Tod des Vaters mußte ich mir eine andere Stelle suchen. Ich wurde Registratorin bei Ukomgolod, dem ukrainischen Komitee für Hungersnot, später hieß es Ukomposledgolod, ukrainisches Komitee für Folgen der Hungersnot. Wir erhielten Pakete aus Amerika und begannen Ausspeisungen zu organisieren. Mama arbeitete als Verteilerin. Es gab einen wässerigen Brei aus schwarzem Mehl. Diese Speise hatte überhaupt keinen Nährwert. Man konnte essen, soviel man wollte, man war so hungrig wie vorher. Im Juni 1922 brach in unserer Stadt die asiatische

На правом снимке — помощник мастера Амир Наджапов. Он ведет наблюдение за давлением в нефтяной скважине. Жители поселка Нефтяные Камни избрали А. Наджапова депутатом поселкового Совета депутатов трудящихся.

лось еще 2 девочки в 1913г. и в 1915 году. Лидочка и Женичка. После смерти отца, пришлось искать другое место. Я поступила регистратором в Укомголод, впоследствии Укомпослецголод. Мы получали посылки из Америки и стали организовываться столовые. Мама поступила раздатчицей. Была затируха из черной муки. Питательности от этой пищи не было. Сколько ни ели, голодно было попрежнему. В июне 1922 года у нас по городу вспыхнула эпидемия азиатской

La Vie humiliée Life as an insult Leben als Erniedrigung Жизнь как оскорбление

La troupe de danse amateur de l'Institut pédagogique du Kazakhstan en concert. Beaucoup de jeunes Ouïgoures suivent des cours aux côtés de jeunes filles d'autres nationalités.

A performance by the amateur dance group of the Kazakh Pedagogical Institute. Many young Uigur girls study at this institute along with girls of other nationalities.

Ein Auftritt der Amateur-Tanzgruppe des Kasachischen Pädagogischen Instituts. Zusammen mit Mädchen anderer Nationalitäten studieren in diesem Institut nicht wenige junge Uigurinnen.

sévit dans la ville. Il y a cinq cas dans notre quartier. Parmi les victimes, ma mère. Diarrhée et vomissements. Je suis impuissante. Personne ne peut m'aider. Je cours à l'hôpital pour chercher l'ambulance, elle arrive et je ne reverrai jamais ma mère. Le lendemain matin, je retourne à l'hôpital où on m'apprend que ma mère est morte. Je pars au cimetière dans un grand chariot qui transporte les morts du choléra, parmi lesquels je reconnais ma mère à ses longs cheveux ; je demande à l'enterrer séparément, je mets une pierre pour marquer l'endroit en me demandant

cholera in our town. There were five cases of it on our block. My mother was one of the victims. Diarrhea and vomiting. I was helpless. No one could help me. I went to the hospital, the ambulance came and I never saw mother again. I left for the hospital in the morning and they told me that my mother had died. I went to the cemetery with a big load of those who had died from cholera, I recognized mother by her long hair, they buried her separately at my request, and I put a stone there to mark the place and began to think about

Cholera aus. In unserem Hof gab es 5 Fälle. Zu den Leidtragenden zählte auch meine Mutter. Durchfall und Erbrechen. Ich war hilflos. Niemand konnte mir helfen. Ich ging ins Krankenhaus, die Rettung kam und ich sah Mama nicht wieder. Am Morgen ging ich ins Krankenhaus und man sagte mir, meine Mutter sei gestorben. Mit einer großen Fuhre von Choleratoten fuhr ich zum Friedhof, die Mutter erkannte ich an den langen Haaren, auf meine Bitte hin begrub man sie getrennt, ich legte einen Stein hin, um den Platz zu kennzeichnen und begann nachzudenken,

Выступление танцевальной группы художественной самодеятельности Казахского педагогического института. Вместе с девушками других национальностей в этом институте учится немало молодых уйгурок.

холеры. Во дворе у нас было 5 случаев. В числе пострадавших была и моя мать. Понос и рвота. Я была беспомощна. Никто не мог мне помочь. Я пошла в больницу, приехала скорая и больше я маму не видела. Утром я отправилась в больницу и мне сказали, что мать моя умерла. Я поехала на кладбище с большим возом умерших от холеры мать я узнала по длинным волосам, ее похоронили по моей просьбе отдельно, я положила камень, чтобы отметить место и стала думать,

Devant l'école L. N. Tolstoï à Yasnaïa Poliana.

Near the building of the Yasnaya Polyana school named after L. N. Tolstoy.

Vor der L. N. Tolstoj-Mittelschule in Jasnaja Poljana.

quel signe mettre sur la tombe. J'y pense longtemps et je finis par voir ces signes en rêve. Sur la tombe de mon père je vois les mots : « L'étoile juive à cinq branches. Il vécut de 1874 à 1922, 48 ans durant. Il vécut paisiblement et mourut en paix ». Et sur la tombe de ma mère : « Paix désirée ». Le matin, je note ces paroles, commande les plaques en fer-blanc que je pose sur les tombes. Nous ne sommes plus que cinq. J'ai 20 ans. La petite, Jénetchka, a 7

what sign to use to mark the grave. I thought about it for a long time, and I even dreamed about these markers. On father's grave I dreamed I saw the words: "A five-pointed Jewish star. He lived from 1874 until 1922, he lived 48 years. He lived quietly and died quietly". And on mother's grave: "the desired peace". And in the morning I wrote these words down and ordered tin plates and placed them on the graves. Five of us remained. I was 20 years old. The youngest Zhenechka was 7

was für ein Zeichen ich aufs Grab setzen sollte. Ich dachte lange nach und dann sah ich diese Zeichen in einem Traum. Auf dem Grab des Vaters sah ich im Traum folgende Worte: » Der jüdische fünfzackige Stern. Er lebte von 1874 bis 1922 — er lebte 48 Jahre. Er lebte ruhig und starb ruhig «. Und auf dem Grab der Mutter: » Ersehnte Ruhe «. Am Morgen schrieb ich diese Worte auf, bestellte blecherne Täfelchen und setzte sie auf die Gräber. Wir blieben zu fünft zurück. Ich war 20 Jahre alt. Schenetschka, die Jüngste, war 7

У здания яснополянской средней школы имени Л. Н. Толстого.

какой знак оставить на могиле. Я долго думала и мне снились эти знаки во сне. На могиле отца я увидела во сне такие слова"Еврейская пятиконечная звезда". Жил с 1874 по 1922 - жил 48 лет. Тихо жил и тихо скончался. А на могиле матери Жила с 1880 по 1922 год на 42 году скончалась. Только в смерти желанный покой. " Я на утро эти слова записала, заказала жестяные дощечки и поставила на могилах. Нас осталось 5 человек. Мне 20 лет. Самой младшей Женичке было 7

La Vie humiliée Life as an insult Leben als Erniedrigung Жизнь как оскорбление

Toute la famille Krapiva s'est réunie pour fêter le 35ième anniversaire de mariage, à l'exception de la fille aînée Nadejda qui habite une autre ville. Sergueï est en train de lire le télégramme de vœux qu'elle leur a envoyé.

To celebrate a 35-year wedding anniversary, the entire Krapiva family gathered together, with the exception of the oldest daughter Nadezhda who lives in another city. A congratulatory telegram has just arrived from her and Sergei is reading it to the others.

An dem Abend, an welchem das 35-jährige Hochzeitsjubiläum gefeirt wurde, versammelte sich die ganze Familie der Krapiwas, ausgenommen die älteste Tochter Nadjeschda, die in einer anderen Stadt lebt. Gerade ist von ihr ein Glückwunschtelegramm eingetroffen, das Sergej den Versammelten vorliest.

ans et mon autre frère 14. Je suis désespérée : comment pourrai-je entretenir les enfants avec mon salaire dérisoire ? Les voisins qui viennent me voir me persuadent d'envoyer les enfants à l'orphelinat, et je finis par le faire. Seule Riva sera acceptée, parce que la plus affaiblie, mais le lendemain, quand je viens la voir, elle éclate en sanglots et m'implore de la reprendre à la maison. Je l'emmène. Elle a 12 ans. Je ne peux pas faire la cuisine ni la lessive et je suis amenée à embaucher une femme de ménage. Nous en changeons souvent. Mais le pire, c'est le manque de nourriture.

years old, the second brother was 14. I was despondent about how I was going to live with the children on my small salary. The neighbors visited and tried to convince me to give the children to an orphanage and I decided to do it. They took only Riva, as the most emaciated, but when I went in the morning to visit she cried bitterly and begged me to take her home. I did. She was 12. I didn't have the strength to cook and wash, and we had to take on some help. The help changed often. The main thing was there wasn't much food.

Jahre alt, der zweite Bruder 14. Ich war verzweifelt — wie sollte ich mit den Kindern mit meinem kleinen Gehalt leben. Die Nachbarn kamen und überredeten mich, die Kinder ins Waisenhaus zu geben. Nur Riva wurde genommen, weil sie am magersten war, aber als ich sie am Morgen besuchte, weinte sie bitterlich und bat mich, sie nach Hause zu nehmen. Ich nahm sie mit. Sie war 12 Jahre alt. Kochen und Wäsche waschen war zuviel für mich, wir mußten eine Bedienerin anstellen. Sie wechselten oft. Die Hauptsache — das Essen war unzureichend.

На вечер, которым был отмечен 35-летний супружеский юбилей, собралась вся семья Крапивы, за исключением старшей дочери, Надежды, живущей в другом городе. Только что от нее пришла поздравительная телеграмма, которую Сергей читает собравшимся.

лет. второму брату 14 лет. Я была в отчаянии, как проживу с детьми на моем малом окладе. Соседи заходили и убеждали меня отдать детей в детдом и я решилась. Приняли только одну Риву, как самую истощенную, но когда я пришла на утром навестить, она горько плакала и умоляла взять ее домой. Я ее забрала. Ей было 12 лет. Приготовить пищу и постирать я была не в силах, пришлось брать домработницу. Они часто менялись. Главное - пища была скудная.

La Vie humiliée Life as an insult Leben als Erniedrigung Жизнь как оскорбление

Une immense pelouse s'étend devant la façade principale du Palais de la Science.

An enormous green lawn sprawled out before the main facade of the Palace of Science.

Vor der Hauptfassade des Palastes der Wissenschaft erstreckt sich ein riesiges grünes Parterre.

Comme au temps de ma mère, je continue de donner tout mon salaire pour le ménage, mais nous sommes 6 et il n'y a pas d'allocations. Une jeune fille qui travaille chez nous suit en même temps des cours de téléphoniste ; les cours terminés, elle nous quitte. Un jour, une vieille femme qui raccommode des bas et des chaussettes, me demande de laisser son coffre chez nous, puis de passer une nuit sur ce coffre et elle finit par s'installer chez nous. Elle a une fille qui l'a chassée. Et la mère est restée sans abri. Elle est

I gave all of my income to the family as I had formerly to my mother, but there were 6 of us, and there were no sources of additional income. One young girl started to study to become a telephone operator, and left once she finished her courses. Once we had an old woman who went from house to house repairing stocking, socks, asked if she could leave her trunk at our place, then she started to sleep on the trunk, and then she just moved in. She had a daughter, but she threw her out. And the mother scurried around from corner to corner. She wasn't

Früher hatte ich Mama mein ganzes Gehalt gegeben, auch jetzt gab ich alles her, aber wir waren 6 Personen, und es gab von nirgendwo Zuschüsse zum Gehalt. Ein junges Mädchen ließ sich zur Telefonistin ausbilden und ging, nachdem sie den Kurs abgeschlossen hatte. Einmal bat mich eine alte Frau, die von Tür zu Tür ging und Strümpfe stopfte, ihre Truhe bei uns einstellen zu dürfen, dann wollte sie auf der Truhe schlafen, dann blieb sie ganz bei uns. Sie hatte eine Tochter, aber die hatte sie hinausgejagt. Und die Mutter versuchte, da oder dort unterzukommen. Sie war nicht ganz richtig im

Огромный зеленый партер раскинулся перед главным фасадом дворца науки.

Я как и маме отдавала все свое жалованье, но нас было 6 человек, а дотации к жалованию ни откуда не было. Одна молодая девушка стала заниматься на телефонистку и закончив курсы, ушла. Однажды старая женщина, которая ходила по домам чинить чулки, носки попросилась поставить только сундучок, потом ночевать на сундуке, а потом и осталась совсем. У нее была дочь, но она ее выгнала. И мать скиталась по разным углам. Она была не совсем в

Cuisine de la cantine universitaire.

The kitchen of the university cafeteria.

Die Küche des Universitäts-Speisesaals.

dérangée. Je lui donne tout mon salaire et elle le dépense comme bon lui semble. Elle maltraite les enfants et lorsque je rentre du bureau, tous s'accusent les uns les autres. Elle se plaint des enfants, les enfants se plaignent d'elle. Je perds l'appétit. Souvent je m'enferme dans les toilettes et donne libre cours à mes larmes. Si je lui demande de laisser notre famille en paix et de partir, elle me répond chaque fois qu'elle ne nous quittera pas parce qu'elle a pitié de nous et qu'elle ne peut pas changer. Que faire ? Je commence une grève de la faim. Je ne touche plus

quite sane. I would give her my pay and she would spend it as she saw fit. She was nasty to the children, and when I came home from work, they always complained about each other. She about the children, the children about her. I didn't even want to eat supper. I would go into the bathroom and let the tears flow. When I asked her to leave my family in peace and to leave, she answered she wouldn't leave me for anything, she was so sorry for us, and wouldn't change for anything. What was there left to do? I went on a hunger strike. I didn't touch a thing,

Kopf. Ich gab ihr mein Gehalt, und sie verwendete es, wie sie es für richtig hielt. Sie kränkte die Kinder und wenn ich von der Arbeit kam, beschuldigten sich alle gegenseitig. Sie beklagte sich über die Kinder, die Kinder beklagten sich über sie. Ich hatte nicht einmal Lust zum essen. Ich ging auf die Toilette und ließ meinen Tränen freien Lauf. Als ich sie bat, meine Familie in Ruhe zu lassen und wegzugehen, antwortete sie, sie wolle mich auf keinen Fall verlassen, wir täten ihr leid, und sie könne sich nicht ändern. Was blieb zu tun? Ich ging in Hungerstreik. Ich rührte nichts

Кухня студенческой столовой.

своем уме. Я отдавала ей своё жалованье и она тратила как находила нужным Детей она обижала и когда я приходила с работы все жаловались друг на друга. Она на детей, дети на нее. Обедать даже не хотелось. Я уходила в туале и давала волю слезам. Когда я просила ее оставить мою семью в покое и уходить, она отвечала, что ни за что меня не оставит, так ее нас было жалко, а измениться она не могла Что оставалось делать? Я объявила голодовку. Но к чему не притра-

La Vie humiliée   Life as an insult   Leben als Erniedrigung   Жизнь как оскорбление

Visite guidée de bacheliers à Moscou: devant le gratte-ciel abritant l'Université. A la rentrée, nombre d'entre eux y commenceront leurs études.

An excursion of graduates from Moscow secondary schools near the University high-rise. In the fall, many of them will come here to study.

Ein Ausflug von Moskauer Mittelschulabsolventen zum Hochhaus des Universität. Im Herbst werden viele von ihnen hierherkommen, um zu studieren.

aux repas et au bout de quelques jours, je me retrouve si affaiblie que je ne peux plus aller au bureau. On appelle des voisins qui jettent son coffre dehors et qui la chassent. Riva promet de faire la cuisine. Mais c'est vite dit. Elle est encore trop jeune et ne sait pas calculer les dépenses. Je pleure souvent et je deviens hystérique. L'étouffement suit les sanglots, les sanglots alternent avec le rire et je ne peux plus m'arrêter. Les enfants s'affolent et se mettent à hurler.

and after a few days I got so weak that I couldn't go to work. The neighbors were called and they tossed out her trunk and chased her from the block. Riva announced that she would cook herself. But we were still far from that. She was still small and wasn't capable of managing the budget. I cried a lot and I began to get hysterical. After all the crying I began to suffocate, the crying turned to laughter and I couldn't stop. The children got frightened, and sobbing filled the whole apartment.

mehr an und nach einigen Tagen war ich so schwach, daß ich nicht mehr zur Arbeit gehen konnte. Man rief die Nachbarn zusammen und sie warfen sie mit ihrer Truhe hinaus und jagten sie fort. Riva erklärte, sie werde kochen. Aber soweit war es noch nicht. Sie war noch klein und konnte noch nicht mit Geld umgehen. Ich weinte sehr viel und begann hysterisch zu werden. Auf das Weinen folgte Atemnot, das Weinen ging in Lachen über und ich konnte nicht aufhören, die Kinder fürchteten sich und es gab Aufruhr in der ganzen Wohnung.

Экскурсия выпускников средних школ Москвы у высотного здания университета. Осенью многие из них придут сюда учиться.

гивалась и через несколько дней так ослабела, что не в силах была идти на работу. Позвали соседей и они выбросили ее сундук и выгнали со двора. Рива заявила, что сама будет готовить. Но до этого еще не было далеко. Она была еще мала и вести расхода еще была не в силах. Я очень много плакала и началась у меня истерика После плача, подступало удушье, плачь переходил в смех и я не могла остановиться. Дети пугались и подумался рев на всю квартиру.

La Vie humiliée Life as an insult Leben als Erniedrigung Жизнь как оскорбление

Le matin, Védiochkine est réveillé par un coup de téléphone. C'est la femme du mineur qui veut savoir comment il se porte au sanatorium et s'il aime bien la station balnéaire.

Vedeshkin was awakened in the morning by a telephone call. The miner's wife inquires about how he feels at the sanatorium, whether he likes the resort.

Am Morgen weckte Vedeschkin das Läuten des Telefons. Die Frau des Bergmanns erkundigte sich, wie er sich im Sanatorium fühle und ob ihm der Kurort gefalle.

Aucun des voisins n'intervient, personne ne s'intéresse à ma vie. Je dois aller voir un médecin. A cette époque, je commence à recevoir des poésies d'un inconnu. Elles ne sont pas fameuses, mais pleines de compassion pour mon triste destin. Plus tard, il me demande la permission de venir me voir. C'est le président des syndicats locaux, un homme marié. Avant de venir, il me téléphone au bureau. Il vient très tard. Reste silencieux. Il me plaint. Nous n'avons presque pas de meubles. Le lit

None of the neighbors dropped by, no one was interested in my fate. I had to go to the doctor. At that time I began to receive poems from a person that I didn't know. They weren't very good, but were full of sympathy for my unhappy lot. Then he asked for permission to visit me. It turned out to be the chairman of the trade union, he was married. He called me first at work to tell me he was coming. He came late. He was mostly silent. He sympathized with me. There was no furniture at home. Mama had

Niemand von den Nachbarn kam vorbei, niemand interessierte sich für mein Schicksal. Ich mußte einen Arzt aufsuchen. Zu dieser Zeit begann ein mir unbekannter Mann mir Gedichte zu schicken. Sie waren nicht besonders, aber voll Mitgefühl für mein unglückliches Los. Dann bat er um Erlaubnis, mich zu besuchen. Es stellte sich heraus, daß er Vorsitzender der Gewerkschaft war, verheiratet. Er rief mich vorher in der Arbeit an, um sich anzukündigen. Er kam spät. Schwieg viel. Zeigte Mitgefühl. Wir hatten keinerlei Einrichtung. Das Bett

Лист — 2/4 №47　　　　　　　　　　　　　　　　　　　　47

Утром Вед... ...шкина разбудил телефонный звонок. Это жена горняка справлялась о том, как он себя чувствует в санатории и понравился ли ему курорт.

Никто из соседей не заходил, никто не интересовался моей судьбой. Пришлось обратиться к врачу. В это время я стала получать от неизвестного мне человека стихи. Они были не важные, но полны со чуствия к моей нерадостной доле. Потом просил разрешения навестить меня. Это оказался председатель совпрофа, женатый. Он звонил предварительно мне на работу, что придет. Приходил поздно. Молчал больше. Сочуствовал мне. В доме никакой обстановки не было. Кровать

Sur la photo de gauche — N. Védiochkine en cure aux bains. L'eau provenant en permanence d'une source est à une température de 34° C.

On the left photo is N. Vedeshkin taking a therapeutic bath. The water which continually flows here from a spring is 34 degrees Celsius.

Auf dem Foto links — N. Vedeschkin nimmt ein Heilbad. Das Wasser aus der Quelle fließt unaufhörlich hierher und hat eine Temperatur von 34° Celsius.

a été vendu du temps de ma mère. On dort par terre. Nous avons un deux-pièces. La première pièce, celle des enfants est plus grande, l'autre, petite, est à moi. Le mur près duquel je dors est toujours humide et donne sur une rue étroite, face à la grande maison de nos voisins. Les médecins me prescrivent le calme et la bonne nourriture qui me font défaut. Mon ami veut m'aider. Il insiste auprès des syndicats pour qu'on m'avance une certaine somme d'argent pour me soigner. Le médecin traitant délivre un certificat attes-

sold the bed. We all slept on the floor. We had a two-room apartment. The first room was big, where the children stayed, the second smaller one was mine. The wall where I slept was all damp, it looked out into a narrow alley where the neighbor's big house was. The doctors prescribed quiet and good food, which I didn't have. My acquaintance decided to help me. He arranged for the union to give me a sum of money for treatment. Having received a certificate from the doctor with a diagnosis

hatte noch Mama verkauft. Alle schliefen auf dem Boden. Unsere Wohnung bestand aus zwei Zimmern. Im ersten, größeren Zimmer befanden sich die Kinder, das zweite war kleiner — das war mein Zimmer. Die Wand, an der ich schlief, war ganz feucht, davor lag eine enge Gasse und das große Nachbarhaus. Die Ärzte schrieben mir Ruhe vor und eine gute Ernährung, was ich nicht hatte. Mein Bekannter beschloß, mir zu helfen. Er setzte durch, daß mir von der Gewerkschaft eine Summe zur Verfügung gestellt wurde. Ich bekam vom Arzt eine Bestätigung mit der Diagnose,

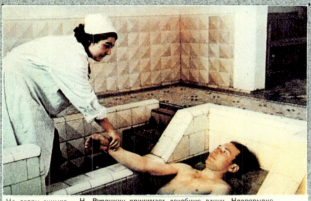

На левом снимке — Н. Ведешкин принимает лечебную ванну. Непрерывно поступающая сюда из источника вода имеет температуру +34° по Цельсию.

еще мама продала. Спали все на полу. У нас была желкоповская квартира из 2х комнат. Первая большая, где находились дети, вторая меньшая — это была моя комната. Стена, где я спала, вся была сырая, она входила в узкий переуклок, где был большой дом соседей. Враче приписывали мне покой, хорошее питание, чего у меня не было Мой знакомый решил мне помочь. Он добился, чтобы профсоюз выделил мне на лечение сумму. Я получив отврача справку с диагно

La Vie humiliée Life as an insult Leben als Erniedrigung Жизнь как оскорбление

Dans la cantine du sanatorium de mineurs. Au premier plan à gauche — N. Védiochkine.

In the cafeteria of a sanatorium for coal-miners. N. Vedeshkin is in the front on the left.

Im Speisesaal des Sanatoriums der Grubenarbeiter. In Vorgergrund links — N. Vedeschkin.

tant que je souffre d'hystérie, et après avoir reçu de la caisse des syndicats 400 roubles pour le traitement je pars à Kharkov que les médecins m'ont conseillé. L'argent est caché dans un petit sac tricoté que je tiens à la main. Dans le train, trois gars m'abordent et me forcent à boire de la vodka. Aucun des voyageurs n'intervient, au contraire, ils trouvent la situation amusante. Que puis-je faire, comment me débarrasser d'eux ? Personne ne prend mon parti et je dois boire un verre plein de vodka. Ensuite je ne me souviens

of hysterics and 400 roubles from the union, I left for Kharkhov, as recommended by the doctors. The money was in a knitted purse which was in my hand. Three guys joined me in the train car and began forcefully to offer me vodka. None of the passengers interfered, on the contrary, it amused everyone to see what I would do to get away from them, no one defended me from them, and there was nothing for me to do but to drink a whole glass of vodka. I don't

daß ich an Hysterie leide, erhielt von der Gewerkschaftskasse 400 Rubel für die Kur und fuhr nach Charkov, wohin mich die Ärzte empfohlen hatten. Das Geld war in einem Häkeltäschchen, das ich in der Hand hielt. Im Zug bedrängten mich 3 Burschen und nötigten mich, mit ihnen Wodka zu trinken. Niemand von den Passagieren mischte sich ein, im Gegenteil, sie hatten alle ihren Spaß daran, was sollte ich tun, wie sollte ich sie los werden, niemand verteidigte mich, und mir blieb nichts übrig, als ein ganzen Glas Wodka auszutrinken. An mehr

Альб — п/н №49

В столовой санатория угольщиков. На переднем плане слева — Н. Ведешкин

зом, что у меня истерия, получив на лечение 400 руб. из кассы совпрофа отправилась в Харьков, куда мне рекомендовали врачи. Деньги были в вязаной сумочке, которая была в руках. В вагоне ко мне пристали 3 парней и стали усиленно угощать водкой. Никто из пассажиров не вмешивался, наоборот это всех забавляло, что было делать, как отвязаться от них, никто не защитил меня от них и мне больше ничего не оставалось как выпить целый стакан водки. Больше я ничего

Dans un des salons du sanatorium. N. Védiochkine joue aux dominos avec des estivants venus à Zkhaltoubo des quatre coins du pays.

In one of the sanatorium's living rooms. N Vedeshkin is playing dominoes with vacationers who have come to Tskhaltubo from various corners of the country.

In einem der Aufenthaltsräume des Sanatoiums. N. Vedeschkin spielt Domino mit anderen Erholungssuchenden, die aus verschiedenenen Teilen des Landes nach Zchaltubo gekommen sind.

plus de rien. Heureusement, on arrive bientôt à une gare, et je garde toujours le sac avec mon argent. Je ne sais plus comment on m'a fait descendre. Une dame veille sur ma valise en attendant que je me dégrise. Elle repart aussitôt. Je demande à tout le monde où est la Direction des affaires sanitaires et je finis par la trouver. Une employée me fait très mauvais accueil et me dit de rentrer chez moi car la Direction ne peut pas m'envoyer dans un sanatorium. Je sors dans le couloir et foudroyée par une crise de nerfs, je m'évanouis. Dieu merci, un médecin

remember anything after that. Fortunately, the station wasn't far, I still had the purse and money. I don't remember how they got me off the train. A woman sat next to my suitcase and waited for me to sober up. She then left immediately. I started to ask where the city Health Committee was, and found it. I was rudely received by an employee of the Health Committee, who told me to go home and that the Health Committee couldn't give me authorization for treatment. I stepped into the hallway, and having given in to hysterics, I fainted. Lucky for me, a doctor

erinnere ich mich nicht. Zum Glück kam bald die Station, das Geldtäschchen hatte ich bei mir. Ich weiß nicht, wie ich ausgestiegen bin. Neben meinem Koffer saß eine Frau und wartete, bis ich nüchtern wurde. Sie ging sofort weg. Ich begann nach dem Gesundheitsamt zu fragen und fand es. Dort wurde ich von einer Mitarbeiterin sehr grob empfangen, sie sagte, ich solle zurückfahren, das Gesundheitsamt könne mir keinen Einweisungsschein für eine Kur ausstellen. Ich ging in den Korridor, bekam einen hysterischen Anfall und fiel in Ohnmacht. Zu meinem Glück kam gerade ein Arzt

В одной из гостиных санатория, Н. Ведешкин играет в домино с отдыхающими, приехавшими в Цхалтубо из различных уголков страны.

не помнила. К счастью скоро была станция, сумочка с деньгами была при мне. Как меня высадили не помню. Рядом с моим чемоданом сидела женщина и ждала моего отрезвления. Она тут же ушла. Я стала спрашивать, где горздрав и нашла его. Меня очень грубо приняла сотрудница Горздрава, сказала, чтобы я ехала обратно, путевки на лечение мне предоставить не может горздрав. Я вышла в коридор и закатив истерику, упала в обморок. На мое счастье, выходил врач

Le mineur Védiochkine et ses nouveaux amis en promenade aux alentours du sanatorium.

The miner Vedeshkin and his new sanatorium acquaintances strolling around the environs of the resort.

Der Bergmann Vedeschkin mit Sanatoriumsbekanntschaften bei einem Spaziergang in der Umgebung des Kurorts.

qui sort des bureaux me fait reprendre mes sens et donne l'adresse de l'hôpital où je pourrai acheter un bon de séjour pour le sanatorium. C'est l'hôpital universitaire où il travaille. Je m'y rends avec son petit mot, je suis bien accueillie, je paye mon séjour et ma cure commence. La nourriture et le traitement sont formidables, et je me rétablis rapidement. On ne me laisse pas sortir seule, sans accompagnateur, même dans la cour, tant je suis affaiblie. Dans ce même sanatorium, un jeune homme d'Ukraine occidentale suit une cure. Son nom est Ilko.

was walking out of the Health Committee, and revived me and gave me the address of a clinic where I could buy a pass to a sanatorium. It was a student clinic where he worked. I went there, where I was seen, I paid my money, and finally ended up in treatment. The food and treatment were excellent, and I quickly began to get well. I was so weak that they didn't let me go even into the courtyard without an escort. In this same sanatorium was a young man from Western Ukraine. His name was Ilko.

aus dem Gesundheitsamt, brachte mich zu Bewußtsein und gab mir die Adresse der Klinik, wo ich die Einweisung ins Sanatorium kaufen konnte. Das war eine studentische Klinik, in der er arbeitete. Ich ging dorthin, wurde aufgenommen, zahlte und begann endlich die Kur. Das Essen und die Behandlung waren ausgezeichnet, ich erholte mich schnell. Man ließ mich nicht einmal ohne Begleitung in den Hof, so schwach war ich. Im selben Sanatorium war ein junger Mann aus der Westukraine auf Kur. Er hieß Ilko.

Шахтер Ведешкин и его новые знакомые по санаторию на прогулке в окрестностях курорта.

из горздрава, привел меня в чувство и дал адрес лечебницы, где я могла бы купить путевку в санаторий. Это была студенческая лечебница, где он работал. Я отправилась по его записке, меня приняли, уплатила деньги и попала наконец на лечение. Питание и лечение были отличны, я быстро стала поправляться. Одну меня не пускали даже во двор без провожатого, такая я была слабая. В этой же санатории лечился один юноша из западной Украины. По имени Илько.

Les sons du clairon retentissent loin dans la forêt. Il est temps de finir la promenade et de rentrer au camp de pionniers : c'est l'heure du déjeuner.

The sound of the bugle resounds all over the forest. It's time to end the outing and return to the pioneer camp : it's time for brunch.

Die Klänge des Horns dringen weit in den Wald. Zeit, den Spaziergang zu beenden und ins Pionierlager zurückzukehren : Zeit fürs zweite Frühstück.

Costaud, il a un problème de bras et on lui permet de m'accompagner. On se lie d'amitié. Au bout d'un mois, je me rétablis et l'hystérie ne me mine plus. Ilko me demande s'il pourra m'écrire et nous nous écrivons régulièrement. Nous sommes très différents l'un de l'autre. C'est un gars de la campagne, il n'a rien de commun avec moi. Il se peut que je lui rappelle une fille de son pays. Il suit des cours à Kharkov, à la faculté de géodésie. Il vient pendant ses vacances

He was well built, he was treating his arm, and they allowed him to escort me. Thus began our friendship. After a month I got a lot better and the hysterics left me in peace. Ilko asked permission to write to me, and we started to correspond. We were different people. He was from a village and had nothing in common with me. I probably reminded him of one of the village girls. He was studying in Kharkhov at the Geodesic Faculty. During vacation

Er war kräftig gebaut, wurde wegen seiner Hand behandelt, und man gestattete ihm, mich zu begleiten. So begann unsere Freundschaft. Nach einem Monat war ich gut erholt und hatte keine hysterischen Anfälle mehr. Ilko bat mich darum, mir schreiben zu dürfen, und wir begannen zu korrespondieren. Wir waren verschiedene Menschen. Er war ein Bauernbub, hatte nichts mit mir gemeinsam. Wahrscheinlich erinnerte ich ihn an irgendein Mädchen aus dem Dorf. Er studierte in Charkov Vermessungswesen. Während der Ferien

Далеко разносятся по лесу звуки горна. Пора кончать прогулку и возвращаться в пионерский лагерь: наступил час второго завтрака.

Он был крепкого сложения, лечил руку, и ему разрешали меня сопровождать. Так начался наша дружба. Пробыв месяц, я хорошо поправилась и истерика оставила меня в покое. Илько просил разрешения писать и мы стали переписываться. Люди мы были разные. Он деревенский парень, совсем ничего не имел общего со мной. Я ему наверное напоминала его нибудь из деревенских девчат. Он учился в Харькове на геодезическом факультете. Во время каникул приезжал

Les jeunes métallurgistes consacrent souvent leur temps libre aux promenades en bateau sur l'Oural ; les plaisanteries, les chansons joyeuses, dont le peuple soviétique est si riche, se succèdent sans fin.

During leisure time the young metallurgists often organize boat outings along the Ural River, and then there is no end to the funny jokes, good, joyful songs, with which the Soviet people are so rich.

In der Freizeit machen die jungen Metallurgen nicht selten eine Bootsfahrt auf dem Ural, und dann hören sie nicht mehr auf mit fröhlichen Späßen und guten, freudigen Liedern, an welchen das sowjetische Volk so reich ist.

dans notre ville et loge dans le foyer du kolkhoze. Pour lui je me fais photographier en costume ukrainien. Plus tard, il m'offre ce même portrait dessiné sur un carton. Je l'ai eu longtemps accroché au mur jusqu'au moment où, lors d'un de ses séjours, Ilko le décroche et le déchire en petits morceaux en me traitant de sale youpine. Après quoi, il file et je ne le reverrai plus jamais. Je ne me rappelle plus pourquoi. Il me semble qu'il me poussait au concubinage. Je travaille à la caisse d'assurances, emploi que j'occupe

he came to visit us in the city, and stayed at the kolhoz. I even had my picture taken in a Ukrainian costume for him. Later he gave me a portrait of this on drawing paper as a gift. The portrait hung on the wall for a long time, until during one of his visits he ripped it off the wall and tore it to pieces, called me a Yid, took off and never showed up again. I don't remember the reason for this. But it seems that he was trying to force me to sleep with him. I worked at an insurance bureau. I worked there

kam er zu uns in die Stadt, er wohnte im Kolchoshof. Ich liess mich sogar für ihn in ukrainischer Tracht fotografieren. Später schenkte er mir dieses Porträt, eine Kreidezeichnung. Es hing lang bei mir an der Wand, bis es Ilko während eines Besuchs von der Wand riß und zerfetzte, mich eine Judensau nannte, verschwand und nie wieder auftauchte. Ich weiß nicht mehr, was der Grund war. Offenbar wollte er mich dazu bringen, mit ihm zusammen zu leben. Ich arbeitete in der Versicherungsanstalt.

В часы досуга молодые металлурги нередко устраивают прогулки на лодках по реке Уралу, и нет тогда конца веселым шуткам, хорошим, радостным песням, которыми так богат советский народ.

к нам в город, останавливался в колхозном дворе. Я даже сфотографировалась для него в украинском костюме. Позже он подарил мне нарисованный на ватмате этот портрет. Долго он висел у меня на стене, пока в один из приездов, Илько не сорвал его со стены, разорвал в клочья, назвав меня жидовкой, укатил и больше не показывался. Что была за причина, не помню. Но кажется он склонял меня на сожительство. Работала я в страховой кассе. Я проработала там

En Crimée, au bord de la Mer Noire, se trouve Artek — station balnéaire qui accueille des pionniers de toute l'Union Soviétique. Ci-dessous — plage d'Artek et vedette pour les promenades maritimes.

There is an all-union pioneer sanatorium — Artek — in the Crimea on the shores of the Black Sea. On the lower photo is the beach in Artek and the boat used by the children in outings on the sea.

Auf der Krim am Ufer des Schwarzen Meeres liegt Artek — das Allunionssanatorium für Pioniere. Auf dem unteren Bild der Strand von Artek und das Motorboot, mit dem die Kinder Spazierfahrten auf dem Meer unternehmen.

de 1925 à 1930. Le travail m'épuise. Nous versons toutes sortes d'assurances : chômage, maladie, primes de maternité et capital décès. Personne ne reste longtemps chez nous. Personne ne travaille plus que moi. Il arrive qu'on nous lance des pierres à travers le guichet. Nous devons alors nous sauver par une autre sortie. Je suis mutée d'un secteur à l'autre et je connais bien le fonctionnement de toute la caisse. Je finis par être nommée déléguée générale et j'accompagne le comptable en mission au port pour verser

from 1925 through 1930. The work was nerve-wracking. You could get all kinds of insurance from us. Unemployment, health insurance, for newborns and life insurance. No one worked there long. No one worked there longer than I did. Sometimes stones would crash through the windows at us. We used a different entrance. I was tossed around to various areas, I knew all the workings of the Insurance Bureau. Finally they gave me authorization, and I went with the cashier to the Port where they gave out

Von 1925 bis 1930 arbeitete ich dort. Es war eine aufreibende Arbeit. Bei uns gab es alle Arten von Versicherungen. Gegen Arbeitslosigkeit, gegen Krankheit, für Neugeborene, für Sterbegeld. Außer mir hielt es niemand dort länger aus. Manchmal flogen auch Steine durchs Fenster. Wir benützten den Hintereingang. Ich wurde in verschiedenen Bereichen eingesetzt, und bald kannte ich die ganze Versicherungstätigkeit. Ich wurde Bevollmächtigte und fuhr regelmäßig mit dem Kassier in den Hafen, wo wir alle möglichen Prämien

В Крыму, на берегу Черного моря, находится всесоюзная пионерская здравница — Артек. На нижнем снимке — пляж в Артеке и катер, на котором дети совершают прогулки по морю.

с 1925 по 1930 год. Работа была нервная. У нас получали все виды страховки. По безработице, по больничным листам, на новорожденных и пособие по смерти. Никто долгое задерживался у нас. Больше меня никто не работал. Бывало и камни летел на нас через окошечки. Ходили мы через другой ход. Меня перебрасывали на разные участки я знала всю работу Стрхкассы. Наконец меня назначили уполномоченной и я вместе с кассиром выезжала в Порт, где выдавали по всем

Les kolkhoziennes Gulnar Osmakhanova (Kirghize), Maria Fimouchina (Russe) et le président du kolkhoze « Dyjchine » Chafour Dagaziev (Doungan) sur les plantations de pavot médicinal. Tous les travaux sur ces plantations sont mécanisés.

Collective farm workers Gulnar Osmakhanova (a Kirgiz woman), Maria Fimushina (Russian) and the chairman of the collective farm "Dyjshin" Shafur Dagaziev (a Dungan) on a medicinal poppy plantation. All work on this plantation is mechanized.

Die Kolchosbäuerinnen Gülnar Osmachanowa (Kirgisin), Marija Fimuschina (Russin) und der Vorsitzende des Kolchos » Dyschin « Schafur Dagasijev (Dschungare) auf einer Schlafmohnplantage. Alle Arbeiten auf dieser Plantage sind mechanisiert.

les prestations. Je fais les calculs, signe les bulletins que le caissier paie. Les dockers m'aiment bien et ne m'insultent jamais. Sauf qu'ils m'encerclent au point de m'étouffer. Mais par malheur, à chaque fois que je descends de l'autobus, je suis prise de nausées à cause des vapeurs d'essence. Je suis obligée de quitter mon service. Mais avant mon départ de la caisse, un événement important se produit. Un jour, une collègue vient me voir avec un jeune homme et me convainc de lui louer ma

the insurance money. I counted and the cashier gave it out after I signed for it. The dock workers liked me. They never cursed me. But they would surround you from all sides and it was hard to breathe. But the bad thing was, that as soon as I got off the bus, I started to vomit from the smell of gasoline. I had to quit. But before I left the insurance bureau, an important thing happened. One of my co-workers came up to me once with a young man and started to persuade me to rent my bedroom to him

ausbezahlten. Ich berechnete alles und der Kassier zahlte gemäß meiner Unterschrift aus. Mit den Transportarbeitern kam ich gut aus. Nie schimpften sie mit mir. Nur umdrängten sie einen immer so von allen Seiten, daß ich keine Luft mehr bekam. Das einzig Dumme war, daß mir sofort übel wurde, wenn ich aus dem Autobus stieg, von dem Benzingestank mußte ich erbrechen. So blieb nur die Kündigung. Aber bevor ich von der Versicherung wegging, geschah etwas ziemlich Wichtiges. Einmal kam meine Mitarbeiterin mit einem jungen Mann zu mir und überredete mich, ihm für 3 Monate mein

Колхозницы Гюльнар Осмаханова (киргизка), Мария Фимушина (русская) и председатель колхоза «Дыйшин» Шафур Дагазиев (дунганин) на плантации лекарственного мака. Все работы на этой плантации механизированы.

видам. Я начисляла, а кассир за моей подписью выдавал. Грузчики хорошо ко мне относились. Никогда не ругали. Только так окружали со все сторон, что нечем было дышать. Но вот беда, как только я сходила с автобуса у меня начиналась рвота от запаха бензина. Пришлось уволиться. Но прежде чем я ушла из страховой кассы, случилось немаловажное событие. Однажды ко мне пришла моя сотрудница с молодым человеком и стала уговаривать, чтобы я сдала ему свою

Coin d'apiculture kolkhozienne. Au premier plan — Claudia Soukhodolova (Russe), stagiaire de l'école d'agriculture de Frounzé, et l'apiculteur du kolkhoze Looussane Mado (Doungan).

A corner of the collective farm apiary. In the forefront: a student from the Frunze Agricultural Institute, Klavdia Sukhodolova (Russian), who has arrived for practical training and bee-keeper of the collective farm, Lousan Mado (a Dungan).

Ein Teil der Kolchos-Imkerei. Im Vordergrund eine Studentin des Landwirtschaftsinstituts von Frunse, die zu einem Praktikum gekommen ist, Klavdija Suchodolowa (Russin) und der Kolchos-Imker Lousan Mado (Dschungare).

chambre à coucher pour trois mois : il est invité par un entrepreneur pour mettre en place une usine d'eaux gazeuses. Il s'agit d'une entreprise privée. Je dis oui ; il me paie 10 roubles par mois. Il mange à part. Il rentre tard et il me réveille pour que je lui ouvre la porte. Peu de temps après, on se met en ménage. Rien ne change dans mon train de vie. Il continue à me verser 10 roubles de loyer, je lui fais la cuisine avec ce budget plus que

for three months since he had come on an invitation to set up a factory for a private employer to make carbonated water. This factory, of course, was a private enterprise. She convinced me, and he paid me 10 roubles a month. He didn't eat with us. He would come home late and wake me up to open the door for him. Soon we became husband and wife. Nothing changed in my life. He paid me the 10 roubles for the apartment as before, and I fed him on that meagre

Schlafzimmer zu vermieten, weil er den Auftrag hatte, für einen privaten Auftraggeber eine Mineralwasserfabrik zu errichten. Nicht direkt eine Fabrik, ein Privatunternehmen. Sie überzeugte mich und er begann mir 10 Rubel im Monat zu zahlen. Er verköstigte sich selbst. Er kam spät nach Hause und weckte mich, um ihm die Tür zu öffnen. Bald lebten wir wie Mann und Frau. Nichts änderte sich in meinem Leben. Er zahlte mir wie früher 10 Rubel im Monat für die Wohnung, und ich gab ihm von diesem wenigen Geld auch

Уголок колхозной пасеки. На переднем плане — прибывшая на практику студентка Фрунзенского сельскохозяйственного института Клавдия Суходолова (русская) и пчеловод колхоза Лоусан Мадо (дунганин).

спальню на 3 месяца, т.к. он приехал по приглашению, поставить завод газовых вод для частного предпринимателя. Завод это конечно не прямо значит, а частное предприятие. Уговорила, он стал платить мне 10 руб в месяц. Питался он самостоятельно. Приходить он поздно и будил меня, чтобы открыть ему дверь. Скоро мы стали мужем и женой. Ничего не изменилось в моей жизни. Он по-прежнему платил мне эти 10 рублей за квартиру, я же подкармливала его из этого бюджета и так

Parmi les mineurs de Tcherta, plusieurs sont passionnés de pêche. Sur la photo — le mineur Stépan Rotkov (devant) pêche avec ses amis dans la rivière.

There are many fans of fishing among the Chertinsky miners. On the photo: the miner Stepan Rotkov (in front) with his comrades are fishing in the river.

Unter den Bergleuten von Tschertinsk gibt es nicht wenige Freizeitangler. Auf dem Bild angelt der Bergmann Stepan Rotkow (vorn) mit seinen Genossen in Fluß.

modeste. J'ai une femme de ménage, une Polonaise âgée qui me demande d'augmenter ses gages, étant donné qu'elle a davantage de linge à laver. Il n'est ni attentif ni délicat à mon égard, ne m'aide pas matériellement et ne s'intéresse pas aux enfants. Chaque mois il envoie 50 roubles de son salaire à ses parents et n'hésite même pas à me demander de le faire à sa place parce que pour lui je suis moins que rien. J'ai 27 ans, ce n'est pas le mariage de mes rêves et je me sens profondément vexée par son comportement.

budget. I had a Polish housekeeper, an elderly woman, who announced that I had to pay her more since she was washing extra laundry. He wasn't very sensitive or caring towards me, he didn't help financially at all, and was indifferent towards the children. He sent his parents 50 roubles a month from his salary, and even sometimes asked me to send his parents this money, and I didn't mean anything to him. I was 27 years old, and never dreamed about this kind of marriage and was deeply offended at his attitude towards me.

noch zu essen. Ich hatte eine polnische Haushaltshilfe, eine ältere Frau, sie erklärte, man müsse ihr mehr bezahlen, weil mehr Wäsche zu waschen sei. Er war weder feinfühlig noch aufmerksam zu mir, half mir materiell überhaupt nicht, die Kinder waren ihm gleichgültig. Von seinem Gehalt schickte er 50 Rubel monatlich seiner Familie, manchmal bat er sogar mich, ihnen dieses Geld zu überweisen, und ich war ihm nichts und niemand. Ich war 27 Jahre alt, so hatte ich mir eine Ehe nicht vorgestellt, ich war zutiefst gekränkt über sein Verhalten.

Среди чертинских шахтеров немало любителей рыболовства. На снимке — горняк Степан Ротков (впереди) со своими товарищами ловит рыбу в реке Ине.

скудно. У меня была домработницей полька пожилая, она заявила, что нужно ей больше платить, т.к. она стирает лишнее бельё. Он не был чуток и внимателен ко мне, ничем материально не помогал, к детям относился безразлично. Из своего заработка он посылал родным по 50 руб. в месяц, даже иногда просил меня переслать родным эти деньги, а я была ему никто и ничто. Мне было 27 лет, о таком замужестве я не мечтала и была глубоко оскорблена его отношением

La Vie humiliée   Life as an insult   Leben als Erniedrigung   Жизнь как оскорбление

Dans la cour des abattoirs de la boucherie A. I. Mikoïan. Chargement de la charcuterie à destination du Magasin de comestibles n° 13 de Kaliningrad.

In the yard of the A. I. Mikoyan meat processing factory. Loading of sausage products intended for the store "Gastronome" No.13 in Kaliningrad.

Im Hof des A. I. Mikojan-Fleischkombinats. Beim Verladen von Wurstwaren für den » Gastronom « Nr.13 in Kaliningrad.

Peu de temps après, je tombe enceinte et quand je lui annonce la nouvelle, il se fâche en disant qu'il ne veut pas de cet enfant. Je ne suis plus si jeune, je désire un enfant, d'autant plus que ma famille m'aiderait à l'élever. Mais puisqu'il n'en veut pas, mon désir n'est pas suffisamment fort et j'opte pour l'avortement. Je cache l'existence du mari, d'autant qu'il ne m'a pas proposé de régulariser notre situation et je déclare à l'hôpital, que je ne suis pas mariée. A vrai dire, c'est tout comme, sur le plan administratif. Je sais

Soon I became pregnant, and when I told him, he became indignant and said that he didn't need a child. I wasn't young and needed a child, especially since the children would help me raise it. But since he didn't want a child my wishes weren't sufficient, and I decided to have an abortion. I hid the fact that I had a husband, especially since he didn't offer to make it legal, and I went to the hospital having stated that I didn't have a husband. Actually, that's how it was officially. I know that

Bald wurde ich schwanger, und als ich ihm davon erzählte, regte er sich auf und sagte, er brauche kein Kind. Ich war nicht mehr so jung, ich brauchte ein Kind, auch hätten mir die Geschwister bei der Erziehung geholfen. Aber da er kein Kind wollte, reichte mein Wunsch nicht, und ich entschloß mich zu einer Abtreibung. Ich verheimlichte die Tatsache, daß ich einen Mann hatte, umso mehr, als wir nicht registriert waren, ging ins Krankenhaus und sagte, ich hätte keinen Mann. Offiziell war das ja auch so. Ich wußte,

Во дворе мясокомбината имени А. И. Микояна. Погрузка колбасных изделий, предназначенных для магазина «Гастроном» № 13 в Калининграде.

ко мне. Скоро я забеременела и когда я ему об этом сказала, он возмутился и сказал, что ребенок ему не нужен. Возраст был не малый, ребенок нужен был, тем более мне помогли бы дети его воспитать Но, раз он не хотел ребенка, мое желание было недостаточно и я решилась на аборт. Я скрыла, что у меня есть муж, тем более, что он не предлагал мне регистрироваться, и я пошла в больницу заявив, что мужа у меня нет. Собственно так официально оно и было. Я знаю, что

La Vie humiliée Life as an insult Leben als Erniedrigung Жизнь как оскорбление

Au rayon « Charcuterie » du magasin. A droite — la vendeuse Sérafima Danilova.

In the grocery department of the store. On the right is the sales clerk Serafima Danilova.

In der Lebensmittelabteilung des Kaufhauses. Rechts die Verkäuferin Serafima Danilowa.

que le premier avortement peut tourner mal, de plus, l'âge compte aussi, mais j'assume le risque. Je me sens profondément blessée et j'accepte le pire. Bien évidemment, cela tourne mal. J'ai une inflammation et j'en souffre longtemps. Quatre ans plus tard, je suis de nouveau enceinte et je lui déclare que je veux garder l'enfant. J'ai 31 ans. Je mets au monde un gros bébé. Dans les premiers temps, il hurle terriblement : il crie de faim. Je suis une mauvaise mère : le lait

the first abortion can end badly, plus my age was a factor, but I consciously took that risk. I was deeply hurt and took the risk. Of course, things didn't go smoothly. I had an inflammation and was ill for a long time. Four years went by before I got pregnant again, and then I told him that I wanted the child. I was 31 years old. I had a healthy child, he screamed terribly at first, but it turned out that he was crying from hunger. I was a bad mother and didn't have

daß die erste Abtreibung oft nicht gut geht, darüber hinaus sprach das Alter für sich, aber ich habe mich bewußt dazu entschlossen. Ich war zutiefst beleidigt und riskierte alles. Natürlich ging es nicht gut aus. Ich bekam eine Infektion und war lange krank. So vergingen 4 Jahre, bevor ich wieder schwanger wurde und da erklärte ich ihm, daß ich das Kind wolle. Ich war 31 Jahre alt. Ich gebar einen kräftigen Buben, der in der ersten Zeit fürchterlich schrie, bis sich herausstellte, daß er vor Hunger schrie. Ich war eine schlechte Mutter und hatte

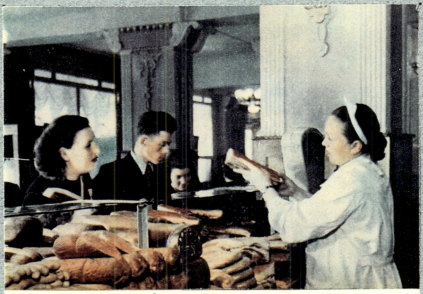
В гастрономическом отделе магазина. Справа — продавщица Серафима Данилова.

первый аборт может не благополучно кончиться, кроме того возраст говорил за себя и я сознательно пошла на это. Я была глубоко оскорблена и шла на все. Конечно это не кончилось благополучно. У меня было воспаление и долго болела. Так прошло 4 года, когда я снова забеременила и тогда заявила ему, что хочу ребенка. Мне было 31 год. Я родила крепыша, он первое время орал ужасно, но оказалось он плакал от голода. Я была плохая мать и молока

La Vie humiliée Life as an insult Leben als Erniedrigung Жизнь как оскорбление

Les bénéfices du magasin s'accroissent de jour en jour, affirme la caissière Maria Nazarova. Cela signifie que les Soviétiques achètent plus de produits et, qui plus est, des produits haut de gamme.

The receipts of the store get bigger and bigger each day, says the cashier Maria Nazarova. And that means that Soviet people are buying more and more products, and of high quality at that.

Die Einnahmen des Kaufhauses steigen jeden Tag, sagt die Kassierin Marija Nasarowa. Und das heißt, daß die Sowjetmenschen immer mehr Waren und immer bessere Qualität einkaufen.

manque. Mais j'y reviendrai plus tard. Je quitte la caisse d'assurances et j'entre comme secrétaire dans une école professionnelle. C'était avant le bébé. Dans les entreprises, on procède à l'épuration du personnel. Mon mari est un « lichéniets », c'est-à-dire qu'il est privé du droit de vote parce que son père était commerçant et que lui, il l'avait aidé. En arrivant à la séance de vérification, je tremble de peur puisque je suis la femme d'un « lichéniets », bien qu'officiellement ce ne soit pas le cas. Mais je m'en tire impeccablement. Les remarques

enough milk. But more about that later. I left the Insurance Bureau and went to work at the vocational school as a secretary. There was a purge of the staff. My husband's status was that of a "disenfranchised person", ie. he didn't have the right to vote since his father was a merchant and he helped him. When I went to the inspection I was shaking all over, after all, I was the wife of a "disenfranchised person", even though I wasn't his wife legally. I passed the inspection impeccably. The comments from the auditorium,

zuwenig Milch. Aber davon später. Ich verließ die Versicherung und begann, in einer Berufsschule als Sekretärin zu arbeiten. Das Kind war noch nicht da. Bei uns fand eine Säuberung aller Angestellten des Sowjetapparates statt. Der Gesetzeslage nach war mein Mann »nicht wahlberechtigt« (und aller bürgerlichen Rechte beraubt), weil sein Vater ein Händler war und er ihm half. Als ich zur Kontrolle ging, zitterte alles in mir, ich war ja die Frau eines »Nichtwahlberechtigten«, obwohl ich offiziell nicht seine Frau war. Die Säuberung durchlief ich makellos. Die Beurteilungen waren ausgezeichnet,

— Выручка магазина с каждым днем становится все больше, — говорит кассирша Мария Назарова. — А это значит, что советские люди покупают все больше продуктов, и притом самого высокого качества.

было недостаточно. Но об этом позже. Я ушла из Страховой кассы и поступила в профессиональное училище секретаршей. Еще ребенка не было. У нас проходила чистка соваппарата. По положению муж был "лишенец", т.е. не имел права голоса, т.к. отец его был торговец а он ему помогал. Когда я вышла на проверку, все во мне дрожало, ведь я была жена "лишенца", хотя официально я не числилась его женой. Прошла я чистку безукоризненно. Отзыва с мест,

Ici, les clients trouvent toujours un grand choix de confiseries et de pâtisseries, des marques allant des plus chères au meilleur marché.

Here consumers always find a large selection of candy and cookies — from the most expensive sort to the cheapest.

Hier finden die Käufer immer eine reiche Auswahl an Konfekt und Backwaren — von den teursten bis zu den billigsten Sorten.

de la salle — et il y a foule — sont des plus favorables. Ainsi, un ouvrier affirme : « si l'on avait davantage d'employés de ce genre »! Personne ne me connaît à mon nouveau lieu de travail. Les vacances approchent et mon mari me propose d'aller dans sa famille qui vient de s'installer pas loin de Dniépropétrovsk. Comme c'est moi qui ai tous les papiers, je prends mes livrets de travail sans autorisation et je pars faire la connaissance de ma nouvelle famille. Parmi mes responsabilités, il y a celle de fournir aux soviets de villages des informations sur les élèves qui entrent à l'école : sur leur origine sociale,

and it was full, were the best, and one worker said: "we need more people like her working for us". No one knew me at this new job. Vacation time approached and my husband suggested I go to the settlement near Dnepropetrovsk where his parents had been relocated. Since I had all my documents, I took my employment record book without permission and went to meet his parents. In my work I had to write to village councils about students who were applying: to what social class

obwohl der Saal voll war, ein Arbeiter sagte sogar: » Wenn wir nur mehr solche Angestellte hätten «. An der neuen Stelle kannte mich niemand. Die Urlaubszeit näherte sich, und mein Mann schlug mir vor, in die Siedlung bei Dnepropetrovsk zu fahren, wo seine Familie hingezogen war. Da ich alle Dokumente bei mir hatte, nahm ich mein Arbeitsbuch ohne Erlaubnis und fuhr hin, um seine Familie kennenzulernen. Meine Arbeit brachte es mit sich, daß ich an die Dorfsowjets schreiben mußte, um Auskünfte über die neuen Schüler einzuholen: welchem Stand sie angehören —

Здесь покупатели всегда находят богатый выбор конфет и печенья — от самых дорогих сортов до самых дешевых.

а зал был полон, самые лучшие, даже один рабочий сказал "побольше бы таких служащих было у нас". На новом месте меня никто не знал. Близилось время отпуска и муж предложил поехать в колонию, куда переселились его родные под Днепропетровском. Так как все документы были у меня, я взяла свои трудовые книжки без разрешения и поехала знакомиться с родными. По роду своей работы мне приходилось писать в сельсоветы о поступающих учениках к какому сословию

La Vendeuse du rayon « Laiterie » Claudia Bouslova met au réfrigérateur électrique des bouteilles de lait livrées du dépôt.

The sales clerk from the dairy department, Klavdia Buslova, arranges bottles of milk delivered from the depot in the electric refrigerator.

Die in der Milchabteilung tätige Verkäuferin Klavdija Buslowa stellt die angelieferten Milchflachen in den elektrischen Kühlschrank.

savoir par exemple, s'ils sont issus de familles de koulaks, de paysans pauvres ou de paysans moyens. Comment puis-je le faire, alors que moi-même, je vis avec un « lichéniets » ? Cela me travaille et je décide de partir. J'ai le papier attestant que je suis en permission ainsi que mes livrets de travail. Pendant le voyage, je fais la connaissance d'une famille — le mari, la femme et leurs filles — qui rentrent chez eux, à Dniépropétrovsk. Ils me demandent qui je suis et où je vais, et je leur cache involontairement que je suis mariée en leur disant que je me rends chez des amis. Ils me laissent leur adresse

they belonged — kulaks (rich peasants), poor or middle. How was I supposed to write this, when I myself lived with a "disenfranchised" person. This was terrible for me, and I decided to quit that job. I had a certificate that I was on vacation, and my employment record. On the way I met one family — husband, wife, and girls, who were going home to Dnepropetrovsk. They asked me who I was and where I was going, and I involuntarily hid the fact that I was married, and said that I was going to visit friends. They gave me their address

Kulaken, Arme, mittlere Bauern. Wie konnte ich solche Brief schreiben, wenn ich selbst mit einem »Nichtwahlberechtigten« zusammenlebte. Das war schrecklich für mich, und ich beschloß, diese Arbeit aufzugeben. Ich hatte eine Urlaubsbestätigung und die Arbeitsbücher. Auf der Reise lernte ich eine Familie kennen, eine Ehepaar mit Mädchen, die nach Hause fuhren, nach Dnepropetrovsk. Sie erkundigten sich, wer ich sei und wohin ich fahre, und unwillkürlich verschwieg ich, daß ich verheiratet war und sagte, ich fahre auf Besuch zu Bekannten. Sie gaben mir ihre Adresse

Работающая в молочном отделе продавщица Клавдия Буслова устанавливает в электрический холодильник доставленные с базы бутылки с молоком.

они приходятся - кулаки, бедняки, середняки. Как же мне было писать, когда я сама жила с лишенцем. Это было для меня ужасно и я решила уйти с этой работы. У меня была справка, что я в отпуске и трудовые книжки. В дороге я познакомилась с одной семьей - муж жена и девочки, которые ехали к себе домой в Днепропетровск. Они меня распросили кто я и куда еду и я невольно скрыла, что я замужняя и сказала, что еду в гости к знакомым. Они дали мне свой адрес

La Vie humiliée Life as an insult Leben als Erniedrigung Жизнь как оскорбление

Vendeuses d'épicerie se préparant à l'ouverture du magasin.

Sales clerks from the dry-goods department prepare for the opening of the store.

Die Verkäuferinnen der Kolonialwarenabteilung bereiten sich auf die Öffnung des Geschäftes vor.

en m'invitant à passer au retour chez eux et à visiter les curiosités de Dniépropétrovsk. Les parents de mon mari m'accueillent bien. J'aime surtout sa mère. Je la trouve si gentille, je fais de mon mieux pour l'aider au ménage. Les frères et la sœur de mon mari travaillent aux champs. L'heure du départ approche. Pendant ce temps, Riva doit tenir la maison toute seule, elle sait déjà faire la cuisine. On n'a plus de femme de ménage. Mon mari vit avec nous. Tout est comme avant. Je leur ai laissé mon allocation de congé et je suis partie pour

and invited me to visit them on the way back to take in the sights in Dnepropetrovsk. My husband's parents treated me well. I particularly liked his mother. She was very cordial, and I helped around the house with whatever I could. My husband's brothers and sister worked in the fields. The time approached for my departure. I left Riva in charge, she could cook by then. We didn't have a housekeeper anymore. My husband was still with us. Nothing had changed. I left my vacation money and went

und luden mich ein, sie auf dem Rückweg zu besuchen und Dnepropetrovsk zu besichtigen. Die Familie meines Mannes empfing mich sehr freundlich. Besonders die Mutter gefiel mir. Sie war so liebenswürdig, ich half ihr im Haushalt, soviel ich konnte. Die Brüder und Schwestern meines Mannes arbeiteten auf den Feldern. Die Abreise rückte näher. Riva führte den Haushalt, sie konnte schon kochen. Haushaltshilfe hatten wir keine mehr. Mein Mann blieb bei uns. Nichts änderte sich. Ich hatte mein Urlaubsgeld zurückgelassen und war für

Продавщицы бакалейного отдела готовятся к открытию магазина.

и просили на обратном пути заехать к ним посмотреть на достопримечательности Днепроптровска. Родные мужа меня хорошо встретили Особенно мне понравилась мать. Такая приветливая, я ей помогала в хозяйстве, чем могла. Братья и сестра мужа работали в поле. Близилось время уезжать. На хозяйстве оставалась Рива, она уже могла готовить. Домработницы больше не было. Муж оставался с нами. Ничто не изменилось Я оставила свои отпускные деньги и поехала на

La Vie humiliée Life as an insult Leben als Erniedrigung Жизнь как оскорбление

Le marbre de Koelga est utilisé pour le revêtement des colonnes et des murs de certaines stations de métro à Moscou. Sur la photo — la station Kourskaïa-ceinture couverte de ce marbre.

Koelga marble was used for the facing on the columns and walls of a few of the Moscow metro stations. On the photo: Kurskaya Station on the ring line, decorated with this marble.

Für die Wandverkleidung einiger Moskauer U-Bahnstationen wurde Koelgin-Marmor verwendet. Auf dem Bild die Station Kurskaja-Kolzewaja mit diesem Marmor.

15 jours. Mais en réalité, les choses prennent une autre tournure. Les vacances touchent à leur fin, il ne me reste que quelques jours et j'ai l'idée d'aller à l'adresse qu'on m'a laissée et voir un peu Dniépropétrovsk. Mes connaissances me reçoivent gentiment et la dame me convainc de rester à Dniépropétrovsk. Elle me permet de vivre chez elle. En face, se trouvent les bureaux d'une entreprise du bâtiment; sur son conseil, j'y vais avec mes papiers, sans me proposer toutefois de demander un emploi. Je demande au chef comptable s'il y a un poste vacant: il

for two weeks. But everything turned out to be quite different. Vacation was ending, only a few days were left, and I decided to visit the address I had and see Dnepropetrovsk. I was well received, and the wife tried to persuade me to stay in Dnepropetrovsk. She would let me live with her, and across from their house they were building a trust, and having listened to her, I grabbed my documents and went to the trust, not thinking that I might go to work there. I asked the head accountant whether there was a vacancy, he

zwei Wochen weggefahren. Aber in Wirklichkeit war alles ganz anders. Der Urlaub ging zu Ende, es blieben noch ein paar Tage, und ich beschloß, nach Dnepropetrovsk zu meinen Bekannten zu fahren. Ich wurde gut aufgenommen, und die Frau begann mich zu überreden, in Dnepropetrovsk zu bleiben. Wohnen sollte ich bei ihnen, gegenüber war eine Großbaustelle, ich hörte auf sie, nahm meine Dokumente und ging ins Baubüro, ohne an Arbeit zu denken. Ich fragte den Hauptbuchhalter nach einer freien Stelle, er

Для облицовки колонн и стен нескольких станций московского метрополитена был использован коелгинский мрамор. На снимке — станция Курская-кольцевая, отделанная этим мрамором.

2 недели. Но все оказалось на самом деле по другому. Заканчивался отпуск, осталось несколько дней и я решила поехать по адресу и посмотреть Днепропетровск. Меня хорошо приняли и хозяйка стала уговаривать меня остаться в Днепропетровске. Жить она разрешила у нее, напротив дома строился строительный трест и я ее послушав захватив документы, зашла в трест, не думая поступать туда на работу. Я спросила главного бухгалтера, есть ли вакансия, он

Il y a toujours une forte demande de primeurs et de légumes. Pour la commodité des clients le magasin organise une vente supplémentaire de légumes à l'extérieur.

There is particularly large demand for the first fresh vegetables. For the convenience of the customers, the store has arranged for the additional sale of vegetables outside on the street.

Nach dem ersten Frischgemüse herrscht besonders große Nachfrage. Um den Käufern entgegenzukommen, hat das Geschäft einen zusätzlichen Gemüseverkauf auf der Strasse eingerichtet.

me prend mes documents, les met dans son tiroir et me dit de commencer le lendemain. Je suis prise au dépourvu par cette proposition inattendue et je le dis à mon hôtesse. Elle est ravie et elle garde mes papiers pour me faire enregistrer. Le lendemain, je me mets au travail, mais en rentrant, je trouve l'appartement fermé. La clé m'attend chez la voisine. Sur la table, je découvre mes papiers avec le permis de séjour et un petit mot, comme quoi ils sont tous partis à la campagne pour 15 jours. Je m'installe donc à Dniépropétrovsk. Je m'acquitte de mon travail. Je tiens

asked for my documents and having placed them in his desk ordered me to report to work the next day. I was taken aback by the unexpected offer and told the wife so. She was thrilled and took my documents to get a living registration. The next day I started work, and upon coming home I found the apartment locked. She had given the key to a neighbor. On the table were my documents with a living permit and a note that they had left for the country for two weeks. And so I became a resident of Dnepropetrovsk. I was capable of the work. I kept

verlangte meine Dokumente und sagte, morgen könne ich anfangen. Ich war verblüfft von dem überraschenden Angebot und erzählte der Frau davon. Sie freute sich und nahm gleich meine Dokumente, um mich anzumelden. Nächsten Tag ging ich zur Arbeit, und als ich nach Hause kam, fand ich die Wohnung verschlossen. Den Schlüssel hatte sie einer Nachbarin gegeben. Auf dem Tisch waren die Dokumente mit der Anmeldung und eine Mitteilung, sie seien für zwei Wochen aufs Land gefahren. So wurde ich eine Bewohnerin von Dnepropetrovsk. Die Arbeit fiel mir nicht schwer. Ich führte

Первые свежие овощи пользуются особенно большим спросом. Для удобства покупателей магазин организовал дополнительную продажу овощей на улице.

попросил документы и положив их в стол, велел на завтра выйти на работу. Я была огорошена неожиданным предложением и сказала об этом хозяйке. Она обрадовалась и взяла мои документы на прописку. На завтра я вышла на работу, а придя домой нашла квартиру запертой. Ключ она вручила соседке. На столе были документы с пропиской, и записка, что они все поехали на 2 недели в деревню. Итак я стала жительницей Днепропетровска. Работа мне была по силам. Я вела

La Vie humiliée Life as an insult Leben als Erniedrigung Жизнь как оскорбление

Lors d'un arrêt du navire diesel-électrique.

During one of the stops of the diesel-electric ship.

Das Dieselmotorschiff bei einem Halt.

le registre de la caisse. Je déjeune à la cantine. Tout d'un coup, se retrouver seule, dans une ville inconnue, sans mari ni enfants — cela me fait peur. J'écoute la radio, je lis. Je crains de sortir seule. Une femme âgée qui vient à la cantine chercher les repas en même temps que moi, me dit bonjour et insiste pour que je vienne chez elle. Elle me raconte qu'elle vit seule avec son mari. Je ne sais plus pourquoi, mais de nouveau, je cache le fait que je suis mariée. Elle fait preuve d'une telle insistance, que je suis

the accounts book. I ate at the trust's cafeteria. After everything I was alone in an unfamiliar city, without my husband, without the children. That was frightening. I listened to the radio, read. I was afraid to go out alone. An elderly woman used to come to the cafeteria at the same time as I did and would take lunch home, she began to greet me and adamantly invited me to visit her. She said that she lived with just her husband. For some reason I also told her that I wasn't married. She was so persistent,

das Kassabuch. Ich aß in der Kantine. Nach all der Zeit war ich allein in einer fremden Stadt, ohne Mann, ohne Kinder. Das war schrecklich. Ich hörte Radio und las. Ich fürchtete mich, allein irgendwohin zu gehen. In der Kantine traf ich mit einer älteren Frau zusammen, die Essen nach Hause mitnahm, wir begannen uns zu grüßen und sie lud mich nachdrücklich zu sich nach Hause ein. Sie sagte, sie lebe allein mit ihrem Mann. Ich erwähnte ihr gegenüber auch nicht, daß ich verheiratet war. Sie war so beharrlich, daß ich

Во время одной из стоянок дизельэлектрохода.

кассовую книгу. Питалась в столовой треста. После всего оказаться одной в незнакомом городе без мужа, без детей. Это было страшно. Я включала радио, читала. Ходить куда нибудь боялась одна. В столовую в одно время со мной приходила пожилая женщина и брала обеды на дом, она стала со мной здороваться и усиленно приглашала к себе в гости. Говорила, что живет только с мужем. Ей я тоже почему то тоже не сказала, что я замужем. Она так была настойчива, что мне

La Vie humiliée Life as an insult Leben als Erniedrigung Жизнь как оскорбление

C'est à bord du « Russie » que se sont rencontrés et ont sympatisé I. I. Abrossimov, président du kolkhoze « Gorchikha » de la région de Yaroslavl (à droite) et V. N. Vlassov, metteur en scène du Théâtre dramatique de Moscou et artiste émérite de la Fédération de la Russie. Le premier va se reposer au sanatorium « Kinechma », l'autre — à « Plios », une maison de repos pour artistes. Les deux sanatoriums sont situés sur la rive de la Volga.

The chairman of the collective farm "Gorshikha" of the Yaroslav region, Hero of Socialist Labor I. I. Abrosimov (on the right) and the director of the Moscow Drama Theater, Honoured actor of the Russian Federation V. N. Vlasov meet and become friends on board the ship "Russia". The first is going to the sanatorium "Kineshma", the second is going to "Ples", house of rest for workers of art. Both of these sanatoria are located on the banks of the Volga.

An Bord der » Rossia « haben sie sich kennengelernt und angefreundet: der Vorsitzende des Kolchos » Gorschicha « im Jaroslavsker Gebiet, I. I. Abrosimov, Held der Sozialistischen Arbeit, und der Regisseur des Moskauer Dramatischen Theaters, V. N. Vlasov, Verdienter Künstler der Russischen Föderation. Der eine fährt ins Sanatorium » Kineschma «, der andere ins » Ples «, Erholungsheim für Künstler. Beide Sanatorien liegen am Ufer der Wolga.

obligée d'accepter son invitation. Je vais la voir d'autant plus volontiers que je ne connais personne dans cette ville. Il se trouve qu'elle a un fils. Divorcé d'avec sa femme. On fait connaissance et on se promène dans la ville. Il est très délicat avec moi. Il me raconte bien des choses intéressantes et on apprécie les moments partagés. Il vient me voir, mais ma propriétaire le prend en grippe, sans raisons apparentes. Je communique mon adresse aux enfants et mon mari vient me rejoindre. Du coup, la propriétaire m'ordonne

that I had to accept her invitation and visit her, all the more since I had no friends. It turned out that she had a son. He was divorced from his wife. We met and started to go about the city together. He was very polite to me. He told me lots of things, and we enjoyed our time together. He visited me, and the wife hated him, although there was no reason for this. I wrote my address to the children, and one fine day my husband arrived. The wife immediately threw

ihre Einladung annehmen mußte und zu ihr ging, umso mehr, als ich keine Bekannten hatte. Es stellte sich heraus, daß sie einen Sohn hatte. Er hatte sich scheiden lassen. Wir lernten einander kennen und gingen in der Stadt spazieren. Er war sehr höflich zu mir. Er erzählte viel Interessantes, und wir genossen die gemeinsame Zeit. Er kam mich besuchen, aber meine Hausfrau konnte ihn nicht leiden, obwohl es keinerlei Grund gab. Ich schrieb den Kindern meine Adresse und an eines schönen Tages kam mein Mann zu mir. Sofort wurde ich aus der Wohnung

На борту «России» познакомились и подружились председатель колхоза «Горшиха», Ярославской области, Герой Социалистического Труда И. И. Абросимов (справа) и режиссер Московского театра драмы заслуженный артист Российской Федерации В. Н. Власов. Первый из них едет в санаторий «Кинешма», второй — в «Плёс», дом отдыха работников искусств. Обе эти здравницы расположены на берегу Волги.

пришлось принять приглашение и пойти к ней, тем более, что знакомых у меня не было. Оказалось у неё был сын. Он развелся со своей женой. Мы познакомились и стали бродить по городу. Он был очень вежлив со мной. Много рассказывал интересного и мы наслаждались проведенным временем. Он заходил ко мне и хозяйка возненавидела его, хотя причин никаких не было. Я написала детям свой адрес и в один прекрасный день муж приехал ко мне. Хозяйка тут же отказала

La Vie humiliée Life as an insult Leben als Erniedrigung Жизнь как оскорбление

A bord du « Russie ». Le tourneur de l'Usine d'appareils électriques de Tcheboksary Nina Spassova et la fonctionnaire du Ministère de la flotte fluviale et maritime, l'ingénieur Nadejda Amélina (à droite).

On the deck of the "Russia". The lathe operator from Cheboksary Electric Appliance Factory, Nina Spasova, and an employee of the Maritime and River Fleet of the USSR, engineer Nadezhda Emelina (on the right).

Auf dem Deck der » Rossija «. Die Dreherin der Elektroapparatefabrik von Tscheboksari, Nina Spasowa, und die Mitarbeiterin des Ministeriums für Meer- und Binnenschiffahrt, Ingenieur Nadjeschda Jemelina (rechts).

de partir. Je me précipite chez mes nouveaux amis en les priant de nous héberger dans les premiers temps, mais ils changent complètement dès qu'ils apprennent que mon mari est là. Ils m'interdisent leur demeure. Dans la même cour, habite une famille juive; je leur demande de nous loger provisoirement et ils me louent leur cuisine d'été. Revoilà donc mon mari à mes côtés. J'ai cru que nous nous étions séparés à tout jamais, eh bien non. Un jour, je croise dans la rue une ancienne copine de Marioupol qui m'aide à

me out. I ran to my new friends for a place to stay in the beginning, but they became unrecognizable when they learned that I had a husband. I was immediately banned from their home. There was a Jewish family on the block, and I asked them to take us in for a while, and they rented me their summer kitchen. And so, my husband was with me again. I thought that we had parted forever, but that didn't happen. I ran into my former girlfriend from Mariupole on the street, and she helped me

hinausgewiesen. Ich eilte zu meinen neuen Bekannten und bat sie, uns für eine kurze Zeit aufzunehmen, aber sie waren nicht wiederzuerkennen, als sie erfuhren, daß mein Mann gekommen sei. Mir wurde sofort das Haus verboten. Im Hof lebte eine jüdische Familie, ich wandte mich an sie, und sie stellten uns ihre Veranda zur Verfügung. Also war mein Mann wieder bei mir. Ich hatte gedacht, wir hätten uns für immer getrennt, aber so war es nicht. Auf der Straße traf ich meine frühere Freundin aus Mariupol und sie half mir,

На палубе «России». Токарь Чебоксарского завода электроаппаратуры Нина Спасова и сотрудница Министерства морского и речного флота СССР инженер Надежда Емелина (справа).

мне в квартире. Я бросилась к моим новым моим знакомым приютить нас на первых порах, но их было не узнать, когда они узнали, что приехал мой муж. Мне тут же было отказано от дома. Во дворе жила еврейская семья, я обратилась к ним приютить нас на время и они сдали мне летнюю кухню. Итак муж был со мной снова. Я думала что мы расстались навсегда, но это не произошло. Я встретила на улице мою бывшую подругу из Мариуполя и она помогла мне

E. P. Bélova fait goûter à ses invités sa propre eau-de-vie de prunes et le miel apporté récemment des ruchers.

E. P. Belova treats her guests to home-brewed plum brandy and honey fresh from the apiary.

E. P. Belowa bewirtet die Gäste mit Pflaumenlikör aus eigener Erzeugung und mit Honig frisch aus der Imkerei.

trouver une chambre. Nous déménageons dans la rue Animée. Une jolie chambre spacieuse. Sauf que le fils des propriétaires, un adolescent, est un fripon. Il dévore toutes nos provisions pendant que nous travaillons car la chambre ne se ferme pas. On hésite à la fermer à clef, mais plus tard, quand je la cadenasse, il dévisse l'anneau et continue à nous dévaliser sans scrupules. Il est impossible de garder des provisions. On ne dit rien à sa mère. Mais une autre famille la persuade de leur louer notre chambre en

find a room. We moved into a place on Bojkaya Street. It was a good, large room. Only the teenage son turned out to be a petty thief. He would eat our food while we were at work, the room wasn't locked. It was awkward to lock it, and then even after I began to do so, he still broke in and stole things shamelessly. It was impossible to keep food. We didn't say anything to the mother. But then a family convinced her to let them have our big room,

ein Zimmer zu finden. Wir zogen in die Bojkaja Straße, in ein schönes großes Zimmer. Nur der halbwüchsige Sohn war ein diebischer Geselle. Es aß immer unsere Vorräte auf, wenn wir in der Arbeit waren, weil sich das Zimmer nicht absperren ließ. Absperren war erstens peinlich, und als ich dann doch absperrte, schraubte er das Schloß ab und stahl unbeirrt weiter. Man konnte nichts Eßbares im Haus lassen. Der Mutter sagten wir nichts. Da begann eine Familie die Hausfrau zu überreden, sie in unser großes Zimmer einziehen zu lassen

Е. П. Белова угощает гостей сливянкой своего приготовления и медом, только что принесенным с пасеки.

найти комнату. Мы поселились по улице Бойкой. В хорошей большой комнате. Только сын подросток оказался мелким воришкой. Он поедал всю нашу провизию, когда мы были на работе, комната не запиралась'. Было неловко ее запирать, а потом, когда уже стала запирать, он выворачивал кольца и все равно тащил без совести. Провизию держать было не возможно. Матери мы ничего не говорили. Но вот одна семья уговорила хозяйку, чтобы она их пустила в нашу большую комна-

Après le bain.

After a swim.

Nach dem Bad.

proposant un loyer plus élevé. Elle nous transfère dans une autre pièce, moins grande, et leur donne notre chambre, mais là, elle se fait avoir : ils versent le premier loyer comme convenu ; ensuite ils la paient selon les tarifs en vigueur, en consignant les sommes. Une façon de la punir de sa cupidité. A cette époque, je suis enceinte à nouveau et me décide à garder l'enfant coûte que coûte, même malgré mon mari. Cela se passe en 1933, le 30.9. Je m'épanouis durant ma grossesse. Je porte l'enfant sans peine et avec beaucoup de joie. Pas d'idées

promising to pay her more than we did. She moved us to another, smaller room, but they tricked her and paid for only one month as agreed and then began to pay according to state standards and to pay in installments. So, they really got her for her greediness. By that time I was pregnant again, and I decided to have the baby, even against my husband's wishes. That was in 1933, 30.IX. I really blossomed during my pregnancy. I had an easy and happy time. I had no bad

und versprachen ihr, mehr als wir zu zahlen. Sie überließ uns ein anderes, kleineres Zimmer, während die in unser Zimmer zogen, aber sie legten sie herein und zahlten ihr nur ein Monat wie abgemacht, dann zahlten den staatlich festgelegten Preis und trugen ihr Geld auf die Bank. So wurde sie wegen ihrer Geldgier hereingelegt. Zu dieser Zeit wurde ich wieder schwanger und beschloß, das Kind zu haben, auch gegen den Willen meines Mannes. Das war im Jahr 1933, 30. Sept. In der Schwangerschaft blühte ich auf, ich fühlte mich leicht und froh. Ich hatte keinerlei schlechte

Альб — ц/н N 70　　　　　　　　　　　　　　　　　70

После купанья.

ту, обещая платить больше чем мы платим. Она переселила нас в другую маленькую комнату, а их пустила, но они еще схитрили, уплатили ей только за один месяц по уговору, а потом стали платить по госуд.стоимости и вносить в депозит. Так они ее перехитрили за ее жадность. К этому времени я снова забеременела и решила иметь ребенка, даже вопреки желанию мужа. Это было в 1933 году, 30. IX Расцвела я во время беременности. Носила легко и радостно. Никаких

Le couple Bélov s'adonne à l'apiculture.

The Belov couple love bee-keeping with a passion.

Das Ehepaar Below widmet sich mit Begeisterung der Bienenzucht.

noires. L'accouchement dure longtemps, deux jours, mais le bébé, dodu et robuste, fait notre joie. Peu après, il a besoin d'une nourriture plus abondante et on passe à l'allaitement mixte. Le congé de maternité terminé, je reprends mon travail. C'est dur. Sans parents. Sans expérience. Je regrette de ne pas l'avoir eu plus tôt, quand mes frères et sœurs étaient à mes côtés. Je travaille loin de chez moi, je ne peux pas allaiter le bébé moi-même, d'autant plus

thoughts. I was in labor a long time, two days, but a healthy baby was born to our joy. He quickly began to demand more food, and I had to supplement his feedings. I went back to work immediately after my maternity leave. It was difficult for me. I had no relatives nearby. I had no experience. How I regretted not having a baby sooner when I had the children with me. I worked far from home and couldn't nurse him, and he gradually was weaned, especially since

Gedanken. Die Geburt dauerte lange, zwei Tage, aber ich gebar einen kräftigten Buben, der uns eine Freude war. Bald forderte er mehr Nahrung und ich mußte ihm zufüttern. Gleich nach dem festgesetzten Urlaub ging ich wieder arbeiten. Es war sehr schwer für mich. Es gab niemand, der mir nahestand. Ich hatte keinerlei Erfahrung. Wie leid es mir tat, nicht früher ein Kind gehabt zu haben, als die Kinder noch bei mir waren. Meine Arbeitsstelle war weit von der Wohnung entfernt, ich konnte ihn nicht stillen, und er entwöhnte sich nach und nach der Brust, umso mehr,

Супруги Беловы с увлечением занимаются пчеловодством.

плохих мыслей не было. Рожала долго, двое суток, но родился крепыш, крупный на радость нам. Скоро начал требовать усиленного питания и пришлось его прикармливать. Работать я пошла сразу после положенного отпуска. Очень трудно мне было. Никого из близких. Опыта никакого.   Как я жалела, что раньше не родила, когда были со мной мои дети. Нработала далеко от дома, кормить его не имела возможности и он постепенно отвык от моего кормления, тем более,

Comme il est bon de faire la sieste en plein air! Mais il ne faut pas oublier l'heure, et Zoïa rappelle à son père qu'ils ont prévu une promenade dans les bois.

How sweet it is to sleep in the fresh air after lunch! But there's a time for everything, and Zoya has decided to remind her father that they had agreed to go for a walk in the woods.

An der frischen Luft schläft es sich gut nach dem Mittagessen! Aber alles hat seine Zeit, und Zoja beschloß, den Vater daran zu erinnern, daß sie zusammen in den Wald spazieren wollten.

que mon lait ne suffit pas. D'abord, la grand-mère des voisins, ceux qui ont emménagé dans notre chambre, le surveille, à condition de ne pas le prendre dans ses bras: il doit rester dans son berceau jusqu'à notre retour du bureau. Il est très vif: ce n'est pas pour rien que nous habitons la Rue Animée! Le père de mon mari insiste pour le faire circoncire. Les femmes de ménage réapparaissent pour garder le petit. Une fois, l'automne est déjà avancé, la femme de ménage ouvre la fenêtre — nous sommes toujours chez la même

my milk wasn't very good. At first the neighbor's grandmother looked after him, who moved into the room next door, and we set the condition that she wouldn't try to lift him, that he would lay in bed until we came home from work. He was very lively, it's no wonder we lived on Lively Street. At the insistence of my husband's father we had him circumcised. We started to take on housekeepers who looked after the baby. Once, in late fall, the housekeeper opened the window, (we still lived at the same place

als die Milch nicht ausreichte. Anfangs sah die Großmutter der Familie, die ins große Zimmer eingezogen waren, nach ihm, aber mit der Auflage, daß sie ihn nicht aus dem Bett nimmt, bevor wir nicht nach Hause kommen. Er war ein sehr lebhafter Bub. Auf Anraten des Vaters meines Mannes wurde die Beschneidung vollzogen. Wieder begannen wir Haushaltshilfen zu haben, die nach dem Kleinen schauten. Einmal, im Spätherbst, öffnete die Haushaltshilfe das Fenster, wir lebten bei derselben

Сладко спится на воздухе после обеда! Но всему свое время, и Зоя решила напомнить отцу, что они условились идти гулять в лес.

что мое молоко было не полноценным. Сначала за ним смотрела бабушка соседей, что поселилась в большой комнате, но с уговором, что она подмывать его не станет, он будет лежать в постели пока мы не придем с работы. Он был очень бойкий, недаром мы жили на улице Бойкой. По настоянию отца мужа совершили обрезание. Начались домработницы, которые смотрели за маленьким. Однажды глубокой осенью, домработница открыла окно, а мы жили у той же

La Vie humiliée Life as an insult Leben als Erniedrigung Жизнь как оскорбление

A. I. Rodionov est venu au kolkhoze « Mémoire d'Ilitch » pour informer les paysans sur les avantages importants prévus par la nouvelle Loi sur la taxe agricole.

A. I. Rodionov has arrived at the collective farm "Memory of Ilich" to tell the peasants about the great advantages provided for in the new Agricultural Tax Law.

A. I. Rodionov kam in den Kolchos » Andenken an Iljitsch «, um den Bauern von den großen Privilegien zu erzählen, welche das neue Gesetz über die Landwirtschaftssteuer vorsicht.

propriétaire, mais désormais nous occupons deux pièces — et moi, qui ne le sais pas, je lave le bébé et j'entre avec lui dans la chambre où la fenêtre est ouverte ; du coup il attrape une pneumonie. Il a six mois. Il tombe souvent malade, je renvoie la fille et je confie l'enfant aux soins de la propriétaire. La peur de retrouver mon enfant malade ne me quitte jamais. Peu de temps après, on le met à la crèche. Il met longtemps à s'habituer aux conditions de la crèche. Je l'arrache de moi à grand-peine et, en larmes, je me précipite

and occupied two rooms), I didn't know it and I bathed the baby and brought him into the room with the open window, and he got pneumonia. He was a half year old. He started to get sick frequently, and I didn't use a housekeeper anymore, leaving the baby in the hands of the landlady. I lived in constant fear that I would come home to find him sick. Soon we had to give him over to nursery school. He couldn't get used to it for a long time. I had a hard time tearing him away from me and would leave for work in tears,

Frau und hatten zwei Zimmer gemietet, und ich badete das Kind und trug es nichtsahnend ins Zimmer mit dem offenen Fenster, und er erkrankte sofort an Lungenentzündung. Er war ein halbes Jahr alt. Er wurde öfter krank, Haushaltshilfe hielt ich keine mehr, ich überließ das Kind nur mehr der Hausfrau. Ich lebte in ewiger Angst, ihn bei meiner Rückkehr krank vorzufinden. Bald mußte ich ihn in die Kinderkrippe bringen. Daran wollte er sich lange nicht gewöhnen. Mit Mühe riess ich ihn von mir los und ging in Tränen aufgelöst

А. И. Родионов приехал в колхоз «Память Ильича», чтобы рассказать крестьянам о больших льготах, которые предусматривает новый Закон о сельскохозяйственном налоге.

хозяйки, и занимали две комнаты, а я, ничего не знаю, выкупала ребенка и внесла в комнату с открытым окном и он тут же заболел воспалением легких. Ему было 1/2 года. Он стал часто болеть, домработницу я больше не держала, оставляя ребенка на руках хозяйки и жила в вечном страхе, что я его не застану здоровым дома. Скоро пришлось его отдать в ясли. Он долго не привыкал к обстановке яслей, и с трудом отрывала его от себя и вся в слезах уходила

La Vie humiliée   Life as an insult   Leben als Erniedrigung   Жизнь как оскорбление

Ensemble de chants et danses « Russie ».

The vocal-choreography ensemble "Russia".

Das Sing- und Tanzensemble » Rus «.

au bureau; mais quand je viens le chercher, je le retrouve par terre, sanglotant au milieu des enfants qui jouent. Les maîtresses me conseillent de le garder à la maison jusqu'à la maternelle, mais mon mari s'oppose farouchement à ce que j'arrête de travailler. C'est une période très difficile. Mon mari ne m'aide en rien. Les jours de repos, je dois être en même temps à la cave et au grenier. Le matin faire les courses au marché, allumer le four, faire le déjeuner et le ménage. Je n'ai plus de jambes. Lui, il ne veut pas m'aider. Il fait la grasse matinée, se repose, et je n'ose rien lui dire. Je crains ses colères, ses cris et ses réprimandes. Mon fils tombe souvent malade et chaque rhume se solde par une pneumonie. Il est très intelligent. Il apprend de longs poèmes, il suffit de les lui lire deux ou trois fois. Il est la gloire de la crèche. Il commence à lire

and when I would come for him I would find him crying on the floor while the other children were playing. The teachers advised me to keep him home, until he could go to kindergarten, but my husband didn't want to hear a word about me quitting my job. It was a difficult time. On my day off I was torn in a million directions. In the morning the market, heating the stove, cooking supper, laundry, cleaning the apartment. I was literally dead on my feet. He didn't want to help me. He would sleep late, relax, I didn't dare say anything to him. I was afraid of his dissatisfaction, yells and reproaches. My son was sick often, and every time it ended in pneumonia. He was mentally well developed. He knew long poems, all you had to do was read them to him a few times. He really brightened up the nursery school. He began to read

zur Arbeit, und wenn ich ihn holen kam, saß er weinend am Boden, während die anderen Kinder spielten. Die Erzieherinnen rieten mir, ihn zu Hause zu behalten, bis er alt genug sei für den Kindergarten, aber mein Mann wollte nichts davon hören, daß ich die Arbeit aufgab. Das war eine schwere Zeit. Mein Mann wollte mir überhaupt nicht helfen. An freien Tagen zerriß es mich fast. Am Morgen auf den Markt, einheizen, kochen, Wäsche waschen, Wohnungsputz. Ich fiel fast um vor Müdigkeit. Er wollte mir nicht helfen. Er schlief lang, faulenzte, und ich traute mich nichts zu sagen. Ich fürchtete seine Gereiztheit, sein Geschrei, seine Vorwürfe. Unser Sohn war oft krank, und jede Krankheit endete mit einer Lungenentzündung. Er war gut entwickelt. Er konnte lange Gedichte aufsagen, man brauchte sie ihm nur ein paar mal vorsagen. Er war eine Zierde der Kinderkrippe. Lesen lernte er früh,

Вокально-хореографический ансамбль «Русь»

на работу, а придя за ним заставала его плачущим на полу, в то время как другие дети играли. Воспитательницы советовали держать его дома, пока подрастет до садика, но муж и слышать не хотел, чтобы я оставила работу. Тяжелое это было время. Муж ничем не хотел мне помочь. В выходной я разрывалась на части. Утром рынок, топка плиты, готовка обеда, стирка, уборка квартиры. Я буквально валилась с ног. Он не хотел мне помочь. Спал поздно, отдыхал, а я не смела ничего ему сказать. Я боялась его недовольства, криков и упреков. Сын часто болел и каждая болезнь заканчивалась воспалением легких. Развит он был хорошо. Он знал длинные стихи, стоило прочесть ему несколько раз. Он был украшением ясель. Читать он

Dans les villages du Kouban sont créés plusieurs types d'agrégats de plantations forestières qui permettent d'élargir la mécanisation de la plantation de zones forestières.

In Kuban villages a few types of forest-planting units have been assembled, permitting expanded mechanization of the planting of forest zones.

In den Kosakendörfern am Kuban wurden einige Typen von Baumsetzaggregaten konstruiert, welche die Mechanisierung der Anlage von Waldstreifen erweitern.

très tôt. Dès la maternelle. J'ai du mal à le porter à la crèche. Nous habitons Tchétchélevka, la crèche se trouve dans la rue Première Tchétchélevka, et nous logeons à l'angle de la Sixième Tchétchélevka et de la Rue Animée. Comme on est tous les deux habillés chaudement, je le porte avec difficulté. L'amener et le ramener, je dois tout faire moi-même. Mon mari part tôt, rentre tard. Il bat l'enfant pour sa désobéissance et ne s'arrête que lorsqu'il a une pneumonie striduleuse et que nous craignons pour sa vie. Les médecins le trouvent très affaibli et lui prescrivent des promenades dans une pinède. Nous partons dans le pays de mon mari, dans la région de Vinnitsa. On y va trois ans de suite et l'enfant reprend des forces. Chaque jour mon mari part avec lui dans la forêt et y reste du matin jusqu'à la tombée de la nuit. Je fais la cuisine et leur porte

early. While he was still in nursery school. It was very hard for me to get him to nursery school. We lived on Chechelevka, the nursery school was on First Chechelevka, and we lived on Sixth Chechelevka which intersected Bojkaya Street. We both were dressed warmly and I carried him to the nursery school with difficulty. Just like I had to take him there alone, I also had to pick him up myself. My husband left early, and came home late. My husband used to beat the child for not listening, and he stopped only when the child got sick with lobar pneumonia, and we doubted that he would survive. The doctors found that he was very weak and recommended we take him to the pine forest. We went to my husband's native region of Vinnitsa. We went there three years in row and our child got stronger. My husband and child would go off to the forest in the morning and stay until dusk. I would cook and take

noch im Kindergarten. Es fiel mir sehr schwer, ihn in die Krippe zu tragen. Wir wohnten in der Tschetschelevka, die Krippe war in der 1.Tschetschelevka, und wir wohnten in der 6.Tschetschelevka, Ecke Bojkaja. Beide waren wir dick angezogen, nur mit Mühe trug ich ihn bis zur Krippe. Sowohl hinbringen als auch abholen mußte ich ihn selbst. Mein Mann ging früh weg und kam spät nach Hause. Wegen Ungehorsam begann mein Mann das Kind zu schlagen und hörte erst auf damit, als das Kind an kruppöser Lungenentzündung erkrankte, und wir schon daran zweifelten, ob er mit dem Leben davonkomme. Die Ärzte fanden, das Kind sei sehr schwach und empfahlen ihm Nadelwald. Wir fuhren in die Heimat meines Mannes ins Gebiet von Winniza. 3 Jahre nacheinander fuhren wir dorthin und kräftigten das Kind. Mein Mann ging mit dem Kind frühmorgens in den Wald und blieb bis zum Abend dort. Ich kochte und brachte

панских станицах сконструировано несколько типов лесопосадочных агрегатов, позволивших расширить механизацию закладки лесных полос.

начал рано. Еще будучи в детском саду. Мне очень трудно было носить его в ясли. Жили мы на Чечелевке. ясли были на 1-й Чечелевке, а жили мы на шестой чечелевке, пересекая Бойкой. Одетые оба тепло я с трудом доносила его до яслей. Как относить так и забирать я должна была сама. Муж уходил рано, приходил поздно. За непослушание муж стал бить ребенка и только прекратил, когда ребенок заболел крупозным воспалением легких и мы сомневались выживет ли он. Врачи нашли, что ребенок очень слабый и порекомендовали ему сосновый лес. Мы поехали на родину мужа в Винницкую область. Ездили 3 года подряд и укрепили ребенка. Муж с ребенком уходили в лес с утра и были там до сумерков. Я готовила и носила

Ci-dessous : le vaisseau amiral « Joseph Staline » entre dans une écluse du premier-né des grands chantiers du communisme — le Canal V. I. Lénine qui réunit le Don à la Volga.

The flagship "Joseph Stalin" passes through one of the sluices of a first in the great constructions of communism, the Volga-Don Shipping Canal named after V. I. Lenin (lower photo).

Das Flaggschiff »Josif Stalin« durchfährt eine der Schleusen des »V. I. Lenin«-Wolga-Don-Kanals, einem der Erstlinge kommunistischer Großbauten (unteres Bild).

à manger dans la forêt. Bien sûr, je ne connais pas de repos. Il faut penser à l'école. D'ailleurs, à la maternelle déjà, on lui découvre un talent de dessinateur. Il dessine mieux que les autres. En 1940, il entre à l'école. Il se fait remarquer dès la première année. Il est le premier de sa classe. Il passe en deuxième, quand la guerre éclate. Je me souviens : on se promène avec mon fils, dans le centre, on entre dans une pâtisserie, il fait très beau, on est le 22.6.1941. Soudain, j'entends par un haut-parleur : la guerre. Tous, comme emportés par le vent, se dispersent, affolés. En rentrant à la maison, on voit sur la table un petit mot : mon mari est mobilisé pour creuser des fossés antichars. Il part peu après. Nous redoutons de sortir dans la rue.

food to them in the woods. Of course, I didn't get a vacation. I got just as tired as before. Nursery school was over and it was time to talk about kindergarten. Yes, his aptitude for painting was discovered in nursery school. He drew better than the other children. In 1940 he entered school. His talents were discovered from the first grade. He was an "A" student. He passed into the second grade, and then the war started. I remember, my son and I were walking around the center of town, we dropped into the bakery, it was a nice day, it was 22.VI.1941. Suddenly I hear over the loudspeaker: war. Everyone, as though whisked away by the wind, scattered in different directions in panic. We got home and there was a note on the table saying that my husband had been mobilized to dig anti-tank ditches. It was frightening on the streets.

das Essen in den Wald. Natürlich war das für mich überhaupt keine Erholung. Ich war erschöpft wie immer. Der Kindergarten ging zu Ende. Es war Zeit, an die Schule zu denken. Ja, im Kindergarten hatte sich seine zeichnerische Begabung gezeigt. Er zeichnete besser als andere Kinder. 1940 trat er in die Schule ein. Seine Fähigkeiten zeigten sich von der ersten Klasse an. Er war ein Vorzugsschüler. Er kam in die zweite Klasse, und da begann der Krieg. Ich erinnere mich, wie ich mit meinem Sohn im Zentrum spazieren ging, wir betraten eine Konditorei, es war ein schöner Tag, es war der 22. 6. 1941. Auf einmal höre ich aus dem Lautsprecher: Krieg. Wie vom Sturm erfaßt, stoben alle in Panik auseinander. Wir kamen nach Hause, da lag auf dem Tisch eine Mitteilung, daß mein Mann zum Ausheben von Schützengräben mobilisiert sei, und bald reiste er ab. Auf den Straßen ging es fürchterlich zu.

Флагманский корабль «Иосиф Сталин» проходит через один из шлюзов первенца великих строек коммунизма — Волго-Донского судоходного канала имени В. И. Ленина (нижний снимок).

в лес в утренних саду. Конечно, для меня отдыха не существовало. Уставала я попрежнему. Кончился детский сад. Нужно было подумывать о школе. Да, в детском саду обнаружились его способности к рисованию. Он рисовал лучше других детей. В 1940 году он поступил в школу. Способности его обнаружились с первого класса. Он был отличник. Перешел во второй класс и тут началась война. Помню мы с сыном гуляли по центру, зашли в кондитерскую, день был хороший это было 2 .УI-1941 года. Вдруг слышу по репродуктору война. Все, как подхваченные ветром, бросились в разные   разные стороны в панике. Пришли домой, а на столе записка, что муж мобилизован на копку противотанковых канав и он вскоре уехал. На улице было страшно.

La Vie humiliée Life as an insult Leben als Erniedrigung Жизнь как оскорбление

Le dimanche, les mineurs font des promenades collectives en car et en voiture de tourisme. Sur la photo — une des promenades dominicales des mineurs à la lisière de la forêt de Botchat.

On Sundays the miners often go for collective outings on buses or in their private cars. In the photo: one Sunday outing on the edge of the Botchatsky Forest.

An Sonntagen machen die Bergleute nicht selten gemeinsame Ausflüge mit Autobussen oder einigen Autos. Auf dem Bild ein sonntägliches Picknick der Bergleute am Rand des Botschatsker Waldes.

Les premiers réfugiés arrivent. Tous les frères et sœurs de mon mari se retrouvent peu à peu à Dniépropétrovsk. Sa sœur est mariée et l'usine où travaille son mari est évacuée à Magnitogorsk. Ils ont le droit d'emmener la famille, car tout le convoi est à leur disposition, ils me mettent sur la liste avec mon fils, mais je refuse, avec une obstination inexplicable, de partir sans mon mari. Lors du départ, je viens à la gare pour leur faire mes adieux, mais je ne veux pas partir. Je panique, mais j'attends toujours mon mari. En effet, il revient quelques jours plus tard. Il travaille dans une coopérative artisanale. Ils évacuent leur matériel et nous nous installons sur un chariot entre des machines-outils et des clous. Ils fabriquent des fusils-jouets. C'est le dernier train à quitter Dniépropétrovsk. Les troupes marchent à côté de nous, la gare est déjà en ruines, derrière nous le pont saute.

The first evacuees arrived. All my husband's brothers and sister gradually moved to Dnepropetrovsk. His sister got married, and the factory where he worked was evacuated to Magnitogorsk. They were allowed to take their families along since they gave them an entire train, and they signed up my son and me, but because of some sort of stubbornness I didn't want to go without my husband. I stood by the train car seeing them off, but wouldn't agree to leave for anything. It was terribly frightening, but I waited for my husband. And he really did come home in a few days. He worked in the artel. They were carrying away equipment and we got on the cart with the machines and nails. They made toy guns. That was the last echelon to leave Dnepropetrovsk. Troops travelled with us, the railway station had been destroyed, behind us the bridge was destroyed.

Die ersten Evakuierten trafen ein. Alle Brüder meines Mannes und die Schwester fuhren nacheinander nach Dnepropetrovsk. Seine Schwester hatte geheiratet und die Fabrik, in der er arbeitete, wurde nach Magnitogorsk evakuiert. Man konnte auch Verwandte mitnehmen, weil sie einen ganzen Zug zusammenstellten, sie schrieben auch mich und meinen Sohn ein, aber aus einer Sturheit heraus wollte ich nicht ohne meinen Mann fahren. Ich stand am Zug und verabschiedete sie, und wollt nicht und nicht mitfahren. Zwar hatte ich schreckliche Angst, aber ich wartete auf meinen Mann. Und wirklich, ein paar Tage später kam er. Er arbeitete in einer Genossenschaft. Man lud die Ausrüstung auf und wir setzten uns in den letzten Waggon mit den Maschinen und Nägeln. Sie erzeugten Kindergewehre. Es war der letzte Transport, der Dnepropetrovsk verließ. Soldaten fuhren mit uns, der Bahnhof wurde zerstört, hinter uns wurde die Brücke zerstört.

По воскресеньям шахтеры нередко совершают коллективные прогулки на автобусах и собственных автомашинах. На снимке — одно из воскресных гуляний горняков на опушке Бочатского леса.

Прибыли первые эвакуированные. Все братья мужа и сестра постепенно переехали в Днепропетровск. Сестра его вышла замуж и завод, где он работал эвакуировался в Магнитогорск. Можно было взять и родственников, т.к. подали целый состав, они меня с сыном записали, но я из какого-то упрямства ни за что не хотела ехать без мужа. Стояла у вагона, провожая их, и ни за что не соглашалась уезжать. Страшно было очень, но я ждала мужа. И действительно через несколько дней он пришел. Он работал в артели. Отвозили оборудование и мы уселись на подводе с машинами, гвоздями. Делали детские ружья. Это был последний эшалон, который выезжал из Днепропетровска. Шли с нами войска, к.д. вокзал был разрушен, за нами был разрушен мост.

La Vie humiliée   Life as an insult   Leben als Erniedrigung   Жизнь как оскорбление

Au rayon « Prêt-à-porter » du grand magasin de l'arrondissement Cherbakovski (Moscou).

In the ready-made dress department of the department store in the Shcherbakovsky region of Moscow.

In der Konfektionsabteilung des Kaufhauses im Schtscherbakov-Bezirk in Moskau.

On prend place sur les plates-formes ouvertes réservées aux réfugiés, et en route pour le Caucase du Nord. On ne veut pas trop s'éloigner, on suppose que la guerre sera bientôt finie. On prend juste une valise avec deux coupons de tissu pour me faire un tailleur et un manteau d'hiver. Je décroche du mur la photo qui m'est si chère, là où je suis photographiée avec la famille en 1923. Je la décroche mais je ne la mets pas dans la valise, va savoir pourquoi, ce que je regretterai toute ma vie. On arrive à la gare la plus proche du Caucase du nord, village de Kamennobrodki. Je commence à travailler dans une école et mon mari — au parc de tracteurs. Je remplis le bulletin de paie, mais on n'a pas le temps de me verser mon salaire. Un mois plus tard, les Allemands sont déjà aux portes d'Armavir qu'ils bombardent. Dans la nuit, mon mari loue un chariot pour quitter le village, on s'embarque sur des plates-formes pour gagner l'intérieur du pays. On va jusqu'à Samarkande et là, on s'arrête.

We boarded the platforms assigned for evacuation, and we went to the Northern Caucasus. We wanted to go someplace close, we thought the war would end soon. We took a suitcase with us, where there were two pieces of material for a suit and winter coat for me. I took the most precious photograph off the wall, the one of me and the children taken in 1923. I took it down but didn't put it in the suitcase, I don't know why, and I have regretted this all my life. We made it to the station, the closest one in the Northern Caucasus, the village of Kamennobrodki. I went to work at the school, my husband at the auto-tank station. I filled out the papers to get paid, but never got it. After one month a German went up to Armavir and shot him. At night my husband got a cart and we left the village and got on the platform and went to the far rear, we went as far as Samarkand, where we got off.

Wir fuhren mit den anderen Evakuierten in den nördlichen Kaukasus. Wir wollten nicht so weit wegfahren, weil wir dachten, der Krieg sei bald zu Ende. Ich hatte einen Koffer mitgenommen mit Stoff für zwei Kostüme für mich und einen Wintermantel. Von der Wand hatte ich die mir liebste Fotografie heruntergenommen, ein Foto von den Kindern und mir aus dem Jahr 1923. Ich hatte sie heruntergenommen, aber nicht in den Koffer gelegt, warum, weiß ich nicht, und mein Leben lang tat es mir leid darum. Wir fuhren bis zur nächsten Station im nördlichen Kaukasus, zum Dorf Kamennobrodki. Ich ging in die Schule arbeiten, mein Mann in die Maschinen-Traktoren-Station. Ich reichte bei der Behörde um mein Gehalt ein, aber das Geld sollte ich nicht mehr bekommen. Einen Monat später rückten die Deutschen bis Armavir vor und beschossen den Ort. In der Nacht mietete mein Mann ein Fuhrwerk, wir verließen das Dorf und fuhren dann mit dem Zug ins tiefe Hinterland, bis Samarkand fuhren wir, und dort stiegen wir aus.

В отделе готового платья универсального магазина в Щербаковском районе Москвы

Сели в поданые для эвакуации платформы и мы поехали на Северный Кавказ. Хотелось поближе, думали что война скоро кончится. Взяли с собой чемодан, где были 2 отреза мне на костюм и зимнее пальто. Сняла со стены самую ценную для меня фотографию, где я в 1923 г. снялась с детьми. Сначала, но не положила в чемодан не зная почему и очень жалела об этом всю жизнь. Доехали мы до станции ближайшей на Северном Кавказе, до села Каменнобродки. Я пошла работать в школу, муж на МТС. Подготовила ведомость на зарплату, но получить деньги не пришлось. И через месяц немец подступил к Армавиру и обстрелял его. Ночью муж нанял подводу, мы выехали из села и сели на платформы и поехали в глубокий тыл, ехали до Самарканда и там выгрузились

Devant le sanatorium de mineurs. A droite — N. Védiochkina.

Near the building of the sanatorium for workers of the coal industry. N. Vedeshkina is on the right.

Vor dem Sanatorium für Arbeiter der Kohleindustrie. Rechts N. Vedeschkina.

Une usine de conserves a été évacuée de Simféropol avec son personnel et on nous embauche. Je travaille à la comptabilité, mon mari — à l'atelier, comme ajusteur. Il a une affectation spéciale et on ne le mobilise pas. On loue aux Ouzbeks une maisonnette crépie d'argile et notre fils va à l'école ouzbek.

This is where the Simferopole factory had been evacuated to, a preserves factory, with its staff, and my husband and I got jobs there. I worked in the accounting office, my husband worked as a metal worker. He had an "exemption" and wasn't mobilized. We rented an Uzbek cottage, a small clay house, my son started an Uzbek school.

Hierher war aus Simferopol eine Konservenfabrik evakuiert worden und zusammen mit meinem Mann fanden wir dort Arbeit. Ich in der Buchhaltung, mein Mann in der Schlosserei. Er wurde freigestellt und nicht mobilisiert. Wir mieteten eine usbekische Lehmhütte und unser Sohn besuchte die usbekische Schule.

У здания санатория для работников угольной промышленности. Справа — Н. Ведешкина.

Здесь был эвакуированный Симферопольский завод консервный со своим штатом и мы вместе с мужем поступили туда работать. Я в бухгалтерию, муж на производство в цех слесарей. Он имел "бронь" и его не мобилизовали. Наняли мы узбекскую мазанку, сын пошел учиться в узбекскую школу. Завод делал консервы овощные и мясные. Столовая пользовалась продуктами из остатков, вообще было не плохо. Мы были устроены. Но вот "бронь" была снята и мужа мобилизовали на фронт. Мы остались с сыном одни. Муж просил директора не оставлять нас без поддержки и меня не оставляли действительно. Подбрасывали иногда продукты. В это время в Самарканд была эвакуирована академия Художеств и среднехудожественная школа из Ленинграда.

A la place des marais asséchés sont construits des villages kolkhoziens.

Collective farm settlements are being built on the site of drained swamps.

Auf dem Areal trockengelegter Sümpfe werden Kolchossiedlungen gebaut.

Mon fils fait connaissance avec le fils d'une secrétaire qui lui parle de l'inscription à l'école des Beaux-Arts en première année spécialisée et dans la quatrième d'enseignement général. Cela tombe bien, parce qu'il est en quatrième. Il prend l'initiative d'apporter ses dessins et il est admis, car il n'y a pas beaucoup de candidats. Les gens du pays ne veulent pas s'inscrire. Mais on lui demande son dossier scolaire et là, je dois intervenir. Je suis prise au dépourvu lorsque mon fils me demande de retirer son dossier de l'école ouzbek et de l'envoyer à l'école des Beaux-Arts de Léningrad. Je demande conseil à notre voisin, membre du parti, et il m'encourage à changer mon fils d'école, disant que cela ne lui fera pas de mal, mais lui sera, au contraire, profitable. Ce que je fais. La directrice de l'école ouzbek est une Russe réfugiée. Elle nous souhaite bonne chance et mon fils entre à l'école

My son met the son of the secretary and found out that they would be accepting students at the art school for the first grade, special group, and the fourth general education grade. He independently took his drawings, was accepted since the recruitment wasn't very big. The local kids didn't want to go there. But they demanded his school documents, and for this he needed me. I was concerned when my son asked me to bring his documents from the Uzbek school to the Leningrad Art School. I asked the advice of my neighbor, a Party member, and he said I should make the transfer, since it wouldn't hurt my son, but would be good for him. So that's what I did. The director of the Uzbek school was a Russian woman, an evacuee. She wished us great success, and my son started to

Unser Sohn lernte den Sohn der Sekretärin kennen und erfuhr, daß in der künstlerischen Mittelschule Aufnahmen stattfänden in die erste spezielle Klasse und in die vierte allgemeinbildende. Alles paßte, er war in der vierten Klasse. Er trug seine Zeichnungen selbständig hin und wurde ohne Schwierigkeit aufgenommen. Von den Ortsansässigen wollte kaum jemand in so eine Schule. Aber man verlangte auch seine Schuldokumente und das ging nicht ohne mich. Ich war ganz verstört, als mein Sohn mich wieder und wieder bat, die Dokumente aus der usbekischen Schule in die Leningrader Kunstschule zu bringen. Ich beriet mich mit unserem Nachbarn, einem Parteimitglied, und er riet zu dem Übertritt, er meinte, es werde meinem Sohn nicht schaden, sondern nützen. Und so machte ich es. Die Direktorin der usbekischen Schule war eine Russin, eine Evakuierte. Sie wünschte uns viel Erfolg, und mein Sohn begann

На месте осушенных болот строятся колхозные поселки.

Сын познакомился с сыном секретарши и узнал, что в средне-художественную школу будет набор в первый специальный и 4й общеобразовательный. Все подходило, он был в 4м классе. Он самостоятельно принес свои рисунки, был принят, т.к. набор был незначительный. Местные не хотели поступать. Но у него потребовали его школьные документы, а тут без меня не обошлось. Я очень растерялась, когда сын просил принести документы из узбекской школы в Ленинградскую худож.школу. Я посоветовалась с соседом, членом партии и он посоветовал сделать перевод, т.к. сыну это не повредит, а только будет на пользу. Я так и сделала. Директором узбекской школы была русская, эвакуированная. Она пожелала нам хороших успехов и сын

Atelier n°30 réalisant les commandes individuelles des Moscovites. Le sculpteur Marianna Yaroslavskaïa choisit le modèle de sa nouvelle robe. On lui fait voir le modèle d'une robe chasuble créé par la directrice artistique de l'atelier L. A. Danilova.

In fashion house No. 30 which fills individual orders for Moscow women. The sculptor Marianna Yaroslavskaya is choosing a style for a new dress. A sarafan-dress created by the artistic director of the studio L. A. Danilina is being shown.

Im Schneideratelier Nr. 30, das individuelle Aufträge von Moskauerinnen anfertigt. Die Bildhauerin Marianna Jaroslavskaja wählt den Schnitt für ein neues Kleid aus. Ein Kleiderrock wird vorgeführt, dessen Modell von der künstlerischen Leiterin des Ateliers L. A. Danilina geschaffen wurde.

des Beaux-Arts de Léningrad. Je travaille toujours à l'usine. Mais l'ennemi chassé, les administrations et les établissements scolaires commencent la réévacuation. Cela concerne également l'école de mon fils. Il tient à y rester et je ne peux pas le laisser partir seul. A l'école, on me propose une place d'économe: dans ce cas-là, je pourrai les suivre. Je vais voir le directeur de l'usine pour ma démission, mais il ne veut pas en entendre parler. Je dois m'assurer l'accord du chef comptable. Originaire d'Odessa, il comprend ma situation et intervient pour qu'on me laisse partir. Il explique qu'il s'agit du destin de mon fils et avec beaucoup de mal

attend the Leningrad Art School. I worked at the same factory as before. But the enemy was repulsed and they started to re-evacuate organizations and educational establishments. The question was now what to do about my son's school. My son insisted on going with them, but I couldn't let him go alone. He was 10 years old. Then my son suggested that I go to work at the school and go with him. At the school they offered me a maintenance job, and then they would take me along. I asked the director of the factory to let me go, but he didn't want to hear about it. I had to get the permission of the head accountant. He was from Odessa and put himself in my position, and insisted that they let me go. He explained that this was for the future of my son, and with great difficulty

die Leningrader künstlerische Mittelschule zu besuchen. Ich arbeitete in der Fabrik, wie früher. Aber der Feind war nun zurückgeschlagen, und die Behörden und Lehranstalten wurden reevakuiert. Welche Schule sollte mein Sohn weiter besuchen? Er bestand darauf, mit ihnen zu fahren, ich aber konnte ihn nicht allein lassen. Er war 10 Jahre alt. Da riet mir mein Sohn, in die Schule einzutreten und mitzufahren. In der Schule schlugen sie mir vor, als Betreuerin einzutreten, dann könnten sie mich mitnehmen. Ich wandte mich an den Direktor der Fabrik und bat ihn, mich gehen zu lassen, aber er wollte nichts davon hören. So mußte ich mich auf die Zustimmung des Hauptbuchhalters verlassen. Er war ein Odessit, versetzte sich in meine Lage und bestand darauf, mich gehen zu lassen. Er erklärte, es gehe um die Zukunft meines Sohnes, mir gelang es unter großen Schwierigkeiten,

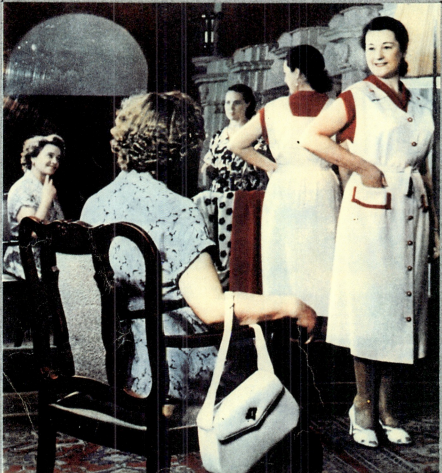

В ателье № 30, выполняющем индивидуальные заказы москвичек. Скульптор Марианна Ярославская выбирает фасон для нового платья. Демонстрируется платье-сарафан, модель которого создана художественной руководительницей ателье Л. А. Данилиной.

стал посещать ленинградскую среднехудожественную школу. Я работала на заводе, где и раньше. Но вот враг был отброшен, стали реэвакуироваться, учреждения и учебные заведения. Стал вопрос и о школе сына. Он настаивал, что поедет с ними, а я не могла его отпустить одного. Ему было 10 лет. Тогда сын посоветовал мне поступить в школу и поехать с ними. В школе мне предложили поступить сестрой хозяйкой и тогда они возьмут меня с собой. Я обратилась к директору завода, чтобы меня отпустили, но он и слушать меня не хотел. Пришлось заручиться согласием главного бухгалтера. Он был одессит, вошел в мое положение, настоял, чтобы меня отпустили. Объяснил, что тут будущее моего сына и с большим трудом я

D'année en année, de quinquennat en quinquennat, le centre industriel du sud de l'Ukraine franchit de nouveaux sommets.

From year to year, from five-year plan to five-year plan, the industrial center of the South Ukraine achieved one success after another.

Von Jahr zu Jahr, von Fünfjahrplan zu Fünfjahrplan hat das industrielle Zentrum der Südukraine immer neue Höhen erreicht.

j'encaisse mon salaire et j'entre à l'école des Beaux-Arts comme économe. Le travail n'est pas trop difficile. Je répare le linge et les matelas. Je suis logée à l'école. Mais trois mois plus tard, l'école et l'Académie reçoivent l'ordre de retourner à Moscou. On part en trois convois. Enfin c'est le tour de l'école. On met à sa disposition un wagon où j'ai aussi une place. Et là mes tourments commencent.
Je dois revenir un peu en arrière. Avant mon mariage, j'ai eu un moment de totale démoralisation : ayant perdu tout espoir d'améliorer mon sort, je décide de mettre fin à mes jours. Je trouve quelques cachets de somnifère, du véronal, si je ne me trompe, et je les avale. Ça rate, mais je dors, sans me réveiller, plusieurs jours de

I settled accounts with the factory and went to work at the Leningrad Art School. The work wasn't particularly difficult. I mended mattresses and linens. Three months went by this way, then the order was received to move all academies and schools to Moscow. We left in three stages. Finally it was the school's turn. The school had its own train car, to which I was assigned. This is when my torment began.
Let me go back a little. Even before I was married I was desperate: there was no hope of improving my position, and I decided to leave this life. I gathered up a few sleeping powders, it seems veronal, and drank it. I didn't achieve my goal, but I slept without waking for a few

mit der Fabrik abzurechnen, und ich trat als Betreuerin in die Leningrader Kunstschule ein. Die Arbeit war nicht besonders schwer. Ich flickte Matratzen und Wäsche. Ich wohnte bei der Schule. Nach 3 Monaten kam die Anordnung, die ganze Akademie und die Schule habe nach Moskau zu fahren. Die Schule hatte einen eigenen Waggon, für den ich zuständig war. Und da begannen meine Qualen.
Ich schweife etwas ab. Schon vor der Heirat war ich verzweifelt: es gab keinerlei Hoffnung auf eine Besserung meiner Lage, und ich beschloß, aus dem Leben zu gehen. Ich sammelte einige Tabletten Schlafpulver, Veronal glaube ich, und nahm sie. Das Ziel erreichte ich nicht, aber ich schlief ohne aufzuwachen einige Tage

Из года в год, от пятилетки к пятилетке, брал высоту за высотой индустриальный центр Юга Украины.

расчиталась с заводом и поступила в Ленинградскую художественную школу в должности сестры-хозяйки. Работа была не особенно трудной Я чинила матрацы и бельё. Жила при школе. Но вот прошло 3 месяца и получен был приказ выезжать в Москву всей академии и школе. Выез жали в 3 этапа. Наконец дошла очередь и до школы. Школа имела отдельный вагон, куда я была прикреплена. Вот когда начались мои мучения.

    Немного вернусь назад. Еще до замужества я дошла ит до отчаяния никаких надежд не было на улучшение моего положения и, я решила уйти из жизни. Собрала несколько порошков отбессоницы, кажется веронала и выпила. Цели я не достигла, но спала беспробудно несколько

La Vie humiliée Life as an insult Leben als Erniedrigung Жизнь как оскорбление

La kolkhozienne Nadejda Trapeznikova se prépare pour aller à une soirée au club.

The collective farm worker Nadezhda Trapeznikova is getting ready to go to a party at the club.

Die Kolchosbäuerin Nadjeschda Trapesnikowa geht zu einem Klubabend.

suite. On appelle un médecin, tout se termine bien et je ne recommence plus. J'ai oublié encore une circonstance. Lorsqu'on est allé déclarer notre fils, j'ai exigé de mon mari de régulariser notre situation, ainsi, l'acte de naissance de l'enfant et celui du mariage sont datés du même jour, le 30 septembre 1933. On ne fête pas l'événement et mon mari ne veut pas acheter d'alliances. On part toujours du principe que je n'ose rien m'acheter moi-même, que ça me plaise ou non. Mon mari ne me demande jamais mon avis, il achète ce qu'il juge nécessaire; je lui donne mon salaire, comme je l'ai autrefois donné à ma famille. Il rabâche avec mépris que mon salaire ne vaut rien. Il me donne de l'argent pour faire les courses et me reproche de

days. They had to send for the doctor, and everything turned out fine, and I didn't attempt such experiments again. One more thing I left out, that is when we registered the baby I announced to my husband that we needed to make the marriage legal, and so the birth certificate and marriage certificate are issued the same day — 30 September 1933. We didn't mark these events in any way, my husband didn't intend to buy rings. In general we had such an arrangement that I didn't dare buy anything for myself, whether I liked it or not. My husband never asked, he bought what he thought to be necessary, and I gave him my pay as I had my parents, and he said with contempt that my pay was just a trifle. He gave me money for expenditures at the market, and always said that I didn't know how to

durch. Man mußte einen Arzt rufen, alles ging gut aus, und mehr solcher Experimente habe ich nicht unternommen. Noch etwas habe ich ausgelassen, als wir das Kind anmeldeten, erklärte ich meinem Mann, unsere Ehe müsse auch offiziell geschlossen werden, und der Geburtsschein und die Heiratsurkunde tragen das gleiche Datum — 30. September 1933. Dieses Ereignis wurde auf keine Weise gefeiert, auch Ringe kaufte mein Mann nicht. Überhaupt ging es bei uns so zu, daß ich nicht wagte, mir etwas zu kaufen, ob mir etwas gefiel oder nicht. Mein Mann frage mich nie, kaufte, was er für nötig hielt, ich gab ihm mein ganzes Gehalt, wie ich es früher meiner Familie gegeben hatte, und er sagte verächtlich, mein Gehalt sei sowieso lächerlich. Er gab mir Geld für die Einkäufe auf dem Markt und wiederholte immer wieder, ich könne nicht

Колхозница Надежда Трапезникова собирается на вечер в клуб.

дней. Пришлось вызвать врача, все окончилось благополучно, больше таких экспериментов я не пробовала делать. Еще одно пропущено было. когда мы регистрировали ребенка, я заявила мужу, что нужно оформить наш брак и у меня свидетельство о рождении ребенка и регистрация брака одним числом 30 сентября 1933 года. Ничем не отмечено было это событие, колец муж и не собирался покупать. Вообще у нас была такая установка, что я ничего не смела себе покупать, нравилось мне это или нет. Муж никогда не спрашивал, покупал что находит нужным, я, как и родным, отдавала ему свою зарплату, а он с пренебрежением говорил, что моя зарплата ерунда. Выдавал мне на расходы на рынок и все повторял не раз, что я не умею

La Vie humiliée Life as an insult Leben als Erniedrigung Жизнь как оскорбление

La jeune pianiste, élève de terminale de l'école centrale de musique auprès du Conservatoire de Moscou, Natacha Youzbachéva.

The young pianist, a tenth-grade student of the Central Music School at the Moscow Conservatory, Natasha Yuzbasheva.

Die junge Pianistin Natascha Jusbaschewa, Schülerin der 10. Klasse der Zentralen Musikschule beim Moskauer Konservatorium.

ne pas savoir marchander comme les autres ménagères. Moi, je fais le tour du marché à la recherche des produits les moins chers, que j'achète ; mais il est vrai que je ne sais pas marchander.
Donc, on prend le dernier convoi pour Moscou. On s'arrête souvent en route. Nous sommes dans la dernière voiture, le reste de l'école et l'administration sont dans la première. Il m'incombe de m'occuper des rations pour les élèves. Dès que le train s'arrête, je me précipite avec deux garçons et deux seaux à la gare, vers l'endroit où l'on distribue la soupe chaude. Combien de temps le train restera en gare, personne ne le sait. Il y a beaucoup de neige partout. Comme je ne suis pas trop rapide, je galope entre le train et la gare. Pire, pendant les arrêts, je cavale

buy things cheaply like other housewives. And I scoured the entire market in search of cheaper things which I bought, but it's true, I didn't know how to haggle.
And so, we left with the last echelon for Moscow. We stopped a lot along the way. Our car was the last one, that is the school's, and all the bosses rode in the first car. I was put in charge of getting food for the schoolchildren. As soon as the train stopped, I would take two boys and two buckets and hurry to the station to get our hot "first course". It wasn't clear how long the train would remain stopped. I'm not particularly quick, and had to gallop from the train to the station and back. In addition, I also had to run

so günstig einkaufen wie andere Hausfrauen. Ich ging aber den ganzen Markt auf und ab und schaute, wo die Lebensmittel billiger waren — handeln konnte ich allerdings wirklich nicht.
Also fuhren wir mit dem letzten Transport nach Moskau. Oft blieben wir stehen. Unser Waggon war der letzte, also die Schule, alle Vorgesetzten fuhren im ersten Waggon. Zu meinen Verpflichtungen gehörte der Empfang von Nahrungsmitteln für die Schüler. Immer wenn der Zug stehenblieb, rannte ich mit 2 Buben und 2 Kübeln in den Bahnhof um heiße Suppe. Man wußte nie, wie lange der Zug stehenblieb. Es gab große Schneeverwehungen. Ich bin nicht besonders flink, mußte aber im Galopp vom Zug zum Bahnhof rennen und zurück. Außerdem mußte ich während der Aufenthalte

Юная пианистка, ученица 10-го класса Центральной музыкальной школы при Московской консерватории, Наташа Юзбашева.

дешево покупать, как другие хозяйки. А я обходила весь рынок в поисках продуктов, какие подешевле и их покупала, но торговаться, правда не умела.

Итак мы выезжали последним эшелоном в Москву. Мы часто останавливались в пути. Наш вагон был последним, т.е. школа, а все начальство ехало в первом вагоне. Мне вменялось в обязанность получать продукты на школьников. Как только поезд останавливался, я с 2 ребятами и 2 ведрами мчалась на станцию, получать горячее "первое". Сколько будет стоять поезд – не известно. Заносы были большие. А не особенно быстрая, должна была галопом мчаться с поезда на станцию и обратно. Кроме того, я должна была еще на остановках летать с

La Vie humiliée Life as an insult Leben als Erniedrigung Жизнь как оскорбление

La Volga. Le bateau longe les monts Jigouli dont les chansons chantent la beauté.

The Volga. The boat is sailing past the Zhiguli Mountains, the beauty of which is glorified in songs.

Die Wolga. Ein Schiff gleitet an den Schigulev-Bergen vorbei, deren Schönheit in Liedern gerühmt wird.

entre le dernier wagon et le premier où voyage le chef comptable à qui je dois rendre compte des dépenses. Le pain, on l'a emporté avec nous et une des mamans le distribue. Comme c'est affreux de voir les élèves, affamés, scruter le pesage du pain. Où donc est mon fils? Pas moyen de le surveiller. Il se sent gêné parce que je fais partie du personnel et essaie de garder ses distances. Finalement, tout se passe bien. Nous, c'est-à-dire les garçons et moi, remontons toujours à temps dans le train et au bout du compte nous arrivons à Zagorsk. On est le 1.11.1944. Nous sommes bien nombreux. Toute l'équipe pédagogique et, de plus, les 6 classes de l'Académie et l'école secondaire. On nous loge dans le monastère. Il fait très froid, à l'extérieur et dans les locaux.

from the last car to the first, where the head accountant was. I had to account for all the money spent on lunch to him. We took our own bread with us, and one of the mothers would pass it out. It was horrible to watch the schoolchildren who would follow the weighing of the bread with their hungry eyes. Who knows where my son was, I didn't even have the chance to watch after him. He was very ashamed of the fact that I worked at the school and tried to stay as far away from me as possible. And so, everything went well. We didn't miss the train, that is, the children and I arrived safely in Zagorsk. That was on 1.II.1944. There were a lot of us. The entire teaching staff and students from six levels of the academy and the artistic school. They housed us in the monastery. It was terribly cold, both outside and in the dwelling.

vom letzten zum ersten Waggon rasen, wo der Hauptbuchhalter saß, mit dem ich die Ausgaben fürs Mittagessen abrechnen mußte. Das Brot führten wir mit uns, es wurde von einer der Mütter verteilt. Es war schrecklich, die Schüler zu beobachten, wie sie mit hungrigen Augen das Abwiegen des Brotes verfolgten. Ich hatte gar keine Gelegenheit, auf meinen Sohn aufzupassen. Es war ihm sehr peinlich, daß ich in der Schule arbeitete und er hielt sich von mir fern. Aber alles ging gut. Wir blieben nicht zurück und der ganze Zug mit allen Kindern kam in Zagorsk an. Das war am 1. Februar 1944. Wir waren viele. Das ganze pädagogische Personal und die Studenten der Akademie und der Mittelschule. Untergebracht wurden wir im Kloster. Es war schrecklich kalt, draußen wie auch drinnen.

Волга. Судно плывет мимо Жигулевских гор, красота которых прославлена в песнях.

последнего вагона в первый, где сидел главный бухгалтер, перед которым я должна была отчитываться за израсходованные деньги на обеды. Хлеб везли с собой и раздавали его одна из мамаш. Это было ужасно следить за учениками, которые голодными глазами следили за развеской хлеба. И Где был сын, я не имела даже возможности за ним проследить. Он очень стеснялся, что я работаю в школе и старался быть от меня подальше. Итак все обошлось благополучно Мы не отстали от поезда, т.е. я с ребятами и и благополучно прибыли в г. Загорск. Это было 1.П-1944 г. Нас было много. Весь педагог. персонал и учащиеся 6 курсов академии и средней худож. школы. Поместили нас в Лавре. Было ужасно холодно. И на улице и в помещении

Devant l'entrée du grand magasin d'arrondissement.

Near the entrance of the regional department store.

Vor dem Eingang zum Gebiets-Kaufhaus.

Les grands apportent du bois que tout le monde scie; les repas à la cantine sont dégoûtants bien que nous ayons remis nos rations, de très bonne qualité. Petit à petit, les étudiants et les enseignants obtiennent l'autorisation et partent. Les mères qui étaient avec nous, partent aussi. Elles sont toutes de Léningrad. Concernant mon fils, le directeur de l'école me dit qu'il peut être autorisé à aller à Léningrad mais pas moi, parce que je ne suis pas de là et qu'ils ne pourront pas me loger. J'ai oublié de noter qu'en route une des mamans est tombée malade et que j'ai dû l'amener à l'hôpital. Je ne peux pas laisser mon fils partir seul et comme un des professeurs reste à Moscou, il m'aide à transférer mon fils de l'école de Léningrad à celle de Moscou. Une collaboratrice du musée de Zagorsk a une chambre dans le monastère. Elle travaille

The older kids carried firewood, everyone chopped it, we ate in the cafeteria pretty badly, even though we gave out our own rations which were very good. Gradually, having received permission, the students and teachers left. The mothers who were with us left, too. They were Leningraders. When the question arose: what to do with my son, the director of the school said that they could take my son to Leningrad but not me, since I wasn't a Leningrader and they couldn't provide me with living space. I forgot to write that on the way one mother got sick and I had to put her in the hospital. I couldn't let my son go alone and since one teacher stayed in Moscow he could transfer my son from the Leningrad school to the Moscow school. One of the workers of the museum in Zagorsk had a room in the Monastery. She worked

Die älteren Burschen brachten Holz und zersägten es, das Essen war furchtbar, obwohl wir gute Rationen ablieferten. Nach und nach erhielten alle, die Studenten und die Lehrer, die Erlaubnis zur Abreise. Auch die Mütter, die mit uns waren, reisten ab. Sie waren aus Leningrad. Als sich die Frage erhob, was mit meinem Sohn geschehen sollte, sagte der Leiter der Schule, ihn könnten sie nach Leningrad mitnehmen, mich aber nicht, weil ich keine Leningraderin sei und man mir keinen Wohnraum zur Verfügung stellen könne. Ich habe vergessen zu erwähnen, daß unterwegs eine der Mütter erkrankte und ich sie ins Spital bringen mußte. Ich konnte mich nicht dazu entschließen, meinen Sohn allein fortzulassen, und da ein Lehrer in Moskau blieb, half er dabei, ihn von der Leningrader in die Moskauer Schule übertreten zu lassen. Eine der Mitarbeiterinnen des Zagorsker Museums hatte ein Zimmer im Kloster. Sie arbeitete

У входа в районный универмаг.

Старшие ребята привозили дрова, все пилили, питались в столовой прескверно, хотя мы сдавали свой паек очень хороший. Постепенно, получив разрешение, уезжали студенты и преподаватели.
Уезжали и матери, которые были с нами. Они были Ленинградки. Когда стал вопрос как быть с сыном, завод. школой сказал, что сына можно взять в Ленинград, а меня нет, т.к. я не ленинградка и обеспечить меня жилплощадью не могут. Забыла написать, что дороге заболела одна мать и мне пришлось её поместить в больницу. Пустить одного сына я не решилась и так как один педагог остался в Москве, то он и помог сделать перевод сына из Лнин. школы в Московскую. Одна из сотрудниц музея Загорского, имела комнату в Лавре. Она работала счет

Mon berceau, ma joie, mon amour et mon rêve,
Comme les oiseaux qui rentrent au pays natal,
J'ai fait le tour du monde, j'ai feuilleté des villes,
Mais chaque fois je reviens chez moi.

My cradle, joy, love and dream —
Birds return to their native lands.
I have knocked about the world, shuffled through cities,
But always, but always I come back here.

Meine Wiege, meine Freude, Liebe und Traum,
Die Vögel kehren in die Heimat zurück.
Ich hab die Welt bereist und viele Städte,
Doch immer, immer bin ich hierher zurückgekehrt.

à la comptabilité. Mais elle veut partir pour Léningrad et elle me recommande à sa place. J'obtiens ainsi un travail et une chambre; mon fils habite dans un foyer à Moscou où il va à l'école, rue Lavrouchinskaïa. A ce moment-là, mon mari nous rejoint. Il m'a écrit que grièvement blessé, il est resté longtemps à l'hôpital et que maintenant qu'il est rétabli, il reviendrait chez nous. Je suis en train de faire le ménage, en blouse noire, me disant que le ménage terminé, j'aurai le temps de m'habiller. Mais tout se passe autrement. Mon mari me surprend la serpillière à la main, en blouse. Lui, il est en pleine forme. Il s'effraie à ma vue. Et il ne me le cache pas : « Qu'est-ce que tu as vieilli ! Et tous ces cheveux blancs ! », dit-il. Pas un mot de compassion ni de joie de me retrouver. Cela me fait mal. Il reste quelques

as an accountant. But she wanted to go to Leningrad and recommended me for her job. In this way I got a job and a room, and my son was in a dormitory in Moscow where he studied on Lavrushkinsky Lane. By that time my husband had arrived. He had written that he was seriously wounded, that he was in the hospital for a long time and recovered, and that he would soon come. I started to clean the room, I was in a black robe and thought that after cleaning I would have time to put myself together. But it turned out not like I thought. He caught me with a rag in my hands, in my work robe. He looked very good. Seeing me, he was horrified. He said right to my face: "How old and gray you are". Not one sympathetic word, no joy at our meeting. It was painful. He stayed for a few

in der Buchhaltung. Aber sie wollte nach Leningrad fahren und empfahl mich für ihre Arbeit. So hatte ich eine Arbeit, ein Zimmer, und der Sohn lebte im Heim in Moskau, wo er auch zur Schule ging, in der Lawruschin-Gasse. Damals kehrte mein Mann zurück. Er schrieb mir, er sei schwer verletzt gewesen, hätte lange im Spital gelegen, sei jetzt geheilt und käme bald. Ich räumte das Zimmer auf, war in einem alten Hauskleid und dachte, nach dem Aufräumen könnte ich auch mich noch schön machen. Aber so war es nicht. Er traf mich mit dem Putzfetzen in der Hand an, im Arbeitskleid. Er sah sehr gut aus. Als er mich sah, erschrak er. Er sagte mir direkt ins Gesicht: » Wie alt und grau du bist «. Kein einziges mitfühlendes Wort, keine Wiedersehensfreude. Es tat mir weh. Er blieb einige Tage

Колыбель моя, радость, любовь и мечта, —
Возвращаются птицы в родные места.
Я мотался по свету, листал города,
Но всегда, но всегда возвращался сюда.

ным работником. Но она захотела поехать в Ленинград и порекомендовала меня на свою работу. Таким образом я имела работу, комнату, а сын находился в общежитии в Москве, где и учился в Лаврушинском переулке. К этому времени приехал муж. Он написал мне, что был тяжело ранен, лежал долго в госпитале и поправился, что скоро приедет. Я стала убирать комнату, была в черном халате и думала, что успею после уборки и себя привести в порядок. Но получалось не так, как я думала. Он застал меня с тряпкой в руках, и в рабочем халате Выглядел он очень хорошо. Увидев меня, он ужаснулся. Прямо так и высказал в лицо "Какая ты старая и седая". Ни одного сочувствующего слова, ни радости от встречи. Больно было. Он пробыл несколько

Sur le grand canal de Fergana, artère majeure d'irrigation.

On the Great Fergana Canal, the main irrigation artery.

Auf dem Großen Fergana-Kanal, der Hauptader der Bewässerung.

jours et il s'empresse de rentrer chez lui, à Dniépropétrovsk. Il compte récupérer l'appartement, bien que nous ne soyons que des sous-locataires, sans aucun droit. On lui propose de rester à Zagorsk où il pourrait avoir un permis de résidence et trouver du travail, mais il ne veut pas en entendre parler et il repart. Il revient de temps en temps, personne n'a l'intention de lui restituer son appartement car le fils de la propriétaire, qui avait divorcé, y a emménagé avec sa nouvelle femme et habite dans nos trois pièces meublées. Un jour, mon mari vient pour me demander de retourner à Dniépropétrovsk. Je démissionne en invoquant des raisons personnelles, je laisse des instructions à une fille qui va me remplacer, je lui loue ma chambre; il ne reste qu'à faire les papiers pour mon fils, c'est à dire pour le retirer de l'école. Mon mari va chercher les billets. Et il revient pour m'annoncer

days and hurried off home to Dnepropetrovsk. He assumed he could take back his old apartment, but we were renters, and had no rights to that apartment. It was suggested that he stay in Zagorsk where he could get a registration and find work, but he didn't want to hear it and left. He would come occasionally, no one was about to return the apartment to him, the landlady's son lived there who had divorced and now lived with his new young wife in our three furnished rooms. Then my husband came and said we had to leave for Dnepropetrovsk. I put in the paperwork to quit for personal reasons, trained a girl for my place, rented the room to her, all that was left was to process my son's documents, that is, to take him out of school. My husband went for the tickets. He returns and says that

in Zagorsk und strebte zu sich nach Hause, nach Dnepropetrovsk. Er wollte die Wohnung zurückhaben, aber wir waren ja nur Untermieter und hatten keinerlei Recht auf die Wohnung. Man schlug ihm vor, in Zagorsk zu bleiben, sich hier anzumelden und eine Arbeit zu finden, aber er wollte nichts davon hören und fuhr ab. Hin und wieder kam er auf Besuch, die Wohnung bekam er natürlich nicht zurück, dort wohnte der Sohn der Eigentümerin, der sich von seiner Frau hatte scheiden lassen und mit der jungen neuen Frau in unseren drei Zimmern samt Einrichtung hauste. Dann kam mein Mann und sagte, es sei notwendig, nach Dnepropetrovsk zu fahren. Ich kündigte meine Stelle, arbeitete ein Mädchen ein, übergab ihr das Zimmer, blieb nur noch, den Sohn aus der Schule zu nehmen. Mein Mann ging die Fahrkarten kaufen. Er kam zurück und sagte,

На Большом Ферганском канале, главной артерии орошения.

дней и заторопился к себе в Днепропетровск. Полагал забрать обратно квартиру, а ведь мы были поднаниматели, и никаких прав на квартиру не имели. Предлагая ему остаться в Загорске, где он бы прописался и нашел работу но он и слушать не хотел и уехал. Стал наезжать временами, квартиру ему никто не собирался возвращать, там жел сын хозяйки, который развелься с женой и с молодой новой женой поселился в наших 2х комнатах с обстановкой. Потом муж приехал и сказал, что нужно выезжать в Днепропетровск.Я оформила увольнение по собственному желанию, подготовила девушку на мое место, сдала ей комнату, оставалось только оформить сына т.е. забрать его из школы. Муж пошел за билетами. Возвращается и говорит, что

Nous visitions maison sur maison, rencontrant des dizaines de gens. Parmi eux, nous découvrions des femmes passionnées de travaux d'aiguille, des amateurs de discussions sur la chasse, la pêche et tous les sujets imaginables.

We visited house after house, meeting dozens of new people. Among them were both fans of handicrafts and fans of talking about hunting, fishing and about everything in the world.

Wir haben Haus um Haus besucht, lernten Dutzende von Menschen kennen. Darunter waren Liebhaber von Handarbeiten ebenso wie Liebhaber von Gesprächen über die Jagd, über Fischfang, über alles auf der Welt.

qu'il a acheté un billet pour lui, mais que moi, je vais attendre encore un peu à Zagorsk. Tout est pourtant réglé définitivement: je n'ai plus d'emploi ni de logement. Il part tranquillement et moi, je reste. Comment appeler ça? Une bassesse, de l'insouciance, de l'égoïsme? De l'égoïsme. Mais pourquoi me faire abandonner ma place, mon appartement? Mon désespoir est sans limites. Je dois déménager au foyer des gardiens du musée. Ils se bagarrent, ils me volent la nourriture. Chaque jour le gérant me rappelle que je dois vider les lieux. J'erre dans les rues à la recherche d'un emploi et d'un appartement. Dans une cour, des chiens me mordent. Mais tôt ou tard, tout a une fin. Je trouve d'abord une chambre, ensuite une place. A l'orphelinat. Comptable. Je reviens un peu en arrière. Quand nous avions été évacués la première fois, c'est-à-dire

he bought a ticket only for himself, and that I would remain in Zagorsk. Everything had been irreversibly done. I had neither a job nor a place to live anymore. He left quietly, and I remained. What was all this? A base act, carelessness, egoism? Egoism. Why did he have to take me out of work, from my apartment? I was interminably depressed. I was moved into a dormitory where janitors from the museum lived. There was cursing, they stole food from me. Everyday the commandant reminded me that I had to leave the dorm. I walked the streets in search of a job and an apartment. In one courtyard I got a painful dog-bite. First I found a room, then a job. In an orphanage. As an accountant. I'll go back a bit. When we were evacuated the first time, that is,

er hätte nur für sich eine Fahrkarte gekauft, ich solle noch in Zagorsk bleiben. Alles war schon endgültig geregelt. Ich hatte keine Arbeit mehr und keine Wohnung. Er fuhr ruhig weg, und ich blieb da. Was konnte das sein? Niederträchtigkeit, Sorglosigkeit, Egoismus? Egoismus. Warum sollte ich kündigen und meine Wohnung aufgeben? Meine Verzweiflung war grenzenlos. Man ließ mich im Heim der Museumswächter wohnen. Dort wurde geflucht, man stahl mir Lebensmittel. Der Kommandant erinnerte mich jeden Tag daran, daß ich das Heim verlassen müsse. Ich ging durch die Straßen und suchte Arbeit und Wohnung. In einem Hof wurde ich von Hunden gebissen. Aber alles hat ein Ende. Erst fand ich ein Zimmer, dann auch eine Arbeit. Im Kinderheim als Rechnungsführerin. Ich schweife ein wenig ab. Als wir erstmals in der Evakuation waren, d.h.

Мы посещали дом за домом, знакомясь с десятками новых людей. Среди них были и любители рукоделия и любители поговорить об охоте, рыбной ловле, обо всем на свете.

он взял только билет себе, а я еще останусь в Загорске. Все было оформлено окончательно. Ни работы, ни квартиры у меня уже не было Он спокойно уехал, а я осталась. Что это было? Низкий поступок, безза ботность, эгоизм ? Эгоизм. Зачем же было снимать меня с работы, с квартиры? Отчаянию моему не было конца. Меня переселили в общежитие, где жили вахтеры музея. Ругань, воровали у меня продукты, Комендант каждый день напоминал чтобы я освободила общежитие Я ходила по улицам в поисках работы и квартиры. В одном дворе меня больно покусали собаки. Новое имеет свой конец. Сначала нашла комнату, потом и работу. В детдоме. Счетоводом.
Вернусь немного назад. Когда мы были первый раз в эвакуации, т.е.

La Vie humiliée Life as an insult Leben als Erniedrigung Жизнь как оскорбление

Aujourd'hui c'est une ville de métallurgistes. Ils fondent l'acier et la fonte, laminent la tôle et le profilé, fabriquent des tuyaux bimétalliques et travaillés à froid, des roues de trains et des tubes destinés aux trous de forage, produisent des articles de quincaillerie et du coke.

Today this is a city of metallurgists. Steel and cast-iron are melted here, sheet and roll-formed metal are rolled, bimetal and cold-drawn pipes, railway wheels and pipes for bore-holes are manufactured, hardware and coke are produced.

Heute ist das eine Stadt der Metallarbeiter. Hier wird Stahl und Eisen geschmolzen, hier werden Walzbleche und Profileisen erzeugt, bimetallische und kaltgeformte Röhren, Eisenbahnräder und Rohre für Erdölbohrungen, Metallwaren und Koks.

dans le Caucase du nord, nous avions commencé à travailler avec mon mari, notre fils allait à l'école. Il était en deuxième année. Personne d'autre parmi les évacués n'envoyait son enfant à l'école, mais moi, je le faisais, en pensant que nous resterions longtemps et que ce n'était pas bien de manquer l'école. Comme les enfants du pays le battaient sans pitié, un jour il a déclaré qu'il n'irait plus en classe. Je l'ai persuadé de ne pas quitter l'école. Se plaindre des enfants ne servait à rien et je lui ai recommandé de trouver des contacts avec eux, ce qu'il a su faire. Il dessinait de très jolis chevaux et les donnait à tout le monde. Les relations ont changé et il est devenu la coqueluche de la classe au point que les garçons venaient le voir chez nous. Encore une lacune dans ces mémoires. Lorsque je suis restée sans emploi, alors que l'Académie et l'école étaient déjà parties pour Léningrad, je suis entrée au

in the Northern Caucasus, my husband and I went to work and we sent our son to school. He entered the second grade. None of the evacuees sent their children to school, but I did, thinking that we would be there for a long time, and that it wouldn't be wise to miss school. The local children beat him, and once he announced that he wasn't going to school anymore. I convinced him not to quit school. It didn't make any sense to complain about the kids, and I suggested that he find his own approach to the children, and he did. He started to draw wonderful horses, and he would give them away as gifts to remember him by. Their attitude changed, and he became the class favorite, and the kids even came to see him at home. There's still one more blank spot in my biography. When I was left without a job and the Academy and school had already left for Leningrad, I went to work

im nördlichen Kaukasus, gingen mein Mann und ich arbeiten, und den Sohn gaben wir in die Schule. Niemand von den Evakuierten schickten ihre Kinder zur Schule, ich schon, da ich dachte, wir würden länger bleiben, und es gehört sich nicht, Schule zu schwänzen. Er ging in die zweite Klasse. Die Kinder vom Ort verprügelten ihn und einmal erklärte er, er werde nicht mehr zur Schule gehen. Ich überredete ihn, die Schule nicht aufzugeben. Es macht keinen Sinn, sich über die Buben zu beklagen, und ich riet ihm, selber einen Zugang zu den Kindern zu finden, und er fand etwas. Er zeichnete wunderschöne Pferde und schenkte jedem eine Zeichnung zur Erinnerung. Die Verhältnisse änderten sich, er wurde der Liebling der Klasse und sogar zu Hause besuchten ihn Mitschüler. Noch eine Lücke habe ich in meiner Biographie entdeckt. Als ich ohne Arbeit war, und die Akademie und die Schule schon nach Leningrad abgereist waren, trat ich

Сегодня это — город металлургов. Здесь плавят сталь и чугун, катают листовой и профильный металл, производят биметаллические и холоднодеформированные трубы, железнодорожные колеса и трубы для буровых скважин, выпускают метизы и кокс...

на Северном Кавказе, мы с мужем поступили работать, а сына отдали в школу. Он пошел во второй класс. Никто из эвакуированных не отдал детей в школу, а я отдала, думая, что мы надолго здесь останемся, а пропускать школу не следовало. Дети местные его били, а однажды он заявил, что больше в школу не пойдет. Я уговорила его не бросать школу. Жаловаться на ребя не имело смысла, а я посоветовала ему самому найти подход к детям и он нашел. Он стал рисовать прекрасных лошадей и каждому дарил на память. Отношения переменились, он стал же любимцем класса, даже домой к нему ходили ребята. Еще один пропуск я обнаружила в своей биографии. Когда я осталась без работы, а Академия и школа уже уехали в Ленинград, я поступила в

La Vie humiliée Life as an insult Leben als Erniedrigung Жизнь как оскорбление

Entrée principale du Palais de la Science.

The main entrance to the Palace of Science.

Die Haupteingang des Palastes der Wissenschaften.

Service social de Zagorsk comme inspecteur des retraites de militaires. Le problème du travail résolu, je n'ai toujours pas où vivre. Vers cette époque, les médecins me déconseillent de mettre mon fils dans un foyer et je m'arrange pour qu'aux Beaux-Arts on lui accorde un congé d'un an. Il fréquente l'école municipale de Zagorsk et passe la nuit avec moi. Comme je n'ai pas d'appartement, la nuit, je le garde dans mon bureau. Mon fils dort sur les chaises, moi — sur le bureau, les dossiers sous la tête. Je me lève à 5 heures, parce qu'une femme vient pour chauffer les locaux et faire le ménage. Je fais les poussières moi-même, elle lave le sol. Cela dure tout l'hiver. Enfin une employée du musée me propose sa place et sa chambre. Ainsi, je me retrouve au musée. Je travaille à la caisse et comme secrétaire. Ma chambre est une ancienne cellule, face au

at the social security office in Zagorsk as an inspector for matters involving military pensions. I had a job but no place to live. About that time the doctors recommended that I didn't place my son in the dormitory, and I arranged for a year's leave of absence from the art school for him. He went to the regular school in Zagorsk and stayed with me at night. We didn't have an apartment, so we would stay at the social security office at night. My son slept on the chairs, and I slept on the table, using document folders as a pillow. I would get up at 5 o'clock, since that's when the cleaning lady used to come to clean and heat the place. I dusted and she washed the floors. So this is how it was for a few winter months. Finally, an employee of the Museum came to visit me and offered me her job and her room. That's how I wound up in the Museum. I worked as a cashier and secretary. The room, a former cell, was opposite the bell-tower

in Zagorsk eine Stelle bei der Sozialfürsorge an, als Inspektor für Heeresrenten. Eine Arbeit hatte ich, aber wo sollte ich wohnen. Zu dieser Zeit rieten mir die Ärzte, meinen Sohn nicht im Wohnheim zu lassen und ich nahm ihn für ein Jahr aus der Kunstschule. Er besuchte die normale Schule in Zagorsk und nächtigte bei mir. Wohnung hatte ich keine, und so übernachtete ich mit ihm im Sozialamt. Der Sohn schlief auf Stühlen, ich auf einem Tisch, mit einer Mappe unterm Kopf. Um 5 Uhr standen wir auf, da die Putzfrau kam, um zu heizen und aufzuräumen. Ich wischte selber den Staub, na und sie wusch den Boden auf. So ging das einige Wintermonate. Endlich kam eine Mitarbeiterin des Museums und bot mir ihre Arbeit und ihr Zimmer an. So fand ich mich im Museum wieder. Ich arbeitete als Kassier und als Sekretärin. Das Zimmer war eine frühere Mönchszelle, gegenüber

Главный подъезд дворца науки.

Загорске в Собес на должность инспектора по военным пенсиям, Служба была, а вот жить было негде. К тому времени врачи посоветовали не отдавать сына в общежитие и я взяла на год ему отпуск из средне худ.школы. Он пошел в обыкновенную школу в Загорске и ночевал со мной Квартиры не было и я с ним оставалась в Собесе ночевать. Сын спал на стульях, я на столе, подложил себе папки под голову. Вставала 5 ч., так как приходила уборщица топить и убирать. Я сама вытирала пыль, ну а полы она мыла. Так продолжалось несколько зимних месяцев. Наконец, пришла сотрудница музея и предложила мне свою работу и комнату. Таким образом я очутилась в Музее. Работала я кассиром, секретарем. Комната была бывшая келья, напротив коло-

Le bâtiment du restaurant « Le Phare » se marie bien avec le profil du rocher de granit.

The building of the restaurant "Lighthouse" fits organically into the coastal granite rock.

Der Bau des Restaurants » Leuchtturm « fügt sich organisch in die Granitfelsen des Ufers ein.

clocher. Elle est impossible à chauffer. Le musée distribue un fagot de bois par jour. Donc, après mon départ du musée, lorsque mon mari est parti, j'entre à l'orphelinat et je loue une chambre chez une femme très sympathique. Elle habite avec sa fille et ses deux fils, son mari est mort à la guerre. Cet orphelinat n'est pas comme les autres. Il dépend de la ville de Moscou pour son approvisionnement, les enfants aussi viennent de Moscou, c'est-à-dire de différents orphelinats de Moscou. Mais comment sont-ils, ces enfants? Un jour ils ont dévalisé un magasin et revendu beaucoup de vêtements chers au marché. Des enfants terribles. L'un d'eux surtout se fait remarquer. Chef de bande des gamins, qui le suivent partout. Sa parole fait loi. Il commande aussi au sein de l'orphelinat: ils pénètrent, par exemple, dans la salle des profs et chipent tout ce qui leur tombe

It was impossible to heat it. The museum gave out a small bundle of firewood a day. And so, after I quit working at the museum and my husband had left, I went to work at the orphanage and rented a room from a very nice landlady. She lived with her daughter and 2 sons, her husband had died at the front. This orphanage was special. It was considered to be a Moscow one in terms of provisions, and the children there were Muscovites, ie. they were from all the orphanages in Moscow, but what kind of kids were they? They stole from the storeroom and they sold a lot of valuable clothing at the market. They were terrible children. One of them especially stood out. He was the ataman of all the younger kids, they followed him around like a gang. His word was law for them. It was his gang in the orphanage, they even got into the teachers' office and stole whatever they laid their

vom Glockenturm. Es war unmöglich zu heizen. Das Museum stellte ein Bund Holz pro Tag zur Verfügung. Also nach der Entlassung aus dem Museum, als mein Mann abgereist war, trat ich beim Kinderheim eine Stelle an und mietete ein Zimmer bei einer sehr netten Eigentümerin. Sie lebte mit ihrer Tochter und zwei Söhnen, der Mann war im Krieg gefallen. Dieses Kinderheim war etwas Besonderes. Es wurde von Moskau aus versorgt und die Kinder dort waren Moskauer Kinder, d.h. aus verschiedenen Moskauer Heimen, aber was für Kinder? Sie stahlen aus der Vorratskammer und verkauften viel wertvolle Kleidung auf dem Markt. Schreckliche Kinder. Einer von ihnen zeichnete sich besonders aus. Er war der Häuptling der Kleineren, ihm folgten sie in Scharen. Sein Wort war für sie Gesetz. Diese Räuberbande herrschte im Kinderheim, sogar ins Lehrerzimmer drangen sie ein und stahlen, was nur

Органично вписалось в прибрежную гранитную скалу здание ресторана «Маяк»

кольни. Натопить её было невозможно. Дров выдавал вязанку в день музей. Итак после увольнения из музея, когда муж уехал, я поступила в детдом и наняла комнату у очень хорошей хозяйки. Она жила с дочерью и 2 сыновьями, муж погиб на фронте. Этот детдом был особенный. Он считался по снабжению московским и дети там были московские, т.е. из всех детдомов Москвы, но какие? Они обворовали кладовую и много ценной одежды перепродали на рынке. Ужасные дети. Особенно отличался один из них. Атаман всех малышей. Они гурьбой ходили за ним. Его слово было для них законом. Эта же его команда была в дет доме даже в учительскую они забирались и воровали чтотольуо попадет

La ville ouvrière compte bien des héros, bien des métiers. Pourtant ce sont les œuvres des architectes et des constructeurs qui ont toujours joui d'une grande célébrité. Elles créent les contours et l'image de la ville.

A working city has many heroes, many professions. However, the works of builders and architects have always remained the most famous and honoured. It is they who create the image of a city, its face.

Viele Helden, viele Berufe hat die Arbeiterstadt. Aber am meisten bemerkenswert und geehrt ist das Schaffen der Bauarbeiter und Architekten. Sie sind es, die das Stadtbild gestalten.

sous la main. Bref, tout à coup ce meneur se met à me manifester des égards. Il tourne autour de moi, dit bonjour avec gentillesse, demande de lui prêter un livre. Si l'on joue un film, il garde toujours une place pour moi. Les professeurs s'en aperçoivent et me prient de le parrainer. Je vais avec lui à Moscou chercher les salaires, je lui achète des sucreries. Quand mon fils vient me voir le dimanche, le gamin se montre très attentif et respectueux à son égard. Il commence à s'assagir, fait moins de bêtises, tout le monde s'en réjouit. A ce moment, on annonce des cours accélérés de fabrication de décorations de Noël. Il y a à Zagorsk la « Maison du jouet » et les cours se déroulent là-bas. Je rêve d'apprendre à fabriquer des décorations et mon directeur y consent. Il paie mon stage et il m'autorise à

eyes on. And so, all of a sudden this ataman turned his attention toward me. He started to appear before my eyes all the time, and politely greeted me, asked to borrow books. And when there was a film, he saved a seat for me. The teachers took an interest in all this, and advised me to take charge of him. I started to go to Moscow with him to pick up our salary, and would buy him treats. And when my son came to visit on Sunday, he would also show him respect. The boy began to straighten up, he misbehaved less often, and we were all happy looking at him. By that time courses had begun on making Christmas tree toys. There was a "House of Toys" in Zagorsk, and the courses were held there. I really wanted to learn how to make toys and my director helped me. He paid for the lessons and let me

ging. Und dieser Häuptling begann mich plötzlich zu verehren. Er paßte mich ab, grüßte mich liebenswürdig, wollte sich Bücher ausleihen. Und wenn ein Film gezeigt wurde, reservierte er für mich einen Platz. Die Pädagogen interessierten sich für diesen Fall, und rieten mir, eine Art Patenschaft für ihn zu übernehmen. Ich begann mit ihm nach Moskau zu fahren, um das Gehalt abzuholen und kaufte ihm Süßigkeiten. Als mein Sohn am Sonntag zu mir kam, erwies er auch ihm Respekt und Verehrung. Der Bub begann sich augenscheinlich zu bessern, stellte weniger an, und wir freuten uns alle. Damals wurden Kurse zur Herstellung von Schmuck für den Neujahrsbaum angeboten. In Zagorsk gab es ein » Haus des Spielzeugs « und dort fanden die Kurse statt. Ich wollte das sehr gern lernen und der Direktor kam mir entgegen. Er zahlte mir den Kurs und verlegte

Много героев, много профессий у рабочего города. Однако самыми заметными и почетными всегда оставались дела строителей, зодчих. Это они создают портрет города, его облик.

на глаза. Так вот этот атаман вдруг проникся вниманием ко мне. Стал попадаться мне на глаза, любезно здоровался, просил почитать книжку. А когда было кино берег для меня место. Педагоги заинтересовались этим явлением и посоветовали взять над ним шефство. Я стала в Москву ездить с ним за зарплатой, покупала ему лакомства Когда сын приезжал ко мне на в скресение, ему тоже оказывал почет и уважение. Парень стал исправляться, меньше шалил все мы радовались, глядя на него. К тому времени открылись кратковременные курсы по выделке елочных игрушек. В Загорске был "дом игрушки" и курсы проходили там. Я оченьзахотела обучиться делать игрушки и директор пошел мне на встречу. Уплатил за обучение, перенес мой

La Vie humiliée Life as an insult Leben als Erniedrigung Жизнь как оскорбление

Au laboratoire de biochimie de la cellule animale. Les lauréats du prix Staline, le professeur V. A. Enguelgardt, membre correspondant de l'Académie des Sciences, membre titulaire de l'Académie de Médecine, et M. N. Lubimova, directeur de recherches, étudient les propriétés mécaniques de l'albumen.

In the laboratory of animal cell biochemistry. Laureates of the Stalin Prize, corresponding member of the Academy of Sciences of the USSR, active member of the Academy of Medical Sciences of the USSR, Professor V. A. Engelgardt, and senior scientific fellow, M. N. Lubimova are studying the mechanical properties of protein.

Im Laboratorium für Tierzellen-Biochemie. Hier erforschen V. A. Engelgardt, Stalinpreisträger und korrespondierendes Mitglied der Akademie der Wissenschaften der UdSSR, und der wissenschaftliche Mitarbeiter M. N. Ljubimova die mechanischen Eigenschaften des Eiweisses.

travailler le soir. Je lui promets de décorer l'arbre de Noël avec l'aide des enfants. Je m'épuise à organiser la fête. Les enfants se montrent insupportables. Ils confectionnent des jouets pour les casser aussitôt. Les matériaux disparaissent et mon protégé s'avère des plus zélés. Avec beaucoup de peine on fait 300 jouets. J'invite des gens de l'Education Nationale qui apprécient la présentation ; ils me félicitent et j'en suis très heureuse, tous mes tracas sont aussitôt oubliés. Je fais moi-même le grand Père Noël et la Fille des Neiges, et les enfants confectionnent tous les autres sujets. Même mon fils, quand il est là, nous donne un coup de main. Quelques mois s'écoulent jusqu'au jour où l'on reçoit un arrêté de Moscou : notre budget est revu à la baisse, l'orphelinat ne sera plus approvisionné par la ville de Moscou, certains emplois sont supprimés et je suis congédiée. Que faire ? Mon fils me donne l'idée de

work at night. I promised to decorate the tree with the help of the kids. I put a lot into organizing a tree trimming. The kids were terrible. They made the toys and then destroyed them right away. All the materials disappeared, and my charge really distinguished himself. But with difficulty we made 300 toys. I invited people from the City Education Council, and they really liked my undertaking, everyone thanked me, and I was happy, having forgotten about all my worries. I made a big Santa Claus and Snow Maiden by myself, and the kids made all the toys. Even my son, when he came, also helped us. And so this lasted for a few months, and then came the order from Moscow that they were cutting our allowable expenditures, the orphanage was no longer to be financially supported by Moscow, there were lay-offs and I lost my job. What was to be done. My son advised me

meine Arbeitszeit auf den Abend. Ich versprach, zusammen mit den Kindern den Neujahrsbaum zu schmücken. Ich gab mir sehr viel Mühe, den Baumschmuck zu organisieren. Die Kinder waren schrecklich. Sie stellten etwas her und ruinierten es sofort. Alles Material verschwand, besonders mein Schützling zeichnete sich aus. Mit viel Mühe brachten sie doch 300 Stück Neujahrsbaumschmuck fertig. Ich lud Vertreter der Städtischen Volksbildung ein, denen meine Idee sehr gefiel, alle dankten mir, ich war glücklich und alle Aufregungen waren vergessen. Die großen Figuren von Väterchen Frost und der Schneeprinzessin hatte ich selbst gemacht. Sogar mein Sohn half uns, wenn er kam. So ging es einige Monate, aber dann kam eine Anordnung aus Moskau, unser Budget wurde gekürzt, das Heim wurde nicht mehr von Moskau versorgt, Personal wurde entlassen und ich wurde gekündigt. Was sollte ich machen. Mein Sohn riet mir,

В лаборатории биохимии животной клетки. Лауреаты Сталинской премии член-корреспондент Академии наук СССР, действительный член Академии медицинских наук СССР, профессор В.А. Энгельгардт и старший научный сотрудник М.Н. Любимова изучают механические свойст...

рабочий день на вечер. Я обещала силами ребят украсить елку. Я много труда потратила, чтобы организовать елку. Ребята были ужасные. Делали игрушки и тут же их портили. Исчезали все материалы, особенно отличался мой подопечный. Но с трудом все же сделали 300 игрушек. Пригласила из ГОРОНО, им очень понравилась моя затея. Все меня благодарили, и я была счастлива, забыв все волнения. Большого деда мороза и снегурочку я сделала сама, а все игрушки сделали дети. Даже сын когда приезжал тоже помогал нам. Так длилось несколько месяцев, но вот пришло распоряжение из Москвы, что нам урезали смету, дом стал уже не Москвой обеспечиваться, настало сокращение штатов и меня уволили. Что было делать. Сын посоветовал

Aujourd'hui c'est une ville de constructeurs de machines. Locomotives et wagons basculants, tracteurs et machines pour l'industrie papetière, équipement pour la métallurgie, équipement de silos et machines de meunerie, moteurs électriques et réfrigérateurs de ménage fabriqués à Dniépropétrovsk jouissent d'une bonne renommée dans notre pays et à l'étranger.

Today this is a city of machine-builders. Electric locomotives and dump-trucks, tractors and paper-manufacturing machines, metallurgical and mill and grain-elevator equipment, electric motors and household refrigerators with the Dnepropetrovsk trade-mark have won popularity in our country and abroad.

Heute ist das eine Stadt der Maschinenbauer. E-Loks und Draisinen, Traktoren und Papierverarbeitungsmaschinen, Werkzeugmaschinen und Aufzugstechnik, Elektromotoren und Kühlschränke aus Dnepropetrovsk sind sowohl bei uns wie im Ausland populär.

partir avec eux en colonie de vacances. Je m'adresse au censeur et je suis admise comme économe et comptable ; nous partons en colonie. C'est très difficile. Il faut calculer les vivres selon les normes. Le linge et la vaisselle font aussi partie de mes attributions. Les gens du pays volent d'une façon effrontée. Embauchés pour travailler aux cuisines et faire le ménage, ils substituent leurs vieilles assiettes et tasses à notre belle vaisselle. Les ustensiles de cuisine, les serviettes, tout est remplacé de sorte que la quantité reste la même, mais la qualité se dégrade. Ces escroqueries m'exaspèrent, mais je n'y peux rien. Heureusement, l'été fini, je rapatrie le matériel à l'école. Je n'ai toujours pas de logement, je continue à payer régulièrement ma chambre à Zagorsk, mais rentrer

to go to summer camps with him. I went to see the director of the school and they made me an administrator and accountant, and we left for camp. It was very difficult. It was necessary to ration out the food. I was responsible for the linens and dishes. The local inabitants stole terribly. They hired locals for work in the cafeteria and for cleaning, and they would switch the nice dishes with their old ones. They switched everything — kitchen pots and pans, towels — the quantity didn't change, but the quality was horrible. My head was spinning from everything I saw, but I couldn't do anything. Luckily the summer season ended, and I transferred the entire inventory to the school. I didn't have anywhere to live, even though I paid regularly for the room in Zagorsk, but I just didn't have the strength to travel to Zagorsk when

mit ihnen ins Ferienlager zu fahren. Ich wandte mich an den Schulleiter und wurde als Betreuerin und Rechnungsführerin eingestellt, und wir fuhren ins Lager. Es war sehr schwierig. Die notwendigen Lebensmittel mußten der Norm entsprechend berechnet werden. Ich war für Wäsche und Geschirr zuständig. Die ortsansässigen Mitarbeiter stahlen fürchterlich. Für die Arbeit im Speisesaal und fürs Putzen wurden Ortsansässige eingestellt, sie tauschten das schöne Geschirr in ihre alten Teller und Tassen um. Küchengeschirr, Handtücher — alles wurde umgetauscht, die Quantität blieb gleich, nur die Qualität war schrecklich. Mir drehte sich der Kopf von all dem, was ich mit ansehen mußte, aber ich konnte gar nichts machen. Zum Glück ging die Sommersaison zu Ende, und ich übertrug das ganze Inventar in die Schule. Ich wußte nicht, wo ich wohnen sollte, obwohl ich regelmäßig für das Zimmer in Zagorsk zahlte, aber täglich nach Zagorsk fahren

Сегодня это — город машиностроителей. Электровозы и думпкары, тракторы и бумагоделательные машины, металлургическое и мельнично-элеваторное оборудование, электродвигатели и бытовые холодильники с днепропетровской маркой завоевали популярность в нашей стране и за рубежом.

поехать с ними в лагеря. Я обратилась к зав.школой и меня зачислили сестрой хозяйкой и счетоводом и мы уехали в лагеря. Было очень трудно. Нужно было вычислять по норме нужные продукты. Белье и посуда были на моей ответственности. Воровали местные жители ужасно Для работы в столовую, на уборку помещения брали местных, они меняли прекрасную посуду на свои старые тарелки, чашки. Кухонную посуду, полотенца все обменивали, количество не менялось, но качество было ужасно. Я теряла голову от всего виденного, но ничего поделать не могла. К счастью летний сезон закончился и я перенесла весь инвентарь в школу. Жить мне было негде, хотя я платила регулярно за комнату в Загорске, но ехать в Загорск, когд а

La Vie humiliée Life as an insult Leben als Erniedrigung Жизнь как оскорбление

A Krasnodar a été inaugurée la première exposition d'inventeurs et de rationalisateurs ruraux.

The first exhibit of works by village inventors and rationalizers was opened in Krasnodar.

In Krasnodar wurde die erste Ausstellung von Arbeiten landwirtschaftlicher Erfinder und Rationalisierer eröffnet.

à Zagorsk, à 1 heure 40 de train, c'est au-dessus de mes forces. Je demande mon compte, sollicite un autre emploi et on me nomme concierge. Je couche là où j'ai stocké le matériel, dans des toilettes qui ne fonctionnent pas depuis longtemps. On m'a donné un lit, un matelas et je vis là. Mon fils habite dans un foyer. Un soir, il vient me voir et comme j'oublie de fermer la porte d'entrée à clef, le directeur de l'école s'en aperçoit. Le lendemain, l'avis de licenciement est signé. Je commence à travailler à Kalantchevka. A l'entrepôt de tissus, lin et coton. J'y reste de 1947 à 1957, année où je prendrai ma retraite. Je loge toujours dans les toilettes. Mais un jour l'intendant surgit, avisé que j'habite dans les locaux de l'école sans plus y travailler et me dénonce au directeur. Aussitôt,

it took 1 hour 40 minutes to get there by train. I settled my accounts and requested other work, and they made me a janitor at the school. I slept where the inventory was kept, in the bathroom which hadn't worked for a long time. They gave me a cot and mattress and I lived there. My son lived in a dormitory. But then one night my son came to me and I forgot to lock the front door after him and the director of the school came in. The next day I was fired. I started to work on Kalanchevka Street. A warehouse for cotton and linen goods. I worked here from 1947 to 1957, when I retired. Just like before, I lived in the bathroom. But then the administrator stopped in somehow, and saw that I was living at the school but didn't work there anymore, and he reported to the director, and they

bei einer Wegzeit von 1 Stunde 40 Minuten, das war zuviel für mich. Ich rechnete ab, bat um eine andere Arbeit und wurde Wächterin an der Schule. Ich übernachtete dort, wo ich das Inventar abgegeben hatte, im Abort, der schon lange außer Betrieb war. Man gab mir eine Bettstelle und eine Matratze, und dort lebte ich. Mein Sohn wohnte im Heim. Aber einmal am Abend kam mein Sohn zu mir und ich vergaß, hinter ihm die Eingangstür abzuschließen, als der Schuldirektor hereinkam. Am nächsten Tag wurde ich entlassen. Ich fand eine Arbeit auf der Kalantschevka. In einer Textilbasis für Baumwoll- und Leinenwaren. Dort arbeitete ich von 1947 bis 1957, als ich in Pension ging. Ich wohnte wie früher im Abort. Aber einmal kam der Hausleiter herein, sah, daß ich in der Schule wohnte, obwohl ich nicht mehr dort arbeitete und erstattete dem Direktor Bericht,

В Краснодаре была открыта краевая выставка работ сельских изобретателей и рационализаторов.

дорога элетричкой была 1ч40 мин. в один конец, это было не в моих силах. Я расчитывалась попросила работу другую и меня зачислили вахтером при школе. Ночевала я куда сдала инвентарь, в уборной, которая не работала давно. Мне дали койку, матриц, и я жила там. Сын жил в общежитии. Но вот как то вечером пришел ко мне сын, я забыла за ним запереть входную дверь и вошел директор школы. На завтра был приказ о моем увольнении. Начала работу на Каланчевке База хлопчато и льняных товаров, Эдесь я проработала с 1947 по 1957 год, когда пошла на пенсию. Жила я попрежнему в уборной. Но вот как тонискокккк наскочил завхоз, увидел, что я живу при школе, а уже там не работаю и доложил директору и у меня

La Vie humiliée Life as an insult Leben als Erniedrigung Жизнь как оскорбление

Les avenues, absorbant les ruisseaux des rues, déferlent sur le quai du Dniepr.

The wide streets, as though engulfing streams of little streets, rush in torrents toward the banks, toward the Dnieper River.

Breite Straßen, in die kleine Gässchen münden wie in einen Strom, streben zum Ufer, zum Dnepr.

on me retire la clef des toilettes. Il faut partir à Zagorsk, alors que je travaille à Moscou. C'est possible, personne ne s'y oppose. Or le rationnement est toujours en vigueur. Il faut que mon CV soit certifié par la propriétaire de ma chambre et tamponné au Comité exécutif. Pendant quelque temps, je fais des allers et retours, mais cela m'épuise. Je prends rendez-vous avec la secrétaire de cellule pour lui expliquer que je ne peux plus continuer comme ça. Je me lève à 5 heures pour attraper le train de 6 heures et être au bureau vers 8 heures. Elle me recommande à sa secrétaire pour qu'elle me loue un lit. Celle-ci accepte. Certes, je n'ai pas de permis de résidence. Cette femme se révèle méchante ; sa fille, une écolière, me vole toutes mes provisions. Je ne peux rien laisser de comestible. Elles dévorent tout. Cela dure un certain temps, jusqu'au jour où l'on trouve

took the keys to the bathroom away from me. I had to travel to Zagorsk, but I worked in Moscow. That was possible, no one objected. But at that time we had the system of ration cards. You had to have the form certified by the person you rented from and then have it stamped in the City Committee. I ran around for a while, but I just wasn't able to keep this up. I went to see the Party organizer, and explained that I couldn't make the trip. I had to get up at 5 o'clock to make the 6 o'clock train and arrive at work by 8:00. She put in a good word for me with the secretary, so that she would allow me to have a cot. She agreed. Of course, I didn't have a residence permit. She turned out to be an awful woman, her daughter, who was a school-kid, stole all my food. I couldn't leave anything edible. Everything was eaten, to the last crumb. This went on for a while, until

und mir wurde der Abortschlüssel abgenommen. So mußte ich nach Zagorsk fahren, obwohl ich in Moskau arbeitete. Das war möglich, niemand hatte etwas dagegen. Aber es gab Lebensmittelkarten. Man mußte ein Formular ausfüllen und vom Vermieter und vom Exekutivkomitee bestätigen lassen. Eine Zeitlang fuhr ich hin und her, aber es ging über meine Kräfte. Ich wandte mich an den Parteiorganisator und erklärte, ich könne nicht hin und her fahren, ich müsse um 5 Uhr aufstehen, um den 6 Uhr zug zu erreichen, damit ich um 8 Uhr in der Arbeit sei. Sie empfahl mich der Sekretärin, die mir eine Schlafstelle vermieten könne. Sie war einverstanden. Anmeldung hatte ich natürlich keine. Sie erwies sich als ganz üble Person, ihre Tochter, eine Schülerin, stahl mir alle Lebensmittel. Man konnte nichts Eßbares liegen lassen. Alles wurde weggegessen. So ging es einige Zeit, bis an allen Türen

Широкие улицы, словно вбирая в себя ручейки улочек, потоками устремляются к набережной, к Днепру.

забрали ключ от уборной. Нужно было ехать в Загорск, а работала я в Москве. Это можно было, никто не возражал. Но была карточная система. Нужно было заверить анкету и у хозяйки, и в Исполкоме поставить печать. Я поездила некоторое время, но это было не в моих силах. Я обратилась к парторгу и объяснила, что не могу ездить. Нужно было вставать в 5 ч чтобы успеть на шестичасовый поезд и приехать к 8 ч. утра на работу. Она порекомендовала меня секретарю, чтобы она пустила меня на койку. Она согласилась. Прописки конечно не было. Она оказалась очень плохой женщиной, дочка школьница воровала все мои продукты. Оставлять ничего съестного нельзя было. Все съедалось до основания. Так продолжалось некоторое время, пока на дверях

Grandes dates, événements tragiques et héroïques de notre époque. Avec le temps ils revêtent une autre dimension. Pour ne pas disparaître, pour ne pas être noyés dans les affaires courantes mais pour être transmis à nos descendants.

Memorable dates in history, tragic and heroic events of our epoch. It's as though they cross into a different dimension with time. So as not to disappear, not to get lost in the fast lane of life, but rather to remain for our descendents.

Historische Daten, tragische und heroische Ereignisse unserer Epoche. Mit der Zeit scheinen sie in eine andere Dimension überzugehen. Mögen sie nicht verschwinden, nicht verlorengehen in der Eile des Lebens, sondern für die Nachkommen erhalten bleiben.

sur la porte une annonce qui menace de sanctions ceux qui sous-louent aux personnes sans permis. Aussitôt après cet avis, la propriétaire me jette dehors. Je m'adresse à nouveau au secrétaire du Parti qui me passe l'adresse d'une ancienne employée de l'entrepôt. Je vais la voir, ce n'est pas loin de mon travail, dans la ruelle Grokholski. Elle me permet d'abord de passer chez elle une nuit et quand elle comprend ma situation, elle consent à me garder. C'est mon bon ange. Elle s'appelle Elisavéta Borissovna. Elle est morte à présent, mais son bon souvenir restera à jamais dans ma mémoire. Je reste chez elle plus d'un an. Plus que chez n'importe quelle autre propriétaire. Entre-temps, mon fils se fait exclure pour un mois du foyer pour je ne sais plus quelle faute.

an announcement appeared on the door saying that everyone who had tenants without residence permits would be punished. Having read this announcement, the landlady threw me out of the apartment. I appealed to the Party chief again, and she gave me the address of a former employee at the warehouse. I went to see her, it wasn't far away from my work on Grokholsky Lane. She allowed me to spend the night only, but then she put herself in my place and didn't refuse me shelter anymore. This was the bright angel in my life. Her name was Elizaveta Borisovna. She has died already, but the bright memory of her has never dimmed in my soul. I lived with her for more than a year. Longer than with all my other landladies. During that time my son was thrown out of the dorm for some sort of offence.

eine Bekanntmachung hing, die eine Bestrafung aller Personen vorsah, die Untermieter ohne Anmeldung hatten. Nach dieser Bekanntmachung verlor ich sofort die Wohnung. Wieder ging ich zum Partorg, und sie gab mir die Adresse einer früheren Mitarbeiterin der Textilbasis. Ich ging zu ihr, das war nicht weit von Arbeit in der Grocholski-Gasse. Erst erlaubte sie mir zu übernachten, aber dann versetzte sie sich in meine Lage und bot mir Unterschlupf. Das war eine Lichtgestalt in meinem Leben. Sie hieß Elisaveta Borisovna. Sie ist schon gestorben, aber ich werde ihr immer ein gutes Andenken bewahren. Mehr als ein Jahr lebte ich bei ihr. Länger als bei all meinen übrigen Unterkunftsgeberinnen. Im Lauf dieser Zeit wurde mein Sohn wegen irgendeiner Verfehlung für einen Monat aus dem Heim ausgeschlossen.

...Памятные даты истории, трагические и героические события нашей эпохи. Со временем они как бы переходят в иное измерение. Чтобы не исчезнуть, не растеряться на быстрине жизни, а остаться для потомков.

не появилось объявление, что будут наказываться те лица, которые будут держать квартирантов без прописки. Прочитав это объявление, хозяйка тутже отказала мне в квартире. Обратилась опять к парторгу и она дала мне адрес бывшей сотрудницы базы. Я пришла к ней, это было недалеко от моей работы по Горохольскому переулку. Разрешила только переночевать и потом вошла в мое положение и не отказала мне больше в пристанище. Это был мой светлый ангел в моей жизни. Ее звали Елизавета Борисовна. Она уже умерла, но светлая память о ней никогда не угаснет в моей душе. Я прожила у нее больше года. Больше чем у всех моих хозяек. В течении этого времени за какую то провинность сына исключали из общежития на месяц.

Depuis longtemps l'homme a choisi ce pays pittoresque, riche en poisson, en gibier et au sol fertile. Des témoignages nous en sont parvenus jusqu'aujourd'hui.

Man selected these picturesque places rich with fish, wild game and fertile black-earth long ago. Evidence of this has remained until our times.

Schon lange liebt der Mensch diese malerischen, fisch- und wildreichen, fruchtbaren Schwarzerdegebiete. Zeugnisse sind bis heute erhalten.

Lui aussi, il vient loger chez E. B. Après les classes, il me rejoint à mon bureau où l'on reste jusqu'à 10 heures du soir avant de rentrer dormir chez elle. Mais rien n'est éternel. Mon fils a déjà regagné le foyer lorsqu'un soir, en sortant dans la cour pour chercher de l'eau à la borne-fontaine, me voilà repérée par une voisine. Immédiatement, elle le fait savoir à qui de droit et dans la nuit, ils font une descente pour contrôler mes papiers, mon permis de résidence. Du coup, ils déclarent que puisque je suis enregistrée en banlieue, je n'ai pas le droit de rester à Moscou. Le lendemain je n'ai plus de toit. Elisavéta Borissovna me case chez une de ses amies qui partage un appartement avec une femme et sa fille écolière. La propriétaire est célibataire, il y a aussi un autre locataire, un mutilé de guerre. Nous sommes disposés de la manière suivante : la pièce n'est pas

He also had to live with El. Boris. He would come to see me after class at school, we would sit until 10:00 at night at work and then go to her place. But nothing under the sun is forever. My son was once again in the dormitory, and one time I went out to bring water from the well in the courtyard and the neighbor saw me. She informed the proper authorities immediately, and in the middle of the night they came to check whether or not I was registered there. They said that I had a registration for a place out of town and that I didn't have a right to live in Moscow. The next day I was already without a roof over my head. Elizaveta Borisovna arranged for me to stay on a cot with her friend. She lived with still another neighbor who had a daughter that was still in school. The landlady herself was alone, and she had yet another tenant — a war invalid. We arranged things in the following way. The room wasn't

So wohnte er auch bei Elisaveta Borisowna. Nach dem Schulunterricht kam er zu mir, wir saßen bis 10 Uhr abends in der Arbeit und gingen dann zu ihr übernachten. Aber nichts auf der Welt dauert ewig. Mein Sohn war schon wieder im Heim, da sah mich eines Abends eine Nachbarin Wasser holen im Hof. Sie machte den zuständigen Stellen sofort Mitteilung und noch in derselben Nacht wurde kontrolliert, ob ich gemeldet sei. Am Morgen hatte ich wieder kein Dach über dem Kopf. Elisaveta Borisovna organisierte mir eine Schlafstelle bei einer Bekannten. Sie lebte mit einer Nachbarin zusammen, die eine schulpflichtige Tochter hatte. Die Bekannte war alleinstehend und hatte noch einen Untermieter, einen Kriegsinvaliden. Wir waren folgendermaßen untergebracht. Das Zimmer war nicht

Давно облюбовал человек эти живописные, богатые рыбой, дичью и тучными черноземами места. Свидетельства дошли до наших дней. В Аптекарской

Пришлось и ему жить у Ел.Борис. Он приходил ко мне после занятий в школе, сидели мы до 10 ч. вечера на работе и приходили ночевать к ней. Но ничто не вечно под луной. Сын уже снова был в общежитии а я вечером однажды вышла занести воды из колонки во дворе и меня увидела соседка. Она тут же дала знать куда следует и ночью пришли на проверку или я прописана. Сказали, что у меня прописка загородняя и я не имею права жить в Москве. Назавтра я уже была без крыши над голой. Елизавета Борисовна устроила меня на койку к своей знакомой. Она жила с еще одной соседкой, у которой была дочь школьница. Сама хозяйка одинокая имела еще квартиранта инвалида войны. Располагались мы следующим образом. Комната была неболь-

Dniépropétrovsk aujourd'hui, ville de la grande science.

Dnepropetrovsk today — a city of great science.

Dnepropetrovsk heute — eine Stadt der großen Wissenschaft.

grande et il y a le lit à deux places de la propriétaire, une table, le lit du mutilé, une commode. Je m'installe sur trois chaises, en travers de la pièce. Heureusement, le mutilé ne se lève pas la nuit, car il ne pourrait pas passer. A vrai dire, ce n'est pas très confortable, mais il n'y a qu'à s'y faire. Je vis de cette manière à peu près un an. Je ne sais plus comment on m'a donné l'adresse d'une femme infirme et je déménage chez elle, bien que la propriétaire regrette mon départ. La nouvelle propriétaire souffre d'encéphalite. Ses mains et ses pieds tremblent, elle est soignée par une infirmière. Elle s'attache à moi, mais je la supporte difficilement. Elle se réveille la nuit et pleure sur son destin malheureux. Impossible de dormir. Je fais la cuisine et mon fils vient dîner. L'appartement est surpeuplé et les voisins s'indignent de me voir

big. There was a double bed that belonged to the landlady, a table, the invalid's bed, a chest of drawers. I slept on three chairs across the room. It's a good thing that he didn't get up at night since there was no passage. You can't say that it was comfortable, but we had to bear it. I lived like this for about a year. Somehow I was given a Moscow address of a sick woman, and I left, though the landlady was sorry to see me go. The landlady had encephalitis. Her arms and legs shook, a nanny took care of her. She got very attached to me, but it was very hard for me. She woke up at night and would cry about her unhappy fate, what kind of sleep could I get. I cooked, and my son would come over for lunch. The apartment was very crowded, and the neighbors began to object that (*continued on the page 211*)

groß. Darin standen das Doppelbett der Hausfrau, ein Tisch, das Bett des Invaliden und eine Chiffonniere. Ich schlief auf 3 Stühlen, die quer im Zimmer standen. Gut, daß er in der Nacht nicht aufstand, denn Durchgang gab es keinen. Man kann nicht sagen, daß es bequem war, aber es ging nicht anders. Dort lebte ich ungefähr ein Jahr. Auf irgendeine Weise bekam ich eine Moskauer Adresse einer kranken Frau, und ich ging fort, obwohl der Hausfrau mein Weggang leid tat. Diese Wirtin litt an Enzephalitis, ihre Hände und Füße zitterten, sie wurde von einer Wärterin betreut. Obwohl sie sehr an mir hing, hielt ich es kaum aus mit ihr. Sie wachte in der Nacht auf und weinte über ihr unglückliches Schicksal, wie konnte ich da schlafen, ich kochte, und mein Sohn kam zu mir essen. Die Wohnung war ziemlich überfüllt, und die anderen Bewohner begannen sich darüber aufzuregen, daß ich (*Fortsetzung S. 220*)

Днепропетровск сегодня — город большой науки.

шая. Стояла 2х спальная кровать хозяйки, стол, койка инвалида, ши-
шифоньер. Я располагалась на 3х стульях поперек комнаты. Хорошо
что он не вставал по ночам, прохода не было. Чтобы было удобно
нельзя сказать. но нужно было терпеть. Так я прожила около года.
Каким то образом мне дали адрес московский к одной больной женщине и я ушла, хотя хозяйка жалела о моем уходе. Хозяйка была
больна инцефалитом. У нее дрожали руки и ноги, за ней ухажива
ля няня. Она очень привязалась ко мне, но мне было ужасно тяжело с
ней. Она просыпалась ночью и плакала о своей несчастной судьбе,
какой же тут был у меня сон, я готовила и сын приходил ко мне обе
дать. Квартира была густо населена и соседи стали возмущаться, что

Le jour s'éteint, la frénésie de la lutte s'apaise. Là où tout récemment, sous la lumière du jour écarlate, glissaient à toute vitesse des barques à voile, tout est calme et le soleil couchant répand sa lueur rosâtre.

The day is dwindling, the thrill of competition has waned. And there, where not long ago ice-yachts raced with enormous speed in the bright, sunny day, now everything has become quiet and is tranquilly turning rosy in the shimmering of the setting sun.

Der Tag erlischt, die Kampfeslust ist eingeschafen. Und dort, wo unlängst bei strahlenden Sonnenschein die Segler mit kolossaler Geschwindigkeit dahinflogen, ist jetzt alles still und erglänzt in einem ruhigen Sonnenuntergang.

utiliser la cuisine sans être enregistrée officiellement. Ces conditions m'épuisent complètement. L'aide soignante m'envie parce que la maîtresse de maison me préfère à elle. Rakhil Borissovna, c'est le nom de la propriétaire, est une femme cultivée. Elle était géologue. Probablement, elle a attrapé son encéphalite dans la taïga. Elle a été mariée trois fois. Magnanime, elle a renoncé à son mari, lui rendant sa liberté. Il vit ailleurs et vient la voir de temps en temps. Elle refuse son aide. Il s'est remarié, il a une nouvelle famille, mais il ne l'oublie pas. Nous habitons dans la petite rue Gnezdnikovski, si je ne me trompe. Dans la cour de notre immeuble se trouve le théâtre Romen où je ne suis jamais allée. Bref, il faut chercher un autre appartement. Une des voisines a une amie, une jeune fille qui dispose d'une pièce. La voisine l'embobine pour qu'elle me loue sa chambre car elle pourrait séduire mon fils et l'épouser. J'emménage chez elle.
Il se trouve qu'elle n'a pas de poêle. On chauffe la chambre depuis le couloir. Une autre chambre est occupée par un ivrogne qui vit seul ; son fils vient le voir et ils se saoulent ensemble. Je dors sur une planche, un battant de porte posé sur deux caisses. Je ne me déshabille pas tant que je reste chez elle, à cause du froid glacial. La chambre est si petite qu'il est impossible d'y mettre un autre lit. A l'endroit où l'on pourrait le placer, se trouve l'armoire. Cela aurait pu durer longtemps, mais un jour, le voisin fait un tel éclat que la milice doit intervenir. Le voisin leur dit que j'habite là sans permis, alors que je ne lui ai rien fait de mal et on m'ordonne de vider les lieux. Le lendemain, je demande à une collègue de m'aider à trouver un coin. Elle me le promet et, vingt-quatre heures après, elle me donne l'adresse de la sœur d'une amie à elle. Je me rends à cette adresse. C'est un ancien immeuble dans la rue Troubnaïa. Quand je monte les étages, je me retrouve nez à nez avec un jeune homme qui veut également louer un lit. Peu après, la propriétaire apparaît, elle a refusé le jeune homme et m'introduit dans sa pièce. C'est une ancienne salle de bains. Sans fenêtre ni vasistas. Une chaleur insupportable. Une véritable fournaise. Mais que puis-je faire ? Elle se propose de faire pour moi la cuisine et les courses. D'abord je dis oui, mais plus tard j'y renonce, car elle ne me rend pas la monnaie et partage mon repas. C'est au-dessus de mes moyens et je refuse ses services. Elle n'a pas d'emploi officiel, bien qu'elle soit en bonne santé. Elle est femme de ménage chez des gens aisés, fait les courses, la cuisine et le nettoyage. Je m'aperçois que des hommes viennent la voir alors qu'elle n'est pas encore rentrée. Ils engagent la conversation avec moi, me questionnent sur ma vie. Une fois, quand elle est déjà là, un vieux Juif se met à se déshabiller devant nous. Elle le chasse. Un monsieur cultivé la fréquente aussi, il nous offre à boire et à manger. Je comprends enfin où je suis tombée : elle a d'autres revenus.

Elle se vante devant moi de l'attention que lui portent les hommes. Je n'en doute pas. Elle finit par me dire d'aller chercher un autre logement. C'est vrai que je ne lui rapporte pas grand chose. Je suis toujours enregistrée à Zagorsk et je continue à payer la chambre que je n'habite pas. Mais je dois renouveler les cartes de rationnement et je demande l'autorisation de m'absenter aux heures de bureau. Je travaille à l'entrepôt d'articles en coton et en lin de 1947 à 1957, année où je prends ma retraite. Donc, un jour, venue renouveler ma carte de pain, j'apprends par ma propriétaire qu'elle a une amie à Moscou qui prend des locataires. Je vais chez elle. C'est au sous-sol. La propriétaire y loge avec sa fille écolière, à côté habite une famille nombreuse. Des bruits, des cris, des bagarres en permanence. Mais on me laisse tranquille. Il y a là un grand lit, un lit d'enfant et un coffre. On me donne le coffre. La première nuit, je me déshabille, ce que je regrette après. L'appartement est humide. Le mur contre lequel je dors, est tout nu, froid et suintant. On allume le poêle du couloir. Je prends froid et je reste longtemps malade. Je ne me déshabille plus. J'apprends que la propriétaire dort avec sa fille dans le petit lit et loue le grand lit pour la nuit. Officiellement, la propriétaire ne travaille pas. Elle vit de menus travaux, ménage ou lessive. Visiblement, elle préfère ça au travail dans une entreprise. Une fois, je vois arriver au milieu de la nuit un couple, ils s'installent dans le lit et repartent le lendemain matin. La propriétaire se vante du drap qu'ils lui ont donné. A l'écouter, tout cela est dans l'ordre des choses. En présence de sa fille mineure. Un spectacle pénible. Je ne suis pas restée longtemps chez elle. Mes employeurs à l'entrepôt louent une maison où logent cinq de nos collègues. Le chef comptable leur demande personnellement de me faire enregistrer là-bas. Mais les gens ne sont pas d'accord, de peur de me voir m'installer chez eux. Ainsi, mon calvaire continue. Mon mari m'envoie 30 roubles par mois, comme convenu. Après le bureau, je vais voir mon fils, à l'école, pour lui apporter à manger. On se met dans un coin du vestiaire et il avale à la va-vite ce que je lui apporte, il a honte devant ses copains. Plus tard, je loge chez une ancienne collègue. Elle habite rue Krasnoproletarskaïa. Elle vit avec sa fille et sa petite-fille. Je suis très embarrassée. Il fait déjà nuit quand je rentre après les visites chez mon fils. Elles se couchent tôt. Elle m'interdisent d'allumer la lumière. Souvent je grignote dans le noir avant d'aller au lit. Peu de temps après, on l'avertit qu'elle doit me mettre à la porte, sinon elle aura des problèmes. Je pars. Je vais de nouveau voir Elisavéta Borissovna et elle me place chez ses amis pour l'été : ils vont habiter chez leurs enfants qui partent dans le Sud pour deux mois. De cette façon je suis propriétaire de l'appartement durant l'été. L'été suivant, même chose : ils mettent à ma disposition leur appartement. Mieux encore, ils

Гаснет день, спал азарт борьбы. И там, где недавно еще ярким, солнечным днем с колоссальной скоростью неслись буера, теперь все затихло и спокойно розовеет отблеском уходящего солнца.

я пользуюсь кухней и не прописана. Да и мне была очень тяжела обстановка. Няня ревновала меня к хозяйке, т.к. они уделяла мне больше внимания, чем ей. Рахиль Борисовна, так звали хозяйку, была культурная женщина. Она была геолог. Вероятно и заболев в тайге анцефалитом. У нее был третий муж. Она великодушно от него сама отказалась, дала ему свободу, у него была своя комата и он приходил временами ее навестить. От помощи она отказалась сама. Он женился, у него уже была своя семья, но он ее не забывал. Жили мы в Гнездниковском переулке, если не ошибаюсь. Во дворе был театр Ромен, где я ни разу не была. И так нужно был искать новую квартиру. У одной из соседок была знакомая девушка, которая имела свою комнату. Соседка ее соблазнила, чтобы она пустила меня к себе, т.к. тут был мой сын и можно было надеяться, что он прельстится ее прелестями и возможно женится на ней. Итак я к ней переселилась. Оказалось, что печки у нее не было. Топили из коридора. Во второй комнате жил пьяница сосед один, а к нему приходил сын и они вместе выпивали. Спала я на доске, т.е. половина двери лежала на двух ящиках. Не раз девалась всю зиму, что у нее прожила, холод был ужасный. Кровати второй бы не поместилось, так мала была комната. Где можно было бы поставить кровать, стоял гардероб. Это могло бы тянуться и долго, но однажды сосед устроил попойку и там громко все ругались, что пришла милиция. Сосед сказал, что я живу без прописки, хотя я ему и ничему плохого не сделала и меня попросили оставить помещение. На следующий день я просила свою сотрудницу помочь мне найти угол. Она обещала и на следующий день дала адрес к сестре своей знакомой И пошла по адресу. Это был старинный дом на Трубной улице, когда я подошла к ее комнате уже ждал ее молодой человек, который тоже хотел снять у нее койку. Вскорости хозяйка пришла, молодому человеку отказала и ввела меня в свою комнату. Это оказалась бывшная ванная комната. Окна там не было и, конечно, форточки. Жара была ужасная. Нечем было дышать. Но что оставалось делать. Она предложила мне готовить и самой ходить за покупками. Сначала я согласилась, но после отказалась, т.к. сдачи она не приносила, обедала со мной. Мне это было не по средствам и я отказалась от ее услуг

me paient 10 roubles par mois. Mais la deuxième année cela tourne mal. Ils décident de faire des travaux. Il n'y a plus où dormir, ils ont tout démonté. On dort par terre, avec mon fils. Un ouvrier vient après son travail et retape l'appartement pendant trois heures. C'est dans ces conditions que mon fils prépare le concours d'entrée à l'Institut. On est en 1951. Il entre à l'Institut Sourikov et s'installe à la cité universitaire. A partir de la troisième année, il commence à gagner de l'argent et le budget augmente un peu. Mon fils a un copain qui habite avec sa mère et sa grand-mère dans un deux-pièces. La mère, professeur d'anglais, encourage cette amitié. Elle persuade sa voisine de me loger sans permis et celle-ci nous loue une pièce. La pièce est minuscule. Il y a un canapé, un lit de camp et une table. Cela ne laisse pas de passage. La dame se donne du mal pour que les garçons travaillent ensemble et partagent les honoraires. Elle nous trouve une table de travail. D'abord ça marche. Mais bientôt les éditeurs disent qu'ils ne pourront plus travailler à deux et que chacun devra avoir sa propre commande. Cyril n'étant pas un bon dessinateur, l'amitié se brise. Sa mère monte la voisine contre nous et elle me refuse la chambre. Me voilà de nouveau sans toit. Sur mon lieu de travail, on m'indique l'adresse d'une femme qui part avec son fils écolier en colonie de vacances et loue son appartement pour l'été. Le logis est au sous-sol, mais je suis quand même contente. Rusée, la propriétaire me cache le fait que son fils, aviateur, va venir en vacances. Il arrive et presque tous les soirs, parfois jusqu'à l'aube, il fait la java. Ils chantent, dansent et font un bruit incroyable. Avec mon fils, nous dormons mal à cause du bruit, mais nous n'y pouvons rien. Cela dure deux mois. Et me coûte 20 roubles par mois. Mon fils s'est adressé à un avocat pour m'obtenir un permis de résidence pour deux ans, jusqu'à la fin de ses études, parce que je suis malade, après quoi il promet de m'emmener là où il sera détaché. On obtient cette permission. Mon fils m'installe à Solnetchnogorsk où nous louons deux chambres à 40 roubles par mois. Peu de temps après, le temps vient pour moi de prendre ma retraite et mon fils termine ses études à l'Institut. C'est en 1957. Je suis très malade, les médecins reconduisent mon arrêt de travail, avec quelques interruptions, pendant presque un an, mais finalement j'atteins l'âge de la retraite. Mon fils porte mon dossier au service social, où l'on m'alloue une pension de 52 roub. 30 kop. Je touche également une majoration de 10%, en faisant valoir 37 ans de travail continu. La même année, mon fils achève ses études. On l'autorise à rester à Moscou et il commence à travailler pour les Editions pour enfants. On se demande où je vais habiter. Acheter un appartement dans une banlieue de Moscou ou descendre chez ma sœur à Berdiansk ? En 1958, je vais rendre visite à ma sœur Riva et je reste là-bas. Berdiansk me plaît et je n'en bouge plus. Au début, je loue une pièce, parce qu'il n'y a pas de place dans l'appartement de sa belle-sœur. Elle occupe une chambrette avec son mari et leurs deux fils chez la sœur du mari. La propriétaire me fait un permis de résidence et mon fils me dit de chercher un appartement en vue de l'acheter. Il en a déjà les moyens. Je visite un certain nombre d'appartements, mais je n'en trouve aucun à mon goût. Enfin, ma propriétaire m'apprend qu'à côté de chez sa mère on met en vente le tiers d'une maison. On y va avec ma sœur, nous le trouvons bien et j'écris à mon fils de venir le voir. Ça lui plaît aussi et nous achetons l'appartement pour 2500 roubles nouveaux. C'était en 1959. Dans le second appartement habite Maria Sémionovna Troufanova, dans le troisième, la famille des gens qui nous ont vendu le nôtre. Ils sont en train de construire une autre maison, celle-ci ne leur convient plus. C'est comme ça que je deviens propriétaire de mon appartement. Je me mets à l'aménager. Le mari de ma sœur, Youri Grigoriévitch, prend la direction des travaux. Il commence par construire, avec des caisses, une cuisine d'été, puis une petite cabane. Je la loue à des vacanciers. Deux personnes. Je m'entends bien avec mes voisins.
Malheureusement, des rumeurs sur la démolition imminente de nos maisons commencent à circuler. De peur de voir leur logement rasé, la fille du troisième appartement se hâte de trouver un acheteur et elle vend l'appartement de ses parents. A cette époque, son père est déjà mort, et sa mère a déménagé chez elle. Ma nouvelle voisine se révèle une femme ignoble. Nous partagions avec les parents de l'ancienne propriétaire une remise au fond de la cour, qu'ils avaient divisée en deux par une cloison. La partie avec la fenêtre appartient à la nouvelle co-propriétaire, mais elle a aussitôt envie de s'approprier l'autre moitié. Elle m'embête pendant plusieurs années, mais je ne veux pas lui céder la remise. Malgré tout, en 1979, elle fait apporter des poutres et bâtit en face de chez moi une remise en bois, après quoi elle me réclame les clés de ma moitié de remise. Je ne peux quand même pas en venir aux mains avec elle. Je lui remets les clés, elle déménage mon bois et mes affaires. Elle fait feu des quatre fers. Elle aménage un deux-pièces qu'elle loue aux estivants. Je porte plainte contre elle devant le tribunal du personnel. On décrète de renvoyer le dossier en correctionnelle. Mon fils arrive et me promet de trouver un appartement coopératif en disant qu'il vaut mieux renoncer au procès. Ce que je fais.
Le président du comité exécutif de la ville propose de me « mettre sous contrôle », c'est-à-dire qu'au cas où il y aurait un logement municipal libre, on me l'attribuerait. Je passe au comité exécutif tous les mois, et la camarade Déeva me répond invariablement : « Il n'y a rien pour vous ». Je fais ce genre d'allées et venues pendant deux ans sans résultat,

Она нигде официально не работала, хотя была здоровой женщиной. Она была приходящая домработница у состоятельных людей, сама ходила за покупками, готовила им и убирала. Что то я стала замечать что к ней приходили мужчины, когда ее еще не было с работы. Они вступали в разговоры со мной, интересовались моей биографией. Однажды когда она была дома пришел старый еврей и стал раздеваться в нашем присутствии. Она его выгнала. Приходил один культурный человек и принес много закуски и питья и нас обоих угощал. Все стало мне ясно,- куда я попала, был у нее дополнительный заработок. Она хвастала передо мной, что мужчины на нее обращают внимание. Я тоже в этом не сомневалась. Наконец она сама предложила мне найти другое жилье. Доходу от меня было действительно мало. Была я прописана в Загорске попрежнему и платила хозяйке комнаты, где фактически не жила. Но нужно было отмечать хлебные карточки и я отпрашивалась с работы. Работала я на базе хлопчато бумажных и льняных товаров с 1947 по 1957 г. когда ушла на пенсию. Так вот однажды, когда я приехала отмечать хлебную карточку у хозяйки была знакомая в Москве, которая пустила к себе жильцов. Я отправилась по указанному адресу. Это было подвальное помещение. Хозяйка жила с девочкой школьницей, рядом жила большая семья. Всегда шумно, крики, драки. Но меня никто из их нижне трогал. Стояла большая кровать, детская кровать и сундук. Мне предложили сундук. Я разделась в первую же ночь и очень пожалела. Квартира была сырая. Стена, у которой я спала ничего не завешанная, была сырая и холодная, печки не было. Топили из коридора. Я ужасно простыла и долго болела. Больше я не раздевалась. Оказывается хозяйка с девочкой спали на детской кровати, а большую сдавала на ночь. Работать официально хозяйка не работала. Выполняла разные работы, то по уборке, то по стирке. Повидимому ее это больше устраивало, чем работа на производстве. Однажды я была свидетельницей, когда ночью пришли двое он и она, заняли кровать и утром ушли. Хозяйка хвасталась, что подарили они ей простыню. Все по ее словам было нормально. Все в присутствии дочери и школьницы. Тяжелая картина. Прожила я не долго у нее. Где я работала на базе, арендовали дом, где жили 5 наших сотрудников. Главный бухгалтер лично всех опросил, чтобы меня кто либо из них у себя прописал, Но никто не соглашался, боясь, что я самовольно вселюсь к ним. Так продолжались мои мытарства. Отец присылал ф 30 руб в месяц по соглашению. Я после работы ходила к сыну в школу и приносила поесть. В раздевалке в углу примостимся и он наскоро съедал, что я приносила, стесняясь своих ребят. Жила я потом у своей бывшей сотрудницы. Она жила по Краснопролетарской. Жила она с дочкой и внучкой. Мне было очень не удобно. Приходила от сына, было уже темно. Они рано ложились спать. Огня не разрешали зажигать. Часто я в темноте что то поем и тоже на боковую. Вскорости хозяйку предупредили, чтобы она мне отказала от квартиры, т.к. ее ждут неприятности, если она будет и дальше меня держать без прописки. Пришлось уйти. Снова я обратилась к Елизавете Борисовне и она меня устроила к своим знакомым на лето, т.к. они переходили в квартиру детей, которые уезжали на 2 месяца на юг. Таким образом я была хозяйкой квартиры летом. На следующее лето повторилось тоже, т.е. они предоставили мне снова свою квартиру. Они еще платили мне 10 руб в месяц. Но второе лето было скверное для меня. Они затеяли ремонт. Спать было негде. Их разобрали. Спали с сыном на полу. Приходил рабочий после работы на 2 часа и ремонтировал квартиру. Сын в такой обстановке готовился в институт. Это было в 1951 г. Сын поступил в инт. им. Сурикова и жил в студенческом городке. Начиная с 3 курса он стал подрабатывать и бюджет немного увеличился. Сын учился с одним студентом, который жил с матерью и бабушкой в 2 х комнатной квартире. Мать учительница английского языка всячески содействовала дружбе сына с моими сыном. И она уговорила соседку пустить меня без прописки и та сдала нам комнату. Комната была крошечная. Стоял диван, раскладушка и стол. Проходу уже не было. Старалась она потому, чтобы ребята вдвоем работали и делили заработок пополам. Стол она дала сама. Сначала это так и было. Но вскорости в редакции заявили, что вдвоем они не разрешают ра-

jusqu'au jour où le président du comité part et un autre est nommé à sa place. Alors Déeva m'annonce : « Recommencez à zéro » et en 1981 mon fils vient voir le secrétaire du Parti de la ville pour lui raconter mes tourments. Ce dernier téléphone au nouveau président, le camarade Verjikovsky, et lui demande d'examiner mon dossier. On conseille à mon fils de faire des démarches auprès du service social. Il les fait. Il accomplit toutes les formalités requises et ils me mettent sur la liste d'attente des appartements coopératifs pour l'année 1983. Si je suis encore de ce monde, ce qui n'est pas sûr. Il est temps de parler de mes petits. Mon frère Matveï a disparu pendant la guerre, ma sœur Jénia et ses deux enfants ont été tués par les fascistes à Jdanov. Lorsque Riva était passée par Jdanov, elle lui avait proposé de partir ensemble. Mais Jénia n'avait pas voulu. Elle est restée dans la ville occupée avec son mari et leurs deux enfants. Tous ont péri. Lisa a fait ses études à l'école de médecine de Kiev. Elle a travaillé à l'hôpital de la station Roubtsovka, dans la région de l'Altaï. Plus tard, cet hôpital a été transformé en sanatorium pour tuberculeux. Elle a contracté la tuberculose et elle est morte en 1946, à l'âge de 33 ans. Nous n'étions plus que deux : Riva et moi. Depuis quatre ans j'habite chez elle pendant l'hiver. Elle a deux fils, tous les deux mariés. L'un, Guéna, habite tout près. Il a une femme enseignante et deux fils. L'un, 17 ans, est à l'école de musique, à Zaporojié, l'autre, 13 ans, en sixième année, joue de la clarinette, l'aîné sera pianiste. Ma sœur vit avec son fils cadet, Valéry, qui a un fils de 6 ans. Un trois-pièces avec tout le confort. Nous vivons en parfaite harmonie. Les brus de ma sœur sont gentilles. Je me sens à l'aise avec elles. Je reste jusqu'au mois d'avril, et en mai je rentre chez moi. Je me sens en pleine sécurité. Je les aide tant que je peux. Je lis, je me repose. Je vais avoir 80 ans. Je fais de la gymnastique, prends une douche tous les jours. Je ne souffre que de douleurs dans le dos et aux reins. Mais pour l'instant c'est supportable, pourvu que cela ne s'aggrave pas.

En tout et pour tout j'ai subi trois interventions. Sinusite, ulcère de l'estomac et deux opérations des yeux, de la cataracte. Durant mon séjour à Berdiansk, je fais du travail social. En 1953, à la bibliothèque pour enfants. En 1959, on m'opère d'un œil et en 1961 — de l'autre. Pendant ce temps j'abandonne le travail social. La vue retrouvée, je le reprends. Je propose de créer un chœur du troisième âge. Je me donne du mal pour l'organiser. Je frappe à toutes les portes. Cela se fait sous la tutelle du club Kirov. Les débuts sont prometteurs. On se produit avec succès. Tant que le chef de chœur travaille avec les retraités, tout va bien, mais dès qu'il introduit des jeunes, tout le monde s'entredéchire et le chœur est dissous. Je propose mes services au théâtre populaire de la maison municipale de la culture. Je tiens le carnet de bord, félicite les participants de la troupe. Quelquefois, je fais une lecture publique. Je suis récompensée par des diplômes d'honneur. Je reste au théâtre de 1965 à 1978 ; lorsque le metteur en scène part, moi aussi, je démissionne. Pendant que j'habite chez ma sœur, je travaille, les deux premiers hivers, à la bibliothèque pour enfants. Puis mon travail social prend fin. Je ne suis plus en mesure de l'assumer. J'ai 80 ans. Mes forces baissent. Je m'essouffle vite. Je ne rentre pas encore chez moi. Je fais faire de petits travaux et le 1.7. j'espère me réinstaller chez moi. Riva me promet de rester un mois avec moi. Elle est toujours malade, elle tousse et se plaint de douleurs cardiaques. Je rentre à la maison le 1.7. avec Riva. On reste ensemble en juillet et août. Le 11.7. Riva part chercher sa pension chez elle ; en rentrant, elle a un malaise à l'arrêt de bus, l'ambulance la transporte à l'hôpital, où elle reste 15 jours. Elle sort de l'hôpital rétablie, mais chez moi, ça ne va pas. Le 3.9. elle revient à la maison et elle y est encore actuellement. Elle ne supporte pas la chaleur, de plus, les conditions chez elle sont meilleures. J'attends mon fils en septembre.

Quelques mots à propos de mon mari. Quand il est parti pour Dniépropétrovsk, me laissant sans emploi ni logement, il n'a pas donné de ses nouvelles pendant longtemps et je ne savais plus que penser. Pourtant, quatre mois plus tard, il m'écrit qu'il ne reviendra plus, parce qu'il a une autre famille. Je l'annonce à mon fils par écrit. Dans une lettre que je lui envoie à la colonie de vacances où il se trouve. Il ne me répond rien. Quelquefois, à ma demande, il va voir son père. Il n'éprouve aucun sentiment pour son père, pas plus alors qu'aujourd'hui. Ils sont étrangers l'un à l'autre. Dans la nouvelle famille, il y a un autre fils. Il est déjà marié, mais les demi-frères ne se lient pas d'amitié. Mon fils accepte les invitations de la sœur de son père, Boussia, mais ne tient pas ses promesses d'aller voir son père. Il n'éprouve aucun sentiment pour lui. J'ai été avec Riva à Dniépropétrovsk chez Boussia après son opération de la cataracte en janvier 1982. Mon mari passe nous voir chez Boussia, mais on n'a rien à se dire. Pour moi c'est un étranger, comme s'il n'y avait rien eu entre nous dans le passé. Sa femme et son fils viennent aussi. Ils me sont aussi étrangers et ne m'intéressent guère. Mon mari me demande de lui envoyer notre fils, mais celui-ci ne veut pas en entendre parler. Je n'y suis pour rien, un père reste un père, je demande à mon fils d'y aller.

Son père a déjà 78 ans. Il souffre des jambes, il ne sort plus. Il a une voiture que son fils conduit. Je crois que nous ne nous reverrons plus. La même année, en avril, on va avec Riva chez mon fils, et on loge chez sa belle-mère, Guida Moïsséevna. C'est une femme pleine d'énergie et de volonté. Elle aime bien mon fils. Elle ne nous permet pas de l'aider pour le ménage, même pas faire la vaisselle. Elle dit qu'elle se

méfie et préfère faire tout elle-même. Elle nous prépare de très bons repas. Nous restons trois semaines et repartons le 3.5. Je pense que je ne risquerai plus un tel voyage. Guida Moïsséevna a attiré notre attention sur le fait que mon fils ne sait même pas laver ses chaussettes. En effet, ce n'est pas bien que sa femme lave ses caleçons et ses chaussettes à sa place. L'homme doit savoir le faire lui-même, il doit y être habitué dès son enfance, mais dans quelles conditions grandissait-il pour pouvoir apprendre tout ça ! Dès l'âge de 10 ans dans des foyers. Sa première femme, Irina, et sa mère se moquaient de lui. Il était entre deux feux. Sa fille est déjà mariée, mais mon fils continue de l'aider matériellement. Il leur a laissé son deux-pièces tout confort quand il est parti habiter son atelier. Il a rencontré Vika qui a un fils, Antocha : elle a quitté son mari et emménagé dans son atelier, jusqu'à ce que mon fils trouve l'appartement coopératif qu'ils habitent actuellement. Mon fils a construit une cloison et Antocha a une chambre à lui. Ils font bon ménage et j'en suis contente. Vika est de 12 ans plus jeune, mais, à mon avis, ils ne se disputent pas. Que le Dieu leur donne du bonheur. Mon fils l'a bien mérité.

8.3.1983.
Beaucoup de temps s'est écoulé avant que je reprenne ma biographie. Riva souffre toujours et le 15.12.82 on l'a hospitalisée à nouveau. Elle est restée là-bas un mois, et de retour à la maison elle ne va pas bien. Il s'est passé encore un mois avant qu'elle ne soit définitivement rétablie. En octobre, mon fils est venu chez moi et je le servais toute seule, même si les repas étaient préparés par Riva. Je réussis à le persuader d'aller voir son père. Il lui rend visite, ainsi qu'aux autres parents, et un mois plus tard son père meurt. C'est bien qu'il ait pu le voir peu avant sa mort. Mon fils est allé aux obsèques avec sa femme. La femme de Iossif a bien accueilli mon fils, elle est venue le chercher et elle l'a raccompagné. Ainsi, Iossif est mort dans sa 78-ème année. Doussia, sa femme, a de la sympathie pour Boussia, la sœur de Iossif, elle l'aide comme elle peut. Je vis chez Riva depuis octobre dernier. On a fêté mon anniversaire en grande pompe. Mon fils est venu avec ma bru. Pendant la fête, mon fils a prononcé un discours : il m'a remerciée avec beaucoup d'amour pour ce que j'avais fait pour lui au temps où il était étudiant. C'est vrai que ses études m'ont coûté cher, mais on oublie les ennuis, et seul le bien reste dans la mémoire. J'attends toujours l'appartement coopératif. Je suis sur la liste, le premier versement doit être effectué à la fin de l'année. Ce serait bien si l'on démolissait ma maison, alors on n'aurait pas besoin de vendre mon appartement. Mais on n'en parle plus et il faut attendre.
Avec ma sœur, on se dit que si j'obtiens cet appartement, on se réunira avec Guéna, l'autre fils de Riva, qui a un deux-pièces. Mais le jour où j'aurai mon appartement n'est pas encore venu. La construction prendra deux ans, et est-ce que je serai encore de ce monde ? Je me porte bien, mais la fatigue me gagne vite. Je fais de la gymnastique, je prends un bain presque chaque jour. Je fais la sieste entre 11 et 13 heures. Une promenade d'une heure quasi quotidienne. Mais par rapport à l'année dernière, mes forces déclinent. Bourdonnement dans la tête, j'entends mal ; après le déjeuner, quand je fais la vaisselle, j'ai toujours mal au dos et aux reins. Un repos, même court, me fait beaucoup de bien. L'année dernière, je balayais les pièces et maintenant je ne le peux plus. Je fais les poussières et je donne un coup de balai dans la cuisine et dans le couloir. Ma main gauche tremble. Je tiens avec peine la cuillère. Les doigts de ma main gauche ne se plient pas entièrement. Mais c'est encore supportable. De nouveau Riva est souffrante. Elle a du mal à faire à manger pour tout le monde, mais elle fait elle-même le ménage. Je ne l'aide pas à cuisiner, elle me l'interdit. Je ne sors pas loin, j'ai peur de tomber. Valéry va chercher le lait avant de partir au bureau. Il a plusieurs obligations maintenant : amener son fils à la maternelle et aller chercher le lait. Tant qu'il ne fait pas beau, je ne veux aller ni faire des courses ni chercher le lait. Pour le moment, il fait mauvais, il y a du vent et du verglas. Il n'est pas tombé beaucoup de neige cette année et c'est presque le printemps. Qu'est-ce qui se passe chez moi ? Est-ce que tout va bien ? Je n'ai pas de contacts avec mes voisins. Avec l'autre voisine, Maria Sémionovna, parce qu'elle m'a interdit le coffre à charbon. Elle l'a utilisé durant toutes ces années et la dernière fois, elle a même passé son charbon au crible sur mon territoire, en face de la cabane que, par conséquent, j'ai dû repeindre.
J'ai décidé de vendre le coffre et je le lui ai proposé. Elle a refusé, alors une autre voisine le prend contre la promesse de réparer la palissade, dans la cour, face à la maison. Pourtant la palissade est toujours cassée. Son fils jure de le faire, mais il ne tient pas parole (à savoir la réparation de la palissade). Quand je serai de retour, il faudra trouver quelqu'un pour le faire, et la voisine proposera, probablement, de payer le coffre. Avec la troisième voisine, celle qui m'a pris la remise, je n'ai pas de contacts non plus. Si elle m'adresse la parole, je lui réponds, sinon je n'engage pas la conversation. Je dois aller chercher ma pension à la poste dans le centre ville ; bien que le facteur habite à côté, il n'a pas le droit de me la délivrer. Quand il fait mauvais, je dois demander à Léna de m'accompagner. Ce n'est qu'une fois par mois, mais elle le fait à contrecœur. Il faut insister. Le linge aussi, il faut demander à Guéna de le porter chez une femme qui le lave, et comme elle habite à côté de la gare, il faut

prendre le bus. J'y suis toujours allée avec Riva, mais désormais elle ne pourra plus m'accompagner. Peut-être, elle se remettra en été et pourra m'aider à porter le linge. Parfois je le lave moi-même, mais le plus souvent, je le donne à laver. Donc, je dois demander.
Le 8.3., 10 personnes sont venues, tous de la famille : Guéna et les siens, ça fait quatre, nous trois, moi, Riva et Léna avec sa fille. Arrivés vers 1 h. et repartis à 4 h. de l'après-midi, une belle fête ; et le même jour, soirée en compagnie de Rina Zélionaïa.

13.3.83
Je continue mes notes. La vie s'écoule normalement, rien à signaler. Grâce à Riva, je suis entourée de soins et d'attentions. J'ai reçu une lettre de mon fils. En avril, il va avoir une exposition personnelle au musée Pouchkine. Comme c'est émouvant. Les temps changent. On s'intéresse à ses œuvres. Il a eu une exposition à l'Union des artistes. Que c'est bien qu'il soit satisfait de son œuvre, qu'on commence à le mettre en avant, c'est très important pour un grand artiste. Matériellement, ça ne lui donne rien, mais moralement il est content qu'on le distingue et qu'on lui propose des expositions. Dommage qu'il m'écrive rarement, ça me fait tellement plaisir de lire ses lettres.
Il promet de venir au printemps. Je voudrais l'accueillir chez Riva. Je suis incapable de le recevoir chez moi. Bouger m'épuise complètement. Le matin, avant 11 heures, je peux remuer un peu, mais à partir de 11 heures, le dos et les reins me font tellement mal que je dois me mettre au lit. Après deux heures de repos, je peux de nouveau faire des mouvements. Malgré tout, j'essaie de me débrouiller dans la mesure du possible. Je fais la vaisselle, je balaie, je fais les poussières. C'est tout ce que je peux faire. Je ne sais pas pourquoi, mais j'ai du mal à écrire. Pourtant j'écris. La main gauche me fait parfois mal : elle tremble tout le temps, j'ai de la chance que la droite fonctionne normalement. Chez nous tout est comme d'habitude. Le petit joue aux échecs deux fois par semaine. C'est un enfant très agité. Mais l'échiquier l'apaise et il peut jouer jusqu'au moment où il va au lit, c'est-à-dire, jusqu'à 9 heures. Comment pourra-t-il tenir en place à l'école ? Il commence cette année. J'écris à une amie en lui demandant de rédiger ses mémoires. Elle a vécu une vie difficile. Elle a été arrêtée, est restée 8 ans en prison, victime des répressions. Les amis avec qui on prenait le thé de longues années durant sont morts. Réguina Pavlovna, Irina Andréevna. Notre cercle n'existe plus. La vieille garde disparaît à tout jamais. Bientôt ce sera mon tour. C'est comme ça. Mais je suis satisfaite de la vie que j'ai vécue. Mon passé pénible est à présent compensé par le calme et le bonheur. Toutes les peines s'oublient, perdent leur intensité et la paix actuelle me rend heureuse. Il est vrai que j'attends toujours l'appartement coopératif que mon fils a tant sollicité, mais qui vivra verra. Mon appartement est occupé et ici, c'est le calme absolu. En juin, je dois réemménager chez moi, faire des travaux. Est-ce que Riva pourra venir chez moi cet été ? Elle est toujours très faible, je devrai donc rester seule un moment. On verra.

27.4.83.
Enfin, les travaux sont finis. C'est quelqu'un de la famille qui les a faits, impeccablement. Le père de l'ex-bru de la sœur défunte du mari de Riva. Il a demandé 150 roub., je lui ai donné une majoration de 10 roub. Maintenant, c'est mon tour d'agir : aménager tout à l'intérieur, ranger les caisses, l'armoire, faire le ménage dans la cabane. Ce n'est pas son travail. Je dois tout arranger moi-même, mais je suis à bout de forces. Aujourd'hui je suis allée voir son travail et je suis rentrée morte. Je compte rester ici en mai et après il faut que je m'en aille chez moi. Et je suis épuisée. J'ai tant de mal à marcher. Je vais clopin-clopant. Le dos et les reins me font mal. Il faudra vendre l'appartement, je ne pourrai pas m'en occuper. Il faut penser aux repas, parce que je ne peux plus faire la cuisine. Je doute que Riva puisse rester chez moi en été. Elle se porte mal, elle aussi, à cause de son cœur, et maintenant ce sont les dents. Il faut aller en ville, chez nous il n'y a pas de dentiste. Et le logement coopératif ? On promet d'autoriser le premier versement vers la fin du mois. Mais combien va durer la construction ? En verrai-je jamais la fin ? Et ensuite il faudra effectuer un échange, pour pouvoir habiter avec Guéna. Aurai-je assez de temps pour faire tout ça ? Mes années sont comptées. Et mes forces déclinent.

5.5.1983
J'ai reçu une convocation du comité exécutif. Il faut renouveler les papiers faits en 1981. Ils doivent être datés de 1983. L'acte d'études du logement, le certificat du syndic et du bureau d'inventaire. Un représentant du comité m'accompagne pour rédiger l'acte, une inspectrice signe le certificat ; le certificat sur les conditions de logement sera prêt le 11.5. Cela fait, il faudra attendre l'avis de versement. Mon fils m'a déjà envoyé 2000 roubles. On ne connaît pas encore le montant exact. Je suis très excitée. J'attends ce studio que je vais pouvoir échanger.

12.5. Aujourd'hui mon fils m'a téléphoné et m'a appris une bonne nouvelle. Gala a bien mis au monde une fille à 5 h. du matin. Elle pèse 3 kg 600, tout va bien, la mère et l'enfant se portent bien. A présent, je suis arrière-grand-mère, et mon fils m'en a félicitée. Un autre événement, mais moins important : enfin j'ai acheté un imperméable dont je rêvais.

ботать, на каждый чтобы брал работу отдельно. Художник Кирилл был не важный и дружба поломалась. Мать его настроила мою хозяйку, чтобы она мне отказала в квартире и я снова без угла. На работе мне дали адрес к одной женщине, которая сдавала свою квартиру на лето, а сама с сыном школьником уезжала в детлагерь. Помещение было полуподвальное, но я и этому была рада. Она схитрила не сказав мне что у нее сын летчик и он приедет на лето в отпуск. Приехал ее сын и почти каждый вечер а иногда и до утра устраивались попойки Пели, танцевали и шумели невероятно. Мы с сыном не высыпались от этого шума, но что было делать. Так продолжалось 2 месяца. Я платила по 20 руб в месяц. Сын обратился к юристу с просьбой составить заявление, чтобы меня прописали на 2 года до окончания института, т.к. я больная после института он возьмет меня с собой куда его направят. Такое разрешение было получено Сын устроил меня в Солнечногорске, где мы сняли 2 комнаты и платили 40 р. в месяц. Скоро подошло время, когда должна была уйти на пенсию, а сын закончил институт. Это было в 1957 году Я очень болела, почти год меня держали с перерывами на больничном, но все же достигла пенсионного возраста. Сын сам отнес мои документы в Собес и мне назначили пенсию в размере 52р30к. Я получала с надбавкой 10%, т.к. имела стаж 37 лет. В том же году сын закончил институт. Его оставили в Москве и он стал работать в Детгизе. Стал попрос, где же мне жить. Толи купить под Москвой квартиру или поехать к сестре в Бердянск. В 1958 году я поехала в гости к сестре Риве и там и осталась. Бердянск мне очень понравился и я уже не уезжала больше никуда. Сначала я наняла комнату т.к. у сестры негде было. Она жила с мужем и 2 сыновьями в крошечной комнате. у сестры мужа. Хозяйка прописала меня постоянно и сын просил меня подыскать квартиру, чтобы купить

Он был уже в состоянии купить мне квартиру. Я смотрела разные квартиры, но все не было подходящей. Наконец моя хозяйка мне сообщила, что рядом с ее матерью продают 1/3 дома. Мы пошли с сестрой, нам понравилось и я написала сыну, чтобы он приехал посмотреть. Ему тоже понравилось и мы купили квартиру за 2500 руб. в новых деньгах. Это было в 1959 году. Во 2х квартире жила одна соседка Труфанова Мария Семеновна, в 3й квартире родители тех, кто продал нам квартиру. Сами они строились, эта квартира их не устраивала. Вот таким образом я стала владелицей собственной квартиры. И стала ее благоустраивать. Муж сестры Юрий Григорьевич взял шефство над моей квартирой и занялся строительством. Построил из ящиков сначала летнюю кухню, потом беседку. В беседку стала пускать курортников. 2челов ка жила с седями хорошо. Но вот беда стали поговаривать, что снесут наши дома и дочка, родители которой жили в 3й квартире, испугавшись, что снесут квартиру, быстренько нашла покупателя и продала квартиру родных. Отец к тому времени умер, а мать она забрала к себе. Новая соседка оказалась совсем скверной женщиной. Дело в том, что у меня с родными бывшей хозяйки был общий сарай в глубине двора, они поставили стенку и разделили его поровну. Часть с окном отошла к новой соседке Но она сразу захотела занять и вторую половину. Она беспокоила меня несколько лет, но я не соглашалась отдать ей сарай. И все же в 1979 г она завезла лес и напротив моего дома построила деревянный сарай и потребовала ключи от моей половины сарая. Не драться же мне было с ней. Я отдала ключ и она перенесла мое топливо и кое какие вещи. Она развила буйную деятельность. Сделала 2х комнатную квартиру и стала пускать курортников. Я подала заявление в товарищеский суд. Они постановили передать дело в народный суд. Приехал сын и сказал мне, что будет добиваться кооперативной квартиры, а заниматься судом не следует. Так и сделали Но предисполкома посоветовал ему взять меня на контроль . т.е. когда освободится площадь, предоставят ее мне. Я ходила в Исполком каждый месяц и мне неизменно отвечала т. Деева " ничего нет" Так я проходила 2 года пока не ушел предисполкома и назначали другого. Теперь мне уже Деева заявила "начинайте сначала" и сын поехал в 1981 г. к секретарю парткома и рассказал о моих мытарствах Он позвонил новому предисполкома т. Вержиковскому и просил разоб

Par hasard, Riva entre dans le grand magasin à côté, et il y a un imperméable, en 48. Il coûte 100 roub. 80 kop. Elle trouve de l'argent aussi. Comme elle est prévenante. Mon fils promet de m'envoyer 200 roub. J'ai payé le manteau 101 roub., les cadeaux 5 x 5 = 25 roub., la fête 16 x 2 = 32 + 5 = 37-10-27 = 153 roub. J'ai donné 30 roubles de ma retraite à Riva pour l'anniversaire. Il me reste 46 roub. pour vivre.

1.6. Je réintègre mes pénates. Il faut faire le ménage et déplacer les meubles. Est-ce que Riva viendra chez moi, et pour combien de temps ? Je vais rester ici 4 mois. Mes horaires sont immuables. Le matin, je fais une promenade pendant une heure, une heure et demi. Puis le déjeuner, la vaisselle. A 11 h. je suis déjà hors service. Le dos et les reins me font mal. Je dois rester au lit jusqu'à 1 h. de l'après-midi. Ensuite je fais quelque chose, je lis. A 5 h. dîner. Et de nouveau, la vaisselle. Je lis le journal, regarde la télé. Tout est réglé comme du papier à musique. Bientôt ça va changer. L'ordre sera perturbé. Je m'accroche désespérément à cette vie réglée que je ne veux pas modifier, pourtant il le faudra. Les travaux dans la maison sont finis, mais il faut tout ranger. Aurai-je le temps de le faire avant le 1er juin ? Mes affaires se trouvent un peu partout. Combien de temps faudra-t-il pour les rassembler ? L'exposition personnelle de mon fils est reportée au juin. Il est un grand-père heureux. Cette année, le 30.9. il aura 50 ans. Il est toujours plein d'attentions et de prévenance envers moi. Le 3.5. il m'a envoyé un colis d'oranges et de gruau de sarrasin. Il promet de m'envoyer du beurre. Comment Gala va-t-elle s'en sortir avec la petite ? Vika, Irina viendront la voir, mais elles habitent loin. Elle a un bon mari. Le plus gros sera à sa charge. Qu'ils soient heureux et que notre relève soit saine et forte.

6.6. Aujourd'hui je déménage chez moi. Je n'ai pas dormi de la nuit, je réfléchissais. Le 30.5. on a fait la réunion de copropriétaires. La prochaine fois, ils nous diront où l'on doit verser l'argent et quand. Ils promettent de construire en un an, mais je n'y crois pas. Ça sera un immeuble de 5 étages, en brique, pour des familles peu nombreuses. En tout 90 appartements. 78 studios, de 12 et 14 m². 12 deux-pièces. Pas loin de chez Riva, là où se trouve l'arrêt du bus n°17. En attendant, je veux proposer à Riva de légaliser la donation, ainsi elle pourra le vendre comme elle voudra. L'idée même de m'occuper de la vente me donne froid dans le dos. Qu'elle fasse toutes les formalités comme bon lui semble, elle-même ou Guéna. Je me sens plutôt mal. Est-ce que je verrai mon nouvel appartement ? J'ai peur de rester seule chez moi. On s'habitue à la vie nomade. Les jeunes viendront et repartiront. Ils raconteront tout en détail. Je pense revenir ici une fois par semaine, prendre un bain. Le samedi. Riva ne restera pas avec moi. Elle viendra peut-être quelques jours et puis elle devra repartir. C'est très dur pour elle, chez moi. Aucun confort.

30.6. Ça fait longtemps que je n'ai rien écrit dans mon journal. Le 27.6. a eu lieu la deuxième réunion de l'immeuble coopératif « Victoire », mais on ne nous a rien dit d'important, on a juste rempli le contrat. J'ai fait la bêtise de le signer de mon nom complet, or ma signature habituelle est différente. Il faudra refaire le contrat. Vers le 10.7. on annoncera à l'ordre de qui verser les 2000 roubles. Le prix global du studio est de 5000 roub. Les pièces sont petites, selon le nombre de personnes. Il y en aura de 12, 14 et 16 m². Moi, j'aurai, à coup sûr, celle de 12 m². Tous les meubles n'y entreront pas. Quand le studio sera fini, je pense en faire don à Riva, si mon fils est d'accord.
Qu'elle le vende pour le prix qu'elle veut. Quand j'aurai le studio, (ils disent avant septembre 1984), je veux l'échanger pour vivre avec Guéna ou Riva. On promet à Guéna un trois-pièces ; s'il l'obtient, Riva aura un quatre-pièces. Mais quand ? Je me sens mal. Je me déplace difficilement. J'ai mal au dos et aux reins. Je me repose de 11 h. à 1 h. de l'après-midi. Ensuite ce sont les choses les plus pénibles à faire : laver, nettoyer. Je peine, mais, après tout, je suis chez moi. Je me souviens que chez Riva, en hiver, je reste toujours à l'écart. Je veux vivre autonome. Je suis habituée à faire le ménage toute seule. Combien de temps pourrai-je continuer ainsi ? Surtout n'être à la charge de personne. Me soigner seule. Jusqu'à maintenant je me suis soignée moi-même. Il est vrai que je donne mon linge à laver. Une femme vient laver le sol. Il faudrait profiter de la vie. Mais je ne vis plus. Je me fais beaucoup de soucis pour ma santé à venir. Je ne sors pas. Riva vient le samedi, et le dimanche nous allons chez elle. Je prends un bain, je couche chez elle et le lundi, je rentre chez moi. Elle m'apporte le dîner que je répartis sur 4-5 jours. Je lui paye 2 roubles par jour. Il fait chaud. Beaucoup d'estivants, chez mes deux voisines aussi. Je ne loue plus depuis l'an dernier. Mon fils s'y oppose, et moi non plus, je ne peux plus supporter des étrangers chez moi. Merci à mon fils qui m'envoie de l'argent, parce que ma pension ne me suffit pas. 52 roub., et les travaux m'ont coûté 176 roub. J'ai acheté un manteau de demi-saison à 100 roubles.

1.8. Enfin tout est réglé pour l'appartement coopératif. Le 19.7. on a eu la dernière réunion. On a rédigé une lettre officielle pour faire le premier versement, et le 2.8. j'ai mis mon argent sur deux livrets. 2000 roub. sur l'un et 1000 sur l'autre. Le 29.6. j'ai rempli le contrat. La somme de 2000 roub. est virée à la banque. Ainsi, tout est réglé pour cet appartement coopératif, il ne me reste plus qu'à attendre

l'appartement, — serai-je encore de ce monde ? — et je dois léguer à mon fils les 2000 roub. Si je meurs avant que le studio soit fini, il pourra récupérer cet argent. Valéry me promet de m'accompagner chez le notaire. Seule, je ne sors plus. Mes jambes ne me portent plus. J'ai du mal à monter et à descendre de l'autobus. Hier, le 31.7. Guéna est venu me chercher. On est parti à 5 h., rentré à 9 h. On est allé prendre un bain chez Riva. J'étais morte de fatigue, n'arrivais presque pas à manger. Le dos et les reins me torturent. Et ma main tremble de plus en plus. J'attends le départ des vacanciers et j'irai voir le neurologue. Cette main m'ennuie. Maintenant je lave le sol moi-même. La femme est venue 2 fois et elle ne veut plus. Je fais la lessive moi-même, mais je donne à laver le gros linge. Mon fils promet de venir en août. Riva a la visite de cinq personnes de Rostov et de Kiev. Tout ça pour Micha. Riva a pris froid. C'est embêtant pour elle, ces invités. Ils partent le 13.8.

16.10.84
Mes chers enfants, chers Guita Moïsséevna et Antochenka ! Comment allez-vous ? Comment vous portez-vous ? Moi, je me porte comme avant. Sans changements. Ma main tremble. Mes jambes aussi. Si je dois aller chez le notaire, je prends un taxi et quelqu'un m'accompagne. La grande épopée de l'appartement coopératif est enfin terminée. Le 13.4. on m'a délivré le permis d'emménager et j'ai vu mon nouveau logement. Il faisait un temps de chien, il pleuvait des cordes. La voie non pavée qui mène vers la maison était noyée dans la boue. On délivrait les permis sur place. Pour le moment, je ne mets plus les pieds dans cette maison. Riva s'occupe de tout. Elle y va tous les jours et guette les ouvriers. On a déjà branché l'eau, l'électricité, installé un réchaud à deux feux. Quant au gaz, personne ne sait quand il sera branché. On a commencé à poncer le parquet dans la pièce. Les ouvriers doivent passer pour calfeutrer la porte, il fera plus chaud dans l'appartement. Dimanche dernier. Valéry et Lussia ont lavé les vitres dans la pièce et la cuisine Tout est minuscule, mais j'espère que mes meubles pourront tenir, à l'exception du bureau. Il faut tout mesurer minutieusement pour faire entrer mon mobilier. Il faut que quelqu'un vienne avec moi dans ma petite maison pour mettre tout dans des sacs, sauf le bureau, les armoires et les chaises. A mon avis, un camion ne suffira pas. On a soumis le dossier de vente de mon appartement à la réunion du comité exécutif. Elle se tiendra le 1.11., la réponse sera donnée le 5.11. Chez moi, on a tout détruit sans pitié. Valéry, Guéna et Micha ont participé à l'opération. Ils ont rasé les deux cabanes et la malheureuse remise. Mais nous ne sommes pas autorisés à vendre la maison tant que nos voisins ont encore leur cabane. Pourtant l'architecte nous a laissé l'espoir d'obtenir l'autorisation de la vendre. C'est Lussia qui se décarcasse. Elle est obligée de partir plus tôt du bureau. Après le comité exécutif, on aura besoin des signatures des voisins, certifiées par le notaire, comme quoi ils ne s'opposent pas à la vente de mon appartement. L'acheteur attend, mais il ne veut pas payer des arrhes sans être sûr qu'il aura le droit d'y loger avec sa famille : mari, femme et leur fils écolier. Tout est à l'état de projet. Riva s'affaire aussi, Dieu la protège, qu'elle n'attrape pas froid. Et puis cette pluie et la température qui baisse de jour en jour. Mes idées s'embrouillent. Les travaux continuent. Des affaires traînent partout, rien n'est plus à sa place. Quand tu viendras, mon cher fils, tu le verras toi-même. On a fait un placard dans le couloir, mais il n'est pas fini, et ils ont entrepris les travaux dans la pièce. D'abord ils mettent le carrelage dans les toilettes et la salle de bains. Appelle-moi quand tu seras de retour.
Je vous souhaite une bonne santé et du bonheur à tous.
Affectueusement
Maman.

I was using the kitchen and wasn't registered there. And the situation was hard for me, too. The nanny was jealous of me because the landlady paid more attention to me than to her. Rachel Borisovna, that was the landlady's name, was a cultured woman. She was a geologist. Most likely she came down with encephalitis in the taiga. She was on her third husband. She nobly left him, gave him his freedom, he had his own room, and he visited her occasionally. She herself refused help. He had married and already had his own family, but he didn't forget her. We lived on Gnezdnikovsky Lane, if I'm not mistaken. The theatre "Roman" was in the courtyard, and I wasn't in it even once. And so, I had to look for a new apartment. One of the neighbors had a girlfriend who had her own room. The neighbor convinced her to take me in, since there was my son and she could hope that he would marvel at her wondrousness and would marry her. And so I moved in with her.
It turned out that she didn't have a stove, and the room was heated from the hallway. A drunkard neighbor lived in the other room, and his son would visit and they would drink together. I slept on a board, that is, a half of a door placed on two crates. I didn't undress the entire winter that I lived with her, it was so terribly cold. A second bed wouldn't have fit, the room was so small. A cupboard stood in the only place that we could have put a bed. This could have gone on for a long time, but once the neighbor had a drinking party and everyone cursed so loudly that the police came. The neighbor said that I was living there without a registration, even though I never did anything bad to him, and I was asked to leave the premises. The next day, I asked a co-worker to help me find a corner. She promised to help, and the next day she gave me the address of the sister of her friend. I went to the address. It was an old building on Trubnaya Street. When I got to her room, a young man was already waiting for her. He also wanted to rent a bed from her. The woman arrived shortly thereafter, turned down the young man, and led me into her room. It turned out that the room was formerly a bathroom. There was no window, and of course no vent. It was terribly hot. It was impossible to breathe. But what else could I do. She suggested that I do the cooking and she would go to the store for food herself. At first I agreed, but then I refused since she would eat with me and never bring me any change. This was beyond my means, and I had to refuse her services. She didn't have an official job. She did various jobs, either cleaning or laundry. Apparently she liked this better than manufacturing. I was once present when a couple came at night — a man and a woman — rented the bed and left in the morning. The landlady bragged that they gave her a sheet. In her words everything was normal. Everything in front of the girl. It was a difficult sight to see. I didn't live with her very long. They rented out a building at the warehouse where I worked, five of my co-workers lived there. The head director asked that one of them allow me to register with them. But no one agreed, fearing that I would then go ahead and move in with them. And so my ordeal continued. My husband sent 30 roubles a month as agreed. I would go see my son at school after work and take him something to eat. We would perch ourselves in a corner of the cloakroom and he would gobble up what I brought, being shy to do so in front of the other kids. Then I lived with my former co-worker. She lived on Krasnoproletarskaya Street. She lived with her daughter and granddaughter. It was awkward for me. I would come from visiting my son and it was already dark. They went to bed early. They didn't allow me to light a lamp. Often I would eat something in the dark, and also in bed. Soon they warned the landlady to throw me out of the apartment or otherwise there would be trouble for her if she let me live there without a registration. I had to leave. Once again I turned to Elizaveta Borisovna, and she fixed me up with her friends for the summer, since they were moving into their children's apartment who were going to the south for 2 months. In this way I became the landlady of the apartment for the summer. The same thing happened the next summer, that is they gave me their apartment. They also paid me 10 roubles a month. But the second summer was horrible for me. They had started to remodel. There was no place to sleep, everything was torn apart. I slept with my son on the floor. Workers would come after work and do repairs for 3 hours. Under such conditions my son was getting ready for the institute. That was in 1951. My son entered the Surikov Institute and lived in the student village. When he was in his third year, he began to moonlight a bit, and our budget grew some. My son studied with a student who lived with his mother and grandmother in a two-room apartment. The mother was a teacher of English, she encouraged the friendship with my son however she could. She convinced her neighbor to let me live there without a registration, and the neighbor rented a room to us. The room was tiny. There was a couch, a cot and a table. You couldn't get through. She tried to arrange it so that the boys would work together and split the money they earned. At first that's how it was. But soon they told them in the publishing house that they weren't allowed to work together, and each one had to take work separately. Kirill wasn't a very good artist, and their friendship broke up. His mother convinced my landlady to refuse to give me the apartment, and I was again without a corner. At work I was given the address of one woman who rented out her apartment for the summer, while she went with her son to the summer camp. The place was a semi-basement, but I was glad about that. She tricked me, and

раться. Сыну сказали хлопотать через Собес. Он так и сделал. Он
быстро все оформил и меня записали на очередь на кооперативную
квартиру на 1983 год. Доживу ли - вот вопрос.
Теперь о своих детях. В войну погиб брат Матвей, погибла сестра Женя
с двумя детьми в г. Жданове от рук фашистов. Когда Рива ехала
через Жданова, она звала ее с собой. Но Женя не захотела. Она осталась
в оккупированном городе с мужем и 2 детьми. Они погибли все. Лиза же
окончила Киевский мединститут. Работала в госпитале на станции Руб
цовка Алтайского края. Потом это был санаторий для туберкулезных
Сама заболела туберкулезом и умерла в 1946 г. 33 лет. Осталась
нас 2-е Я и Рива. Вот уже 4й год я на зиму перехожу к ней. У нее
2 сына, оба женаты. Один Гена живет на той же территории. Имеет
жену учительницу и 2х сыновей. Один 17 лет учится в музыкальном учи
лище в г. Запорожье, другому 13 лет учится в 6 классе, тоже посе
щает музык. школу по классу кларнета, старший пианист. Живет сестра
с младшим сыном Валерием, который имеет сына 6 лет. Квартира
3х комнатная со всеми удобствами. Живем все дружно. Невестки у
сестры хорошие. Мне с ними легко. Пробуду еще апрель, а на май нуж
но вернуться к себе. Живу как за каменной стеной. Помогаю чем могу.
Читаю, отдыхаю. Мне скоро будет 80 лет. Занимаюсь физкультурой, об
мываюсь каждый день. Жалуюсь только на боли в спине и
пояснице. Но это еще можно терпеть, не было бы хуже

За свою жизнь перенесла 3 операции. Гайморита, язву желудка и
2 операции глаз, катаракта. За время приезда в Бердянск занималась общественной работой. В 1953г. в библиотеке детской. В 1959г.
мне сделали операцию одного глаза, а 1961 г. операцию другого глаза
В этом промежутке не занималась общественной работой. Когда
стала видеть началась общественная работа снова. Я предложила
организовать хор ветеранов. С большими трудностями я организовала
Ходила по домам. Прикрепили их к клубу им. Кирова. Начало было хо
рошим. Выступили. Но пока руководитель хора занимался только пенсио
нерами все было хорошо, но вот руководитель объединил пенсионеров
с молодежью и все переругались и хор был распущен. Я предложила
свои услуги народному театру при город. доме культуры. Я была
старостой. Вела журнал, поздравляла участников театра. Сама несколько раз выступала с чтением. Имела несколько грамот. Находилась
при народном театре с 1965 г. до 1978 г. когда ушла режиссер театра
и я ушла. За время пока жила у сестры, зимой 2 года работала в
дет. библиотеке. Так закончилась моя общ. работа. Больше я не в
состоянии заниматься общ. работой. Мне 80 лет. Силы мои убывают.
Быстро устаю. Домой еще не вернулась. Сделала небольшой ремонт и с
1.УП думаю пойти домой. Рива обещала пойти на месяц ко мне. Она все
болеет. кашляет жалуется на боли в сердце. Приехала
домой к себе с 1.УП вместе с Ривой. Жили вместе июль и август.
11.УП Рива ездила домой за пенсией и на обратном пути ей стало
плохо на остановке и ее забрала скорая и положили в больницу, где о
на пробыла 2 недели. Вышла из больницы поправившись, но дома у
меня опять болела. С 3.IX она пошла домой и сейчас пока дома. Не
переносили жару, а дома у нее лучшие условия. Жду сына в сентябре

Подробнее о муже. Когда он уехал в Днепропетровск, оставив меня
без работы и жилья он долго не писал и я не знала, что подумать,
но через 4 месяца он написал, что больше ко мне не вернется у
него другая семья. Я сообщила об этом сыну, написала. Письмо в
лагеря, где он отдыхал. Он ничего мне не ответил. Несколько раз,
по моей просьбе, он ездил к отцу. Никаких чувств у него к
отцу не было и нет их сейчас. Они чужие друг другу. В новой семье
есть еще сын. Он уже женат, но привязанности братья не испытывают
друг к другу. На все просьбы сестры Буси, чтобы приехал сын по
видаться с отцом, сын обещает, но не выполняет. Нет у него никаких
чувств к отцу. Была я с Ривой у Буси в Днепропетровске после
того, как ей сделали операцию катаракты в январе 1962 г. отец
приходил к Бусе повидаться с нами, но не о чем было говорить
с ним. Он мне чужой, будто ничего не было в прошлом. Приходила и е
ж его и сын. Чужие и не интересные люди они для меня. Отец
просил, чтобы я прислала сына повидаться, но тот и слушать не
хочет. Моей вины тут нет, отец есть отец, я его прошу поехать.

didn't tell me that her son was a pilot and that he came home for vacation in the summer. He soon arrived and he had drinking parties almost every night which sometimes lasted until morning. They sang, danced, and made unbelievable noise. My son and I didn't get enough sleep because of the noise, but what could we do. And so this continued for 2 months. I paid 20 roubles a month. My son went to a lawyer to request that he draw up an appeal that the authorities register me for 2 years, until he finished the institute, since I was sick, and that after he finished the institute he would take me with him to where he was sent. Permission for this was granted. My son set me up in Solnechnogorsk, where we rented 2 rooms and paid 40 roubles a month. Soon the time approached when I was supposed to retire, and my son finished the institute. That was in 1957. I was very sick, I was on sick leave for almost a year, on and off, but I still reached retirement age. My son took my documents to the proper Committee, and they assigned me a pension of 52 roubles 30 kopeks a month. I got an additional 10% since I had worked for 37 years. My son finished the institute the same year. They left him in Moscow, and he began to work in the Detgiz. The question now was where was I going to live. Either we would buy an apartment near Moscow, or should I go to my sister in Berdyansk. In 1958 I went to visit my sister Riva and stayed there. I really liked Berdyansk, and I never left after that. At first I rented a room, since my sister didn't have room. She lived with her husband and two sons in a tiny room at her husband's sister's place. The landlady gave me a permanent registration, and my son asked me to look for an apartment to buy. He was already in a position to buy me an apartment. I looked at lots of apartments, but none of them were suitable. Finally my landlady told me that next to her mother's place they were selling 1/3 of a house. My sister and I went to look at it, we liked it, and I wrote to my son to come and look at it. That was in 1959. In the second apartment lived one woman, Trufanova, Maria Semyonovna, in the third apartment lived the parents of the people who sold us the apartment. They had built a house for themselves and this apartment didn't suit them anymore. In this way I became the owner of my own apartment. I began to set up the apartment. My sister's husband, Yuri Grigorevich, took charge of my apartment and began construction. First he built a summer kitchen from crates, then a summer room. I started to rent the summer room to vacationers. Two people, I got along well with the neighbors. But then misfortune came, and they began to say that they were going to tear down our buildings, and the daughter, whose parents lived in the third apartment, afraid that they would take away the apartment, quickly found a buyer and sold her parents' apartment. The father had died by then, and the mother moved in with her. The new neighbor turned out to be a totally wretched woman. The thing is, that I shared a small shed in the yard with the relatives of the previous landlady, who had built a wall and divided the shed evenly. The part with the window went to the new neighbor. She immediately wanted to occupy the second half, too. She bothered me about it for a few years, but I wouldn't agree to give her the shed. And all the same, in 1979 she brought in some wood and across from my house built a wooden shed and demanded a key to my side of the shed. I didn't want to fight with her. I gave her the key, and she transferred my fuel and a few other things. She was as busy as a bee. She made a two-room apartment and started to rent to vacationers. I brought a case against her in the local court. They decided to transfer the case to the Peoples' Court. My son came to visit and said that he would try to get a cooperative apartment and that it wasn't wise to get tangled up in court. That's what we did. But the chairman of the Executive Committee advised my son to "keep an eye on me", since some living space was being freed up and they would give it to me. I went to the Executive Committee every month, and every time comrade Deeva would tell me "there's nothing for you". That's how I spent 2 years, until the chairman of the Executive Committee left and they appointed a new one. Now this Deeva tells me "start from the beginning", and in 1981 my son went to the secretary of the Party Committee and told him of my ordeal. He called the new chairman of the Executive Committee, comrade Verzhikovsky, and asked him to get to the bottom of this. My son was told: appeal to the social security department. That's what he did. He quickly filled out all the papers, and put me in line for a cooperative apartment in 1983. Whether I'll live till then — that's the question.

Now about my children. My brother Matthew died in the war, so did my sister Zhenya along with two children in Zhdanov at the hands of fascists. When Riva was travelling through Zhdanov, she asked Zhenya to go with her. But Zhenya didn't want to. She stayed in the occupied city with her husband and two children. They all perished. Liza graduated from the Kiev medical institute. She worked at the hospital at Rubtsovka Station in the Altajsky Region. Then it became a sanatorium for tuberculosis patients. She herself got tuberculosis and died in 1946 at 33 years old. Two of us remained — I and Riva. This is already the fourth year that I am moving in with her for the winter. She has two sons. Both are married. One of them, Gena, lives in the same area. He has a wife, a teacher, and two sons. One is 17 and studies in the music school in the city of Zaporozhe, the other is 13 and is in the sixth grade, he also goes to the

music school in the clarinet class, the older one plays the piano. My sister lives with the younger son, Valery, who has a son 6 years old. It's a three-room apartment with all the conveniences. We live together harmoniously. My sister's daughters-in-law are good girls. I get along well with them. I will stay here for April, and in May I'll have to go back to my place. I am well taken care of. I help with what I can. I read, rest. I will be 80 years old soon. I do exercises and take a bath every day. The only thing I can complain about is the pain in my spine and lower back. But that's bearable, it could be worse.
I had three operations during my life. Arthritis, an ulcer in my stomach, and two eye operations, cataracts. During my time in Berdyansk I have been involved in community service. In 1953 I worked in the children's library. In 1959 I had an operation on one eye, and in 1961 on the other. I didn't do community work in the interval. Once I could see, my activities started again. I offered to organize a choir of veterans. I did so with great difficulty. I went house to house. They attached it to the Kirov club. The beginning was good. We performed. But as long as the choir director had only pensioners, everything was fine, but the director united the pensioners with the young people, and everyone fought, and the choir broke up. I offered my services to the people's theatre at the city house of culture. I was a monitor. I kept the comment book, congratulated the theatre participants. I myself performed a few times by reading poems. I had a few commendations. I was with the people's theatre from 1965 to 1978 when the director left the theatre and so did I. During the time that I lived with my sister for 2 winters I worked at the children's library. That's how my community service ended. I'm not able to do so anymore. I'm 80 years old. I'm losing my strength. I get tired quickly. I still haven't returned home. I did a little remodeling, and I think I'll go home from the first of July. Riva promised to live with me for a month. She's still sick, coughs, and complains of pain in her heart. I came home from the first of July with Riva. We lived together for July and August. 11.VII Riva went home for her pension, and on the way back she got sick at the bus stop, and the ambulance took her away to the hospital, where she spent 2 weeks. She came out of the hospital well, but got sick again at my place. From the third of September she went home and is there now. She couldn't take the heat, and she has better conditions at home. I'm waiting for my son to come in September.
More details about my husband. When he left for Dnepropetrovsk, leaving me without a job or place to live, he didn't write for a long time, and I didn't know what to think, but after 4 months he wrote that he wasn't coming back to me, that he had another family. I told my son about this, I wrote it in a letter. I sent the letter to the summer camp where he was on vacation. He didn't answer me. At my request he went to see his father a few times. He didn't have any feelings for his father and doesn't have any now. They are strangers to one another. There's another son in the new family. He's already married, and the brothers don't feel close to one another. The sister, Busya, keeps asking the son to come visit his father, and the son keeps promising to but never does. He has no feelings at all for his father. I was with Riva at Busya's in Dnepropetrovsk after she had a cataract operation in January 1982. The father came to visit us at Busya's, but there was nothing to talk about with him. He is a stranger to me, as though there was nothing between us in the past. His wife and son came also. They are strangers to me, and very boring people. Father asked me to send his son to see him, but my son doesn't even want to hear about it. I am not at all to blame here. After all, it is his father. I ask him to go.
His father is 78 years old also. His legs were bad and he didn't go anywhere. He has a car which his son drives. I don't think we'll see each other again. In April of that same year, Riva and I went to my son's and stayed with his mother-in-law — Gida Moiseevna. She is a very energetic and willful woman. She liked my son. She wouldn't let us do anything around the house, not even wash the dishes. In her words she doesn't trust anyone and did everything herself. She fed us very well. We stayed for 3 weeks and left on 3.V. I don't think I'll risk such a trip again. Gida Moiseevna brought my attention to the fact that my son couldn't even wash his own socks. And really, it is awkward that the wife washes socks and underwear. A man should do this himself, but he must be taught this from childhood, and what conditions did my son live in that he could be taught this. From the age of 10 he lived in a dormitory. His first wife, Irina, mocked him along with his mother-in-law. He was between two flames. His daughter is already married, and my son helps financially as before. He left a two-room apartment with all the conveniences, and when he left he lived in the studio. He met Vika, who had a son, Antosha, and she left her husband and moved into the studio, also, until my son could get a cooperative room where the three of them still live now. They live harmoniously, I am happy for them. Vika is 12 years younger than my son, but I don't think they have any disagreements. May God give them happiness. My son deserves it.

8.III.1983.
A lot of time passed before I picked up my biography again. Riva got sick again, and they put her in the hospital again from 15.XII.82. She was there for a month, and when she

came home she felt bad again. Another month passed before she felt better and everything returned to normal. In October my son came to visit, and I waited on him alone, though they did bring lunch from Riva. I managed to convince my son to go see his father. He saw his father and other relatives, and a month later his father died. How good that he saw his father before he died. My son and his wife went to the funeral. Joseph's wife received my son well, she met him and saw him off. And so, Joseph died at the age of 78. Dusya, his wife, likes Busya, Joseph's sister, helps with what she can. I have been living with my sister Riva since October. We really marked my birthday very festively. My son and his wife came. My son gave a speech at the table and with great love thanked me for the help I gave him while he was studying. Yes, his studying was difficult for us, but all the bad things are forgotten and only the good things are remembered. In the future I am waiting for a cooperative apartment. I'm on the list, the first down payment will be collected at the end of the year. Wouldn't it be good if they were to tear down my building and I didn't have to sell my apartment. But there's no rumor of such things, and we have to wait. My sister and I dream, that if I get a room, then we'll combine it with Gena's, my sister's second son, two-room apartment. But it's still a long way off before I get an apartment. After all, they'll be building for another 2 years still, will I live that long? I feel good, but I get tired quickly. I do exercises, and take a bath almost daily. I sleep from 11 to 1. I take a walk for an hour almost daily. But compared to last year, I'm losing strength. I hear noise in my head, I hear badly, and without fail, my spine and lower back aches after I eat breakfast and do the dishes. Last year I would sweep the rooms, but this year I no longer can. I just shake out the dust and sweep only the kitchen and hallway. My left hand shakes badly. It's hard to hold a spoon. I can't clench my left fist all the way. But this is still bearable. Riva doesn't feel well again. It's hard for her to cook for the whole family, but she does everything around the house herself. I don't help her with the cooking at all, she won't let me. I don't go very far from home, I'm afraid of falling. Valery goes for milk before work. He has to do more now, to take his son to nursery school and to go buy milk. Until the weather gets better I won't go for milk and groceries. The weather's terrible, windy and slippery. There hasn't been much snow this year, and it's already spring. What's going on at home? Is everything alright? I don't see the neighbors. Things have happened so I don't even speak to them. With the second neighbor, Maria Semyonovna, it's because she wouldn't let me use the coal box. Not only has she been using it all these years, but last time she dumped the coal on my spot across from the gazebo, and the gazebo had to be painted. Then I decided to sell the box, and I first offered her the chance to buy it. She refused, and then the other neighbor took it, promising to fix the little fence across from the house. However, that ramshackle fence is still standing to this day. Her son promised her, but he doesn't fulfill his promises, ie. to fix the fence. When I get home I'll have to find some-one to fix it, and the neighbor will most likely offer to pay for the box. I also don't have anything to do with the third neighbor who took my shed. If she speaks to me I'll answer, but I never start up conversations. I have to go to the town post office to get my pension, the mailman lives nearby but can't give me my pension. When the weather is bad I have to ask Lena to go with me. Once a month, but she does this grudgingly. I really have to beg. And I have to ask Gena to take my laundry to the woman who does it for me, and she lives near the station. I used to go all the time with Riva, but she's not in any condition to go with me now. Maybe she'll get stronger in the summer and will go with me to drop off my laundry. I also do some laundry, but I send the big things out. And here I asked.

8. III. There were 10 people, all close to me: Gena with his family, 4 people, the three of us, I, Riva, Lena with her daughter. They arrived at 1:00 in the afternoon and left at 4:00, it was a nice gathering, and in the evening was the meeting with Rina Zelenaya.

13. III. 83
I continue my notes. Life is going normally, nothing in particular is happening. Thanks to Riva I am surrounded by care and attention. I received a letter from my son. There's to be a personal exhibit of his works in the Pushkin Museum in April. How that inspires him. Times are changing. They now pay attention to his work. There was an exhibit at the Artists' Union. It's so good that he gets satisfaction from his work, that they started to promote him, and that's the main thing for a professional artist. This still doesn't give him anything financially, but it boosts his morale that they notice him and promote his exhibits. It's a shame that he writes about it so rarely, and it's so nice to read his letters. He promised to come closer to spring. I want to receive him at Riva's. I don't have the strength to receive him here. I get exhausted from moving around. In the morning until 11:00 I still move around, but from 11:00 my back and spine ache so and I have to lay down. After two hours of rest I can move again. Nonetheless, I do what I can around the house. I wash dishes, sweep, dust. I can't do anything more than that. It's somehow become hard for me to write. I write nevertheless. My left hand aches and shakes constantly, it's good that my right one is still o.k. Everything here is the same as before.

Отцу тоже 78 лет. Он болел ногами, никуда не ходит. У него машина, которую ведет его сын. Больше я думаю мы не увидимся.
В апреле того же года мы с Ривой ездили к сыну и находились у его тещи Гиды Моисеевны. Это очень энергичная и волевая женщина К сыну она хорошо относится. Нам она ничего не давала делать по дому, даже помыть посуду. По ее же словам она не доверяет и все делала сама. Кормила отлично. Мы пробыли 3 недели и уехали З.У. Больше думаю я не рискну на такую поездку. Вот Гита Моисеевна обратила мое внимание, что сын не может даже постирать себе носки. И действительно, как это не удобно, чтобы жена стирала носки и трусы. Мужчина должен сам это делать, но его приучить должны с детства, а в каких условиях жил сын, чтобы его научить этому. С 10 лет в общежитии. Первая жена Ирина издевалась над ним вместе с тещей. Он был между двух огней. Дочка его уже замужем, но сын попрежнему помогает материально. Он оставил 2х комнатную квартиру со всеми удобствами, а сам жил, когда ушел, в мастерской Встретился он с Викой, у которой сын Антоша и она ушла от мужа и переселилась тоже в мастерскую, пока сын не достал кооперативную комнату, где они втроем живут и сейчас. Сын сделал перегородку и Антоша имеет отдельную комнату. Живут дружно, я рада за них. Вика на 12 лет моложе сына, но разногласий по моему у них нет Дай боже им счастья. Сын его заслужил.

8.Ш-1983 г.

Прошло не мало времени пока я снова взялась за биографию Рива снова болела и ее с 15.ХII-82 снова положили в больницу. Пролежала она месяц, а придя домой опять плохо себя чувствовала Прошел еще месяц, пока ей стало легче и все вошло в норму. В октябре сын приезжал ко мне и я его одна обслуживала, хотя обед привозили от Ривы. Удалось сына уговорить поехать к отцу. Он виделся с отцом и другими родственниками, а через месяц умер отец. Как хорошо, что он повидался с ним перед смертью. На похороны приехал сын с женой. Жена Иосифа хорошо приняла сына, встретила его и проводила. Итак Иосиф умер на 78 году жизни. Дуся жена его хорошо относится к Бусе сестре Иосифа, помогает чем может. Я живу у сестры Ривы с октября. Очень торжественно отмечали мой юбилей. Приехал сын с невесткой. За столом сын держал речь и с большой любовью благодарил меня за помощь, когда он учился. Да тяжело нам досталась его учеба, но все забывается похоже, остается только хорошее. Впереди жду кооперативную квартиру. В списке я состою, деньги первый взнос будут собирать в конце года. Хорошо бы если бы меня снесли и не надо было бы продавать мою квартиру. Но слухов таких нет о сносе и нужно все предоставить времени. Мечтаем с сестрой если получу комнату соединиться с Геной, вторым сыном сестры. у которого 2х комнатная квартира. Но еще так далеко до того как у меня будет квартира. Ведь строить ее будут 2 года, а доживу ли до этого времени % Самочувствие хорошее, но быстро устаю. Делаю физкультуру моюсь, почти ежедневно в ванне. Сплю с 11 до 1 ч. Гуляю по часу почти ежедневно. Но против прошлого года силы уходят. Шум в голове плохо слышу, обязательно после завтрака, помыв посуду, разбаливается спина и поясница. После отдыха чувствую себя гораздо лучше. В прошлом году подметала в комнатах, а теперь уже не в состоянии. Только пыль вытру и подметаю только в кухне и коридоре, Сильно дрожит левая рука. Трудно держать ложку. Пальцы левой руки не сжимаются до конца. Но это еще терпимо. Рися не важно опять себя чувствует...Готовить на всю семью. Ей тяжело, но она делает сама все по дому. Ничем ей в готовке не помогаю, она не раз решает. Выходить из дому далеко не хожу, боюсь упасть. За молоком ходит Валерий до работы. У него теперь увеличилась нагрузка и отводит сына в садик и ходит за молоком. Пока не установится погода, я замолоком и покупками не хожу. Погоды не хорошие, ветры, скользко Снегу выпало совсем немного в этом году, а ведь весна. Что то у меня дома? Благополучно ли. С соседями не общаюсь. Так получилось, что с ними не разговариваю. Со второй соседкой Марией Семеновной по причине, что не разрешила пользоваться ящиком для угля. Она не только все годы им пользовалась, но и последний раз просевала уголь на моей территории, напротив беседки и пришлось красить

The little one goes to the chess club 2 times a week. He is a very nervous child. But at the chessboard he is calm, and can play with anyone until bedtime, that is until 9:00. Somehow he will sit through school. He goes to school this year. I wrote to my friend and told her she should start writing her memories. She has lived a difficult life. She was arrested, was imprisoned for 8 years, was repressed. My friends whom I used to meet for a cup of tea for years have died. Regina Pavlovna, Irina Andreevna. Our circle is no more. Our guard is leaving permanently. Soon my turn will come. That's how it should be. But I am satisfied with my life. After the hard past I have now acquired peace and happiness. All the hard things are forgotten, they lose their intensity, and only the present peace is happiness. True, I am waiting for a cooperative room which my son did so much to get, but what will be will be. My apartment is occupied, and here there is total peace. In June I'll have to go to my apartment to do repairs. Will Riva be able to come to me for the summer? She is still so weak, I'll have to stay alone. We'll see.

27.IV.83
The repairs are finally finished. An excellent job was done by our distant relative. He is the father of the former daughter-in-law of Riva's husband's late sister. He charged 150 roubles. I gave him my subsidy and 10 roubles. Now I have work to do with the boxes and the closet inside, and I have to straighten up and clean up the gazebo. That's not his job. I have to do this myself, but I don't have the strength. Today I went to pick up some work and barely made it home. I think I'll stay here for May, and then I'll have to go back to my own apartment. And all my strength is completely exhausted. It's terribly difficult to walk. I can barely move my legs. My back and spine hurt. I should sell the apartment, I can't take care of it.
I have to worry about food, and I'm in no condition to cook for myself. It's unlikely that Riva will come live with me for the summer months. She doesn't feel well either — heart trouble, and now her teeth. She has to go to the city, we don't have a doctor here. Who knows what's going to happen with the cooperative. They're promising to accept the down payments at the end of this month. And then they'll finish building it. Will I live to see the completion of the construction, and then we need to combine with Gena. Do I have enough time left for all this? After all, my years left on this planet are numbered. I'm losing strength.

5.V.1983.
I received a notice from the Executive Committee. I have to update the documents submitted in 1981. Because of the 1983 Inspection Act a certificate is required from the house management and inventory bureau. The representative of the Executive Committee came to see me at home and drew up the paper, and will give me a certificate of availability of living space on 11.V. Now all the formalities have been taken care of, and all that's left is to wait for a notice about the down payment. My son has already sent 2000 roubles. It's still not clear how much the first payment will be. My mood is heightened. I am waiting for a room that I can then combine with Gena's.

12.V. My son called today and made me happy. Galya's been freed of her pregnancy and a daughter was born at 5:00 am. Weight — 3600 grams, everything is fine, mother and daughter are well. Now I am already a great grandmother, for which my son congratulated me. One more thing happened, though of less importance. I finally bought the raincoat I was dreaming about. Riva just happend to drop into our store and there was one coat in size 48. It costs 100 r. 80 k. She got the money. She cares so much about me. My son promised to send 200 roubles. I gave 101 roubles for the coat, for those celebrating their name days 5 x 5 = 25 roubles, for the food 16 x 2 = 32 + 5 = 37 — 10 = 27 r. = 153 roubles. I gave Riva 30 roubles from my pension for her birthday. That leaves me 46 roubles to live on.

1.VI. I am moving into my own apartment. It still needs to be cleaned and the furniture arranged. Will Riva come with me, and for how long? After all, I'm going for 4 months. Here is the established order. I take a walk in the morning for 1 — 1 1/2 hours. Then there's breakfast. I wash the dishes and at 11:00 I become a casualty. My spine and back begin to ache. Then during the day I lay down for 1 hour. Then I do something, I read. At 5:00 there's supper. Then I wash the dishes again. I read the paper, watch the television. Everything is all set, it goes according to plan. Now everything will change. The order of things will be violated. When I get used to a set way of life, I don't want to change it, but it's necessary. The repairs were done in the house, and now things have to be straightened up. Will I manage by 1 June? My things are in different places. Somehow I'll gather it all in one place. My son's personal exhibit has been moved back to June. He is a happy grandfather. This year on 30.IX he will be 50 years old. He is so attentive and caring toward me. On 3.V he sent me a package, oranges, buckwheat. He promised to send butter, too. How will Galya and the baby manage? Vika and Irina will visit, but everyone lives so far from her. She has a good husband. Most of the help will come from him. May they be happy and may a healthy, strong new generation grow.

6.VI. Today I am moving back to my place. I didn't sleep all night, I kept thinking. 30.V was an organizational meeting for the cooperative. They'll tell us at the next meeting how much to pay and where. They promise to build it in a year, but you can't believe that. It will be a five-storey building, brick, for small families. There will be 90 apartments in all. 78 one-room ones, 12 meters by 14 meters. 12 apartments — are two-room ones. It's not far from Riva, where the closest stop is for bus No.17. I am thinking of offering to register it as a gift to Riva, and then let her sell it for as much as she wants. It scares me to even think about selling. Let her register it herself or let Gena do it. I don't feel so well. Will I live to see a new apartment? It's frightening to be home all alone. We got used to living out of a suitcase. The young people will come, and will go. They'll tell me about everything. I am thinking I'll go once a week to bathe. On Saturdays. Riva won't stay with me. Maybe she'll come for a few days and then leave. It's hard for her to be at my place. There aren't any conveniences.

30.VI. I haven't written in my diary for a long time. 27.VI was the second meeting of the cooperative "Victory", they didn't say anything important, but we filled out our promissory notes. Stupidly I signed my full name, and my signature is completely different. I'll have to redo the note. On 10.VII where to pay the 2000 roubles will be announced. The total cost of the room is 5000 roubles. The rooms are small depending on the number of people. There will be 12-14-16 square meters. I, of course, will get 12 meters. All my furniture won't fit. I think that when I get the room, I'll give Riva my apartment, with my son's consent.
Let her sell it for as much as she wants. And once I get the room, they promise to combine it with either Riva or Gena (by September 1984). Gena is promised a 3-room apartment, and if he gets it, then Riva gets a four-room one. But when will that be. I don't feel so well. It's difficult to walk. My spine and lower back ache. I rest from 11:00 to 1:00 in the afternoon. Then the more difficult things come, laundry, cleaning. It's hard for me, but at least I'm home. I remember how I felt out of place at Riva's in the winter. I want to live independently. After all, I'm used to living alone with my own ways. How much time do I have? I just don't want to be a burden to anyone. I want to take care of myself. So far I'm taking care of myself. True, I send the laundry out. A woman comes to wash the floors. To live and to be happy. But this happiness doesn't exist. I am alarmed over what will happen with my health. I don't go anywhere. Riva comes on Saturday and on Sunday we go to her place. I bathe, spend the night, and go home on Monday. She brings me supper, which lasts 4-5 days. I pay from the same account — 2 roubles a day. It's still hot. There are lots of vacationers, at both neighbors, too. I don't rent to anyone, since last year. My son objects, and I can't stand strangers in my house anymore. I am grateful to my son for sending me money, since my pension isn't enough. 52 roubles, I did repairs in the apartment, it cost 176 roubles. I bought a summer coat for 100 roubles.

I.VIII. Finally everything is set with the cooperative. 19.VII was the last meeting. We got the papers for sending the payments to the account in the bank, and 2.VII I divided my money into 2 accounts. 2000 roubles in one, 1000 in the other. 29.VI I filled out the promissory note. 2000 roubles were transferred to the bank. In this way all is set with the cooperative, all that's left now is to wait for the apartment, whether I'll make it or not, and I still have to make out a will for my son for 2000 roubles. If I don't live to get the room, they'll at least return the 2000 roubles to my son. Valery has promised to come and get me so we can go to the notary. I don't go anywhere by myself. My legs aren't too stable. It's hard to get on and off the bus. Gena came for me yesterday, 31.VII. We left at 5:00 and came back at 9:00. We went to Riva's to take a bath. I was terribly exhausted. I could barely eat. My spine and lower back are overpowering me. And my hand shakes badly. I'll wait for the vacationers to leave, and I'll go to the neurologist. My hand bothers me. I now wash the floor myself. The woman washed it twice and doesn't want to do it anymore. I do the laundry myself, but I send the big things out. My son promised to come in August. Riva has guests — 5 people from Rostov and Kiev. All on account of Misha. Riva's got a cold. It's hard for her to be around strangers. They're leaving 13.VIII.

16.X.84.
My dear children, Gita Moiseevna and Antoshenka!
How are you? Are you all healthy? My health is still the same. There are no changes. My hand shakes. My legs, too. If I have to go to the notary I take a taxi and someone goes with me. The epic with the apartment has finally ended. 13.X they gave me the move-in order, and I looked over my future residence. The weather was horrible, it rained the whole time. The unpaved road leading up to the building was all mud. That's when they gave out the move-in orders. I haven't been back to the building. Riva is taking care of everything. She goes everyday to find the workmen. They turned on the water, lights, and installed a two-burner stove. No one knows when they'll turn on the gas. They began to polish the floor in the room. The workmen will come for a few days, they'll insulate the door for warmth. On Sunday Valery and Lusya washed the windows in the room

and the kitchen. Everything is so small, but I think all my furniture will fit except for the desk. First we need to carefully measure everything in order to fit all my belongings in. Also we need to go to the old little house to put everything in sacks, except for the table, wardrobe, and chairs. I don't think it will all fit in one car. As far as selling my apartment is concerned, they still haven't applied to the executive committee. That will be on 1.XI and we'll get an answer on 5. XI. They mercilessly tore down everything. Valery, Gena and Misha participated in this operation. They tore down both the gazebo and the ill-fated shed. But so far we can't sell because the neighbors also have a gazebo, and this is also supposed to be taken away. But the architect reassures us that we'll be able to sell. Lusya is taking care of all this. She has to take off time from work. After the executive committee we still need the notarized signatures of the neighbors that they don't object to the sale of my apartment. The buyer is waiting, but he hasn't given us any money yet, not knowing whether they'll give them a registration or not. There is a husband, wife, and they have a young son. Everything is planned. Riva runs around taking care of my things, Lord, don't let her catch cold. It rains and gets colder everyday. Things are chaotic. Repairs are being done. Everything is all scattered around nothing is in place. You'll see when you come, son. They made a closet in the hallway, but they haven't finished it yet, but they finished with the room. First they're putting the tiles in the bathroom and toilet. Call when you arrive.
Stay healthy, happy.
Your loving mama.

die Küche benütze und nicht angemeldet sei. Und auch für mich war dieser Zustand schwer erträglich. Die Wärterin war eifersüchtig auf mich, weil die Hausfrau mir mehr Aufmerksamkeit schenkte als ihr. Rachil Borisovna, so hieß sie, war eine gebildete Frau. Sie war Geologin. Wahrscheinlich war sie in der Taiga an Enzephalitis erkrankt. Sie war zum dritten Mal verheiratet. Großzügig gab sie ihrem Mann die Freiheit, er hatte ein eigenes Zimmer und kam sie manchmal besuchen. Sie verzichtete auf Unterstützung. Er heiratete und hatte eine eigene Familie, aber er vergaß sie nicht. Wir wohnten in der Gnesdnikovskij-Gasse, wenn ich mich nicht irre. Im Hof war das Theater « Romen », wo ich kein einziges Mal war. Also mußte ich mir ein neues Quartier suchen. Eine der Nachbarinnen kannte ein Mädchen, die ein eigenes Zimmer hatte. Die Nachbarin überredete sie, mich aufzunehmen, weil ich einen Sohn hatte und man hoffen konnte, er werde sich von ihren Vorzügen blenden lassen und sie möglicherweise heiraten. Also zog ich zu ihr.
Es zeigte sich, daß sie keinen Ofen hatte. Das Zimmer wurde vom Korridor beheizt. Im anderen Zimmer lebte ein Trunkenbold, dessen Sohn ihn besuchen kam, und dann tranken sie zusammen. Ich schlief auf einem Brett, d.h. die Hälfte einer Tür war über zwei Truhen gelegt. Den ganzen Winter, während ich bei ihr wohnte, habe ich mich nicht ausgezogen, so eine fürchterliche Kälte war da. Ein zweites Bett hätte auch gar keinen Platz gehabt, so klein war das Zimmer. Wo ein Bett Platz gehabt hätte, dort stand die Garderobe. Das hätte noch lang so gehen können, aber einmal veranstaltete der Nachbar ein Gelage und alle fluchten dermaßen laut, daß die Miliz kam. Der Nachbar sagte, daß ich nicht angemeldet sei, obwohl ich ihm nie etwas angetan hatte, und ich mußte die Wohnung verlassen. Am nächsten Tag bat ich meine Mitarbeiterin, ob sie mir nicht helfen könne, einen Winkel zu finden. Sie versprach es und gab mir am nächsten Tag die Adresse der Schwester einer Bekannten. Ich ging hin. Das war ein sehr altes Haus in der Trubnaja-Strasse. Als ich zu ihrem Zimmer kam, wartete schon ein junger Mann auf sie, der auch einen Schlafplatz mieten wollte. Bald kam die Wirtin, sagte dem jungen Mann ab und führte mich in mein Zimmer. Es war das frühere Bad. Es hatte kein Fenster und natürlich auch keine Lüftung. Es war furchtbar heiß. Man konnte nicht atmen. Aber was sollte ich tun. Sie schlug mir vor, sie werde selbst kochen und einkaufen. Anfangs war ich einverstanden, aber dann nahm ich davon Abstand, da sie mir das Retourgeld nicht zurückgab und mit mir mitass. Das überstieg meine Mittel, und ich verzichtete

беседку. Тогда я решила продать ящик, предложив ей сначала купить. Она отказалась, тогда другая соседка его взяла, обещав починить заборчик напротив дома во дворе. Однако так разрушенной забор стоит и по сей день. Сын ее обещал, но не выполняет обещание, т.е. починить забор. Когда буду дома, придется найти человека, чтобы починил, и соседка вероятно предложит уплатить за ящик. С третьей соседкой, которая забрала мой сарай, тоже не общаюсь. Если заговорит, отвечаю, сама не завожу никаких разговоров. Приходится ехать за пенсией на городскую почту, а почтальон живет рядом, но выдать мне пенсию не может. Плохие поводы и нужно просить Лену пойти со мной. Раз в месяц, но она не охотно это делает. Нужно очень просить. Вот и белье нужно просить Гену отнести к женщине, которая мне стирает, а живет она возле вокзала, нужно ехать. Все время ездила с Ривой, а теперь она не в состоянии со мной ездить. Может летом она окрепнет и будет со мной отвозить белье. Сама я тоже стираю, но большей отдаю. Вот и просила. 8.Ш. Собрались 10 человек, все свои: Гена со своей семьей, 4 чел, наши 3 человека, я, Рива, Лена с дочерью. Пришли к 1ч. дня ушли в 4 ч. дня, хороший "огонек" был, а вечером встреча с Риной Зеленой.

13.Ш-83г.

Продолжаю свои заметки. Жизнь течет нормально без особенных происшествий. Благодаря Риве я окружена заботой и вниманием. Получила от сына письмо. Ожидается в апреле его персональная выставке в музее им. Пушкина. Как его это вдохновляет. Время меняется. На его работы обращают внимание. Была выставка в Союзе художников. Как хорошо, что он имеет удовлетворение от своих работ, что его начали выдвигать, а это главное для большого художника. Материально это ничего пока не дает, но морально он удовлетворен, что его замечают и выдвигают на выставки. Жаль что он редко об этом пишет, а как приятно читать его письма. Обещал к весне приехать. Хочется встретить у Ривы. У меня я не в силах его принять. Совсем выдыхаюсь от движений. Утром до 11 ч я еще двигаюсь, а с 11 невероятно разбаливается спина и поясница и я должна лечь. После 2х часового отдыха я снова смогу двигаться. Все же я по мере возможности что-то делаю по дому. Мою посуду, подметаю, вытираю пыль. На большее я не способна. Что то писать стало затруднительно. Все же я пишу. Левая рука побаливает и дрожит беспрерывно, хорошо что правая еще в норме. У нас все по-старому. Малыш ходит 2 раза в неделю в шахматный кружок. Он очень нервный ребенок. Но за шахматной доской он спокоен, может играть с кем угодно до сна т.е. до 9 ч. Как то он высидит в школе. А в этом году он идет в школу. Написала своей знакомой, чтобы она занялась писать свои мемуары. Она прожила тяжелую жизнь. Была арестована, сидела 8 и была репрессирована. Умерли мои друзья с кем встречалась на чашке чая много лет. Регина Павловна, Ирина Андреевна. Нет теперь нашего кружка. Уходит наша гвардия безвозвратно. Скоро дойдет и мой черед. Так надо. Но жизнь своей я довольна. За все тяжелое прошлое я обрела сейчас покой и счастье. Все тяжелое забывается, утрачивает свою остроту и только теперешний покой есть счастье. Правда жду кооператив.комнату, о которой так хлопотал сын, но как получится. Квартира моя занята, а тут полный покой. В июне придется пойти на свою квартиру, делать ремонт. Сможет ли Рива пойти ко мне на лето? Она еще такая слабая мне придется побыть одной. Видно будет.

27.1У-83.

Наконец уже закончился ремонт. Отлично сделан ремонт дальний родственник. Ривинова мужа покойной сестры быв. невестки - отец. Взял 150 руб. дал дотацию, дала 10 руб. Ж Теперь моя работа внутри в ящиках в шкафу, убрать, убрать беседки. Это его не касается, это мне нужно самой проделать, а сил нет. Сегодня пошла принять работу и еле дошла домой. Думаю еще май здесь пробыть, а потом нужно пойти на свою квартиру. А силы совсем истощились. Ходить ужасно трудно. Ноги еле переставляю. Болит спина и поясница. Нужно уже продать квартиру, я не могу за ней присмотреть. Нужно и о

auf ihre Dienste. Sie arbeitete nirgends offiziell, obwohl sie eine gesunde Frau war. Sie war Bedienerin bei wohlhabenden Leuten, ging selbständig einkaufen für sie, kochte und räumte auf. Irgendwann merkte ich, daß zu ihr Männer kamen, als sie von ihrer Arbeit noch nicht zurück war. Sie unterhielten sich mit mir, interessierten sich für meine Biographie. Einmal, als sie zu Hause war, kam ein alter Jude und begann sich vor uns auszuziehen. Sie jagte ihn hinaus. Ein gut erzogener Mensch kam und brachte Delikatessen und Getränke, er bewirtete uns beide. Mir wurde alles klar, wo ich hingeraten war, das war ihr Nebenverdienst. Sie prahlte vor mir, daß sie den Männern gefiele. Daran zweifelte ich auch gar nicht. Endlich schlug sie mir von sich aus vor, einen anderen Platz zum Wohnen zu suchen. Viel verdiente sie wirklich nicht an mir. Ich war wie früher in Zagorsk gemeldet und zahlte der Wirtin für das Zimmer, in dem ich faktisch nicht wohnte. Aber ich mußte meine Lebensmittelkarten für Brot abstempeln lassen und nahm mir einen Tag frei. Ich arbeitete in einer Textilwarenbasis, von 1947 bis 1957, bis ich in Pension ging. Einmal, als ich die Brotkarten stempeln ging, war bei der Wirtin eine Bekannte aus Moskau, die Untermieter bei sich wohnen ließ. Ich ging dorthin. Es war eine Kellerwohnung. Die Hausfrau lebte dort mit ihrer schulpflichtigen Tochter, nebenan lebte eine große Familie. Immer gab es Krach und Streitereien. Aber mir tat niemand etwas. Im Zimmer stand ein großes Bett, ein Kinderbett und eine Truhe. Mir wurde die Truhe angeboten. In der ersten Nacht zog ich mich aus, was mir sehr leid tat. Die Wohnung war feucht. Die Wand, an der ich schlief, war nicht abgedeckt, sie war feucht und kalt, Ofen gab es keinen. Geheizt wurde vom Korridor. Ich erkältete mich schrecklich und war lange krank. Nie wieder zog ich mich aus. Es zeigte sich, daß die Hausfrau und das Mädchen in dem Kinderbett schliefen, das große Bett vermietete sie für die Nacht. Offiziell arbeitete die Frau nicht. Sie arbeitete da und dort als Putzfrau, übernahm Wäsche zum Waschen. Offensichtlich lag ihr das mehr, als in der Produktion zu arbeiten. Einmal war ich Zeugin, als in der Nacht zwei kamen, er und sie, das Bett mieteten und in der Früh gingen. Die Wirtin prahlte, sie hätten ihr ein Leintuch geschenkt. Nach ihren Worten war das alles ganz normal. Alles in Gegenwart ihrer Tochter. Ein schwer erträglicher Zustand. Ich wohnte nicht lange dort. Von der Textilbasis, wo ich arbeitete, wurde ein Haus gemietet, in dem 5 unserer Mitarbeiter wohnten. Der Hauptbuchhalter fragte jeden von ihnen persönlich, ob mich nicht jemand von ihnen anmelden könne bei sich. Aber niemand stimmte zu, sie hatten Angst,
ich würde dann eigenmächtig einziehen. So nahm meine Not kein Ende. Der Vater schickte nach Übereinkunft 30 Rubel im Monat. Nach der Arbeit ging ich zu meinem Sohn in die Schule und brachte ihm zu essen. Im Umkleideraum setzten wir uns in die Ecke und er aß schnell, was ich mitgebracht hatte, er genierte sich vor seinen Freunden. Danach wohnte ich bei einer früheren Mitarbeiterin. Sie wohnte auf der Krasnoproletarskaja. Sie lebte dort mit ihrer Tochter und ihrer Enkelin. Es war mir sehr unangenehm. Wenn ich von meinem Sohn nach Hause kam, was schon alles dunkel. Sie gingen früh schlafen. Licht machen war nicht erlaubt. Oft aß ich auch nur schnell schnell im Dunkeln. Bald wurde die Wirtin gewarnt, sie bekäme Unannehmlichkeiten, wenn sie mich weiter unangemeldet bei sich wohnen ließe. Ich mußte ausziehen. Wieder wandte ich mich an Elisaveta Borisovna, und sie brachte mich über den Sommer bei ihren Bekannten unter, da diese in die Wohnung der Kinder gezogen waren, welche den Sommer im Süden verbrachten. So war ich über den Sommer selber Wohnungsinhaberin. Nächsten Sommer wiederholte sich das, d.h. sie stellten mir wieder ihre Wohnung zur Verfügung. Sie bezahlten mir sogar 10 Rubel dafür im Monat. Aber der zweite Sommer war sehr lästig für mich. Sie ließen die Wohnung renovieren, man konnte nirgends schlafen, alles war verräumt. Mein Sohn und ich schliefen auf dem Boden. Der Arbeiter kam nach 3 Uhr, nach seiner offiziellen Arbeit, und begann mit dem Renovieren. Unter diesen Umständen bereitete sich mein Sohn auf das Institut vor. Das war im Jahr 1951. Mein Sohn trat ins Surikov-Institut ein und lebte im Studentenheim. Vom dritten Studienjahr an begann er dazuzuverdienen und das Budget vergrößerte sich ein wenig. Mein Sohn studierte zusammen mit einem Studenten, der mit seiner Mutter und Großmutter in einer Zweizimmerwohnung wohnte. Die Mutter, eine Englischlehrerin, förderte diese Freundschaft ihres und meines Sohnes auf jede Weise. Und sie überredete ihre Nachbarin, mich ohne Anmeldung bei sich wohnen zu lassen, und die vermietete uns ein Zimmer. Das Zimmer war winzig. Es gab einen Diwan, ein Feldbett und einen Tisch. Man konnte sich kaum bewegen. Sie hatte sich deshalb bemüht, damit die Burschen zusammenarbeiteten und ihr Honorar teilten. Den Tisch stellte sie zur Verfügung. Am Anfang war das auch so. Aber bald erklärte man ihnen in der Redaktion, sie könnten nicht zusammen arbeiten, jeder müsse seine Arbeit allein abliefern. Kirill war auch kein besonderer Künstler, und die Freundschaft zerbrach. Seine Mutter beeinflußte meine Vermieterin, mir abzusagen, und wieder war ich ohne Bleibe.

von Serge
für Felix

8.8.1995

In der Arbeit gab man mir die Adresse einer Frau, die ihre Wohnung über den Sommer vermietete, weil sie mit ihrem Sohn ins Ferienlager fuhr. Die Wohnung war im Tiefparterre, aber ich war trotzdem froh. Nur leider hatte sie mir nicht gesagt, daß ihr zweiter Sohn, ein Pilot, seine Sommerferien in der Wohnung verbringen werde. Der Sohn kam und jeden Abend gab es Trinkgelage, manchmal bis in den Morgen. Wir konnten bei diesem Lärm nicht schlafen, aber was sollten wir machen. Ich zahlte 20 Rubel im Monat dafür. Mein Sohn wandte sich an einen Juristen mit der Bitte, ein Ansuchen zu verfassen, man möge mir doch die Anmeldung für 2 Jahre geben, bis er sein Institut abgeschlossen habe, da ich krank sei, nach Studienabschluss werde er mich mitnehmen, wo immer er eine Stelle bekäme. Die Erlaubnis wurde erteilt. Mein Sohn brachte mich in Solnetschnogorsk unter, wo wir zwei Zimmer mieteten und 40 Rubel im Monat zahlten. Die Zeit meiner Pensionierung rückte näher, und mein Sohn beendete das Institut. Das war im Jahr 1957. Ich war sehr krank, fast ein Jahr war ich mit Unterbrechungen im Spital, trotzdem erreichte ich das Pensionsalter. Mein Sohn brachte meine Dokumente aufs Sozialamt, und mir wurde eine Pension in der Höhe von 52 Rubel 30 Kopeken zuerkannt. Ich bekam einen Zuschlag von 10%, da ich 37 Arbeitsjahre nachweisen konnte. Im selben Jahr schloß mein Sohn das Institut ab. Man beließ ihn in Moskau, und er begann für den Kinderbuchverlag Detgis zu arbeiten. Es erhob sich die Frage, wo ich leben sollte. Sollten wir in der Nähe von Moskau eine Wohnung kaufen, oder sollte ich zur Schwester nach Berdjansk ziehen. Im Jahr 1958 fuhr ich meine Schwester Riva besuchen und blieb dort. Berdjansk gefiel mir sehr, und ich reiste nirgendwo mehr hin. Erst mietete ich ein Zimmer, weil bei meiner Schwester kein Platz war. Sie lebte mit ihrem Mann und zwei Söhnen in einem winzigen Zimmer, bei der Schwester des Mannes. Die Vermieterin meldete mich für ständig an, und mein Sohn bat mich, eine Wohnung zu suchen, um sie zu kaufen. Er war schon in der Lage, mir eine Wohnung zu kaufen. Ich schaute mehrere Wohnungen an, aber es war keine passende darunter. Endlich teilte mir meine Wirtin mit, neben ihrer Mutter werde das Drittel eines Hauses verkauft. Ich ging mit meiner Schwester hin und es gefiel uns. Ich schrieb meinem Sohn, er solle es sich ansehen kommen, und ihm gefiel es auch. Wir kauften diese Wohnung für 2500 Rubel in neuer Währung. Das war im Jahr 1959. In der zweiten Wohnung wohnte eine Nachbarin, Trufanowa Marija Semjonowna, in der dritten Wohnung die Eltern von denen, die uns die Wohnung verkauft hatten. Sie bauten ein Haus,

diese Wohnung sagte ihnen nicht zu. Auf diese Weise wurde ich Besitzerin einer eigenen Wohnung. Ich begann sie herzurichten. Der Mann meiner Schwester, Jurij Grigorevitsch, nahm sich dieser Angelegenheit an und befaßte sich mit dem Umbau. Aus Kisten baute er zuerst eine Veranda, dann ein Gartenhäuschen. Das Gartenhäuschen vermietete ich an Sommerfrischler. 2 Personen, mit den Nachbarn vertrug ich mich gut. Unglücklicherweise kam das Gerücht auf, unsere Häuser würden abgerissen und die Tochter, deren Eltern in der dritten Wohnung wohnten, erschrak und suchte in aller Eile einen Käufer für die Wohnung der Eltern. Der Vater starb zu dieser Zeit und die Mutter nahm sie zu sich. Die neue Nachbarin erwies sich als äußerst unangenehme Person. Die Sache war die, daß im Hof ein Schuppen stand, den ich mit den Eltern der früheren Besitzerin zu gleichen Teilen benützte. Sie stellte eine Wand auf im Schuppen und teilte ihn ab. Der Teil mit dem Fenster ging an die neue Nachbarin. Sie wollte aber gleich auch die zweite Hälfte. Einige Jahre beunruhigte sie mich deswegen, aber ich stimmte nicht zu. Und dann, im Jahr 1979, errichtete sie doch gegenüber von meinem Haus einen hölzernen Schuppen und verlangte die Schlüssel von meiner Schuppenhälfte. Ich konnte ja nicht mit ihr raufen. Ich gab ihr die Schlüssel, und sie übersiedelte mein Heizmaterial und noch ein paar Sachen. Sie entwickelte stürmische Aktivitäten. Sie richtete eine Zweizimmerwohnung her und vergab sie an Sommerfrischler. Ich wandte mich ans Kameradschaftsgericht. Sie überwiesen die Sache ans Volksgericht. Mein Sohn kam und sagte, er werde sich um eine Genossenschaftswohnung bemühen, ich solle nicht prozessieren. So machten wir es auch. Aber der Vorsitzende des Exekutivkomitees riet ihm, mich für eine staatliche Wohnung anzumelden, sobald etwas frei werde, käme ich an die Reihe. Jeden Monat ging ich zum Exekutivkomitee, und Genossin Dejeva antwortete mir unausweichlich « Es gibt nichts ». Zwei Jahre ging ich hin, bis endlich ein neuer Vorsitzender des Exekutivkomitees bestellt wurde. Jetzt sagte Dejewa « Fangen Sie von vorn an » und mein Sohn ging im Jahr 1981 zum Parteisekretär und erzählte ihm von meinen Qualen. Dieser rief den neuen Vorsitzenden des Exekutivkomitees, Genossen Verschikovskij, an und ersuchte ihn, die Sache zu klären.

Meinem Sohn sagte man: Machen Sies übers Sozialamt. Und so machte er es auch. Schnell erledigte er die Formalitäten und ich wurde in die Warteliste für Genossenschaftswohnungen für 1983 eingetragen. Ob ich das noch erlebe.

Jetzt zu den Kindern. Mein Bruder Matwej fiel im Krieg, meine Schwester Schenja und ihre zwei Kinder kamen in Schdanov durch die Faschisten um. Als Riva durch Schdanov fuhr, wollte sie sie mitnehmen. Aber Schenja wollte nicht. Sie blieb mit ihrem Mann und den zwei Kindern in der besetzten Stadt. Sie kamen alle um. Lisa hingegen schloß das Kiewer Medizinische Institut ab. Sie arbeitete im Spital von Rubzovka im Altai-Gebiet. Später war das ein Sanatorium für Lungenkranke. Sie erkrankte selber an Tuberkulose und starb 1946 im Alter von 33 Jahren. Nur wir zwei blieben übrig — ich und Riva. Schon das vierte Jahr bin ich den Winter über bei ihr. Sie hat zwei Söhne, beide sind verheiratet. Gena, der eine, wohnt ganz in der Nähe. Seine Frau ist Lehrerin, sie haben zwei Söhne. Einer ist 17 Jahre alt, besucht die Musikschule in Saporoschje, der andere ist 13 Jahre alt, er geht in die 6. Klasse, auch er besucht die Musikschule, er lernt Klarinette, der ältere ist Pianist. Die Schwester lebt mit dem jüngeren Sohn Valerij zusammen, der einen sechsjährigen Sohn hat. Sie haben eine 3-Zimmerwohnung mit allem Komfort. Wir kommen gut miteinander aus. Die Schwiegertöchter meiner Schwester sind sehr nett. Ich habe viel Spaß mit ihnen. Mein Leben ist sehr behütet. Ich helfe, wo ich kann. Ich lese und ruhe mich aus. Bald werde ich 80. Ich mache Gymnastik, wasche mich jeden Tag. Nur Rückenschmerzen habe ich und das Kreuz tut mir weh. Aber es soll mir nichts Ärgeres passieren.

Ich habe in meinem Leben 3 Operationen durchgemacht. Nebenhöhlen, Magengeschwür und 2 Augenoperationen, grauer Star. Seit meiner Ankunft in Berdjansk bin ich ehrenamtlich tätig. Im Jahr 1953 in der Kinderbibliothek. 1959 wurde ich am einen Auge operiert, 1961 am anderen. In dieser Zeitspanne habe ich nicht ehrenamtlich gearbeitet. Als ich wieder sehen konnte, begann ich wieder damit. Ich schlug vor, einen Veteranenchor zu organisieren. Unter großen Schwierigkeiten gelang mir das auch. Ich ging von Haus zu Haus. Man stellte uns den Kirov-Klub zur Verfügung. Der Anfang war gut. Wir traten auf. Solange der Chorleiter sich nur mit Pensionisten befaßte, war alles gut, aber dann vereinte der Leiter die Pensionisten mit der Jugend, und alle zerstritten sich, der Chor wurde aufgelöst. Ich trug meine Dienste dem Volkstheater im städtischen Kulturhaus an. Ich wurde Sprecherin des Kollektivs, führte Buch, begrüßte die Mitglieder des Theaters. Einige Male bin ich selbst mit Lesungen aufgetreten. Einige Urkunden wurden mir verliehen. Am Volkstheater war ich von 1965 bis 1978, als die Regisseurin das Theater verließ, ging ich auch. Während ich bei der Schwester lebte, arbeitete ich im Winter in der Kinderbibliothek. So endete meine ehrenamtliche Tätigkeit. Jetzt bin ich dazu nicht mehr imstande. Ich bin 80 Jahre alt. Meine Kräfte lassen nach. Ich werde schnell müde. Nach Hause bin ich noch nicht zurückgekehrt. Ich habe einiges herrichten lassen und werde um den 1.7. nach Hause zurückkehren. Riva hat versprochen, einen Monat zu mir zu ziehen. Sie ist oft krank, hustet, klagt über ihr Herz. Am 1.7. bin ich zusammen mit Riva zu mir gefahren. Juli und August lebten wir zusammen. Am 11.7. fuhr Riva nach Hause, um ihre Pension abzuholen und am Rückweg wurde ihr an der Haltestelle schlecht, die Rettung kam und man brachte sie ins Spital, wo sie zwei Wochen verblieb. Sie verließ das Spital gesund, aber bei mir wurde sie wieder krank. Am 3.9. ging sie nach Hause und zur Zeit ist sie dort. Wir ertragen die Hitze schlecht, aber bei ihr zu Hause ist es weniger schlimm. Ich erwarte meinen Sohn im September.

Noch etwas über meinen Mann. Als er nach Dnepropetrovsk gefahren war und mich ohne Arbeit und Wohnung zurückgelassen hatte, schrieb er lange nicht, und ich wußte nicht, was ich denken sollte, aber 4 Monate später schrieb er, er werde nicht mehr zu mir zurückkehren, er habe eine andere Familie. Ich teilte das meinem Sohn mit, schrieb ihm in das Ferienlager, wo er auf Erholung war. Er antwortete mir nichts. Auf meine Bitte fuhr er einige Male zum Vater. Er brachte dem Vater keinerlei Zuneigung entgegen, weder früher noch jetzt. Sie sind einander fremd. In der neuen Familie gibt es noch einen Sohn. Er ist schon verheiratet, aber die Brüder empfinden nichts für einander. Auf alle Bitten der Schwester Busja, mein Sohn solle den Vater besuchen kommen, reagiert er mit Versprechungen, erfüllt sie aber nicht. Er hat für den Vater keinerlei Gefühle. Ich war mit Riva bei Busja in Dnepropetrovsk, nachdem sie im Jänner 1982 an grauem Star operiert worden war. Der Vater kam zu Busja, um uns zu treffen, aber es gab nichts zu reden. Er ist mir fremd, so als hätte es in der Vergangenheit nichts gegeben. Auch seine Frau und sein Sohn kamen. Fremde und uninteressante Leute für mich. Der Vater bat, ich solle dem Sohn ausrichten, er möge ihn besuchen, aber der will nichts davon hören. Meine Schuld ist es nicht, Vater bleibt Vater, ich bitte ihn zu fahren. Der Vater ist auch 78 Jahre alt. Er war an den Beinen krank, geht nirgendwo hin. Er hat ein Auto, mit dem sein Sohn fährt. Ich glaube nicht, daß wir uns noch einmal sehen. Im April dieses Jahres fuhr ich mit Riva zu meinem Sohn, wir wohnten bei seiner Schwiegermutter Gida Moissejewna. Das ist eine sehr energische und willensstarke Frau. Zu meinem

питании позаботиться, а я не в состоянии готовить себе. Рива навряд ли ко мне придет на летние месяцы. Она тоже плохо себя чувствует сердце, а теперь и зубы. Нужно ехать в городу у нас нет врача. Как то будет с кооперативом. Обещают в конце этого месяца принять взнос. А потом пока построят. Дождусь ли окончания стройки, а потом нужно соединиться с Геной. Хватит ли у меня времени на все это. Ведь считанные годы мне осталось жить на этом свете. Силы убывают.

5.У-1983 г.

Получила извещение из Исполкома. Нужно обновить документы, сданные в 1981г. Теперь нужно за 1983 г. Акт обследования, справку из домоуправления и инвентарьбюро. Представитель исполкома пошел со мной ко мне домой и составил акт, квартальная подписала справку, за н   даст справку о наличии площади на 11.У. Теперь будто все формальности соблюдены и можно ждать извещения о взносе первой суммы. Сын уже выслал 2000 руб. Сумма пока не известна взноса. Настроение повышенное. Жду комнату, с которой будут соединяться.

12.У- Сегодня позвонил сын и обрадовал меня. Галя разрешилась от беременности и родила дочку в 5 ч. утра. Вес - 3600 Все благополучно мать и дочь чувствуют себя хорошо. Теперь я уже прабабушка в чем меня и поздравил сын. Еще одно событие, но менее важное. Купила наконец плащ, о чем мечтала. Рива зашла случайно в наш универмаг и там было одно пальто 48 размер. Стоит 100р.80коп. Она и деньги достала. Какая же она внимательная ко мне. Сын обещал выслать 200 руб. Я отдала за пальто 101р. на именинников 5х5=25руб за стол 16х2=33+5=37-10-27р.=153руб.. Риве я отдала 30 руб. на день рождения из пенсии. Останется 46 руб. на жизнь.
6.У1 - я перехожу на свою квартиру. Еще нужна уборка и перестановка мебели. Перейдет ли Рива со мной, на сколько? Ведь я перехожу на 4 месяца. Здесь уже заведенный порядок. Гуляю утром 1 1/2 - 2 часа. Потом завтрак. Мойка посуды и уже в 11 ч выбываю из строя. Разбаливается спина и поясница. Ложусь отдых на 1 ч дня. Потом что то делаю, читаю. В 5 ч обед. Опять мойка посуды. Читаю газету, телевизор. Все налажено все как по нотам. Теперь все изменится. Порядок будет нарушен. Как я цепляюсь за постоянный образ жизни, не хочется его изменять, а нужно. В доме сделали ремонт но нужно еще навести порядок. Успею ли к 1 июня. Вещи в разных местах. Когда то соберу все в одно место. Персональная выставка у сына откладывается на июнь. Он счастливый дедушка.
Ему в этом году 30.IX- будет 50 лет. Какой он заботливый и внимательный ко мне. Послал 3.У - посылку, апельсины, гречневую крупу, Обещал еще прислать масло. Как то будет управляться Галя с малышом. Будут приходить Вика, Ирина, но все далеко от нее живут. Муж у нее хороший. Основная помощь будет исходить от него. Пусть будут счастливы и пусть вырастет здоровая, крепкая смена.

1.У1 - Сегодня переселяюсь к себе домой. Ночь не спала все думаю. 30.У- было организационное собрание кооператива. Следующее собрание сообщат сколько вносить и куда. Обещают построить за год, но этому верить нельзя. Будет 5 этажный дом каменный для малосемейных. Всего 90 квартир. 78 однокомнатных, 12 метров и 14 метров 12 квартир 2х комнатных. Недалеко от Ривы, где ближайшая остановка 17 номера. Теперь в ожидании думаю предложить Риве дарственную оформить, а путь продает сама за сколько хочет. Мне даже страшно подумать, чтобы заняться продажей. Пусть как хочет оформляет сама или Гена. Самочувствие не важное. Доживу ли до новой квартиры? Страшно одной быть у себя. Привыкли жить на стульях. Приедут, уйдут молодые. Расскажут обо всем. Думаю раз в неделю приезжать купаться. По субботам. Риса не будет у меня. Может на несколько дней пойдет и уедет. Ей трудно быть у меня. Удобств нет.

30.XI. Долго не писала в своей дневник. 27.У1- было второе собрание кооператива "Победа" ничего существенного не говорили, но заполнили обязательство. Я по глупости подписалась полной

Sohn hat sie ein gutes Verhältnis. Sie ließ uns nichts im Haushalt machen, nicht einmal Geschirr waschen. Nach ihren eigenen Worten hat sie kein Zutrauen zu jemand anders und macht alles lieber selber. Die Bewirtung war ausgezeichnet. Wir blieben 3 Wochen und reisten am 3.5. ab. Ich glaube nicht, daß ich noch einmal so eine Reise riskiere. Nun hat mich Gida Moissejewna darauf aufmerksam gemacht, daß mein Sohn sich nicht einmal selber die Socken waschen könne. Und wirklich, wie unangenehm ist das, wenn einem die Frau Socken und Unterhosen wäscht. Ein Mann muß das selber machen, aber man muß ihm das von Kind auf beibringen, und unter welchen Umständen hat mein Sohn gelebt, daß man ihm sowas hätte beibringen können. Mit 10 Jahren ist er ins Heim gekommen. Irina, seine erste Frau, hat sich über ihn lustig gemacht mit ihrer Mutter. Er war zwischen zwei Feuern. Seine Tochter ist schon verheiratet, aber er unterstützt sie nach wie vor. Er überließ ihr eine Zweizimmerwohnung mit allem Komfort, selbst lebte er, nachdem er auszog, in seinem Atelier. Er lernte Vika kennen, die einen Sohn namens Antoscha hat, sie verließ ihren Mann und zog zu ihm ins Atelier, bis mein Sohn eine Eigentumswohnung bekam, wo sie auch jetzt zu dritt wohnen. Eine Zwischenwand wurde eingezogen, und Antoscha hat ein eigenes Zimmer. Sie leben gut zusammen, ich freue mich für sie. Vika ist 12 Jahre jünger als mein Sohn, aber ich glaube, sie haben keine Meinungsverschiedenheiten. Gott gebe ihnen Glück. Mein Sohn hat es verdient.

8.3.1983
Einige Zeit ist vergangen, bis ich mich wieder meiner Biographie widmen kann. Riva ist wieder krank geworden und kam am 15.12.82 wieder ins Spital. Sie war einen Monat dort, und als sie heimkam, ging es ihr wieder schlecht. Ein Monat verging, bevor es ihr besser ging und sie sich wieder normal fühlte. Im Oktober kam mein Sohn zu mir und ich sorgte allein für ihn, obwohl das Mittagessen von Riva gebracht wurde. Es gelang, meinen Sohn zu einem Besuch bei seinem Vater zu überreden. Er traf seinen Vater und die anderen Verwandten, und nach einem Monat starb der Vater. Wie gut, daß sie sich vor seinem Tod noch sahen. Zum Begräbnis kam mein Sohn mit seiner Frau. Die Frau Josifs hat meinen Sohn gut aufgenommen und begegnete ihm freundlich. So starb Josif im 78. Lebensjahr. Dusja, seine Frau, hat ein gutes Verhältnis zu Busja, der Schwester Josifs, sie hilft, wo sie kann. Ich lebe seit Oktober bei Riva. Mein Jubiläum wurde sehr feierlich begangen. Mein Sohn und die Schwiegertochter kamen. Mein Sohn hielt eine Tischrede und dankte mir mit viel Liebe für meine Hilfe während seiner Schulzeit. Ja, seine Schulzeit war nicht leicht für uns, aber alles Schlechte ist vergessen, nur das Gute bleibt. Jetzt warte ich auf eine Eigentumswohnung. Ich stehe auf der Liste, die erste Rate wird Ende des Jahres einbezahlt. Gut wärs, wenn man mich abtragen würde und meine Wohnung nicht verkauft werden müßte. Aber darüber ist nichts zu hören, über einen Abriß, und man muß alles der Zeit überlassen. Mit der Schwester träumen wir davon, mit Gena zusammenzuziehen, dem zweiten Sohn der Schwester, der eine Zweizimmerwohnung hat. Aber das liegt noch in weiter Ferne, wenn ich eine Wohnung haben werde. Der Bau wird ja zwei Jahre dauern, ob ich das noch erlebe? Ich fühle mich gut, nur werde ich schnell müde. Ich treibe Gymnastik und bade jeden Tag in der Wanne. Ich schlafe von 11 bis 1 Uhr. Fast jeden Tag gehe ich eine Stunde spazieren. Aber im Vergleich zum letzten Jahr haben meine Kräfte nachgelassen. Lärm im Kopf, ich höre schlecht, nach dem Frühstück, wenn ich Geschirr wasche, tut mir unweigerlich das Kreuz weh. Nach einer Erholung fühle ich mich wesentlich besser. Im vergangenen Jahr habe ich die Zimmer noch aufgeräumt, jetzt bin ich dazu nicht mehr imstande. Nur Staub wischen kann ich noch und in der Küche und im Korridor zusammenkehren. Die linke Hand zittert stark. Den Löffel zu halten ist schwer. Die Finger der linken Hand lassen sich nicht schließen. Aber das ist noch auszuhalten. Riva fühlt sich schon wieder nicht gut... Es fällt ihr schwer, für die ganze Familie zu kochen, und sie macht alles allein im Haus. Ich helfe ihr nicht beim Kochen, sie erlaubt es nicht. Ich gehe nicht mehr weit vom Haus weg, ich habe Angst, hinzufallen. Valerij geht vor der Arbeit Milch holen. Er ist jetzt mehr belastet, bringt den Kleinen in den Kindergarten und geht Milch holen. Bevor sich das Wetter nicht bessert, gehe ich nicht Milch holen und einkaufen. Das Wetter ist nicht gut, windig und rutschig. Geschneit hat es dieses Jahr nur wenig, und jetzt ist ja schon Frühling. Wie steht es bei mir zu Hause? Ob alles in Ordnung ist? Mit den Nachbarn habe ich keinen Kontakt. Es hat sich so ergeben, daß ich mit ihnen nicht rede. Mit der zweiten Nachbarin Marija Semjonovna aus dem Grund, daß ich ihr nicht die Benützung der Kohlenkiste gestattete. Sie hat sie nicht nur die ganzen Jahre über benützt, letztes Mal hat sie auch noch Kohle auf mein Territorium verstreut, vor der Laube, und ich mußte die Laube streichen lassen. Dann beschloß ich, die Kiste zu

verkaufen, zuerst bot ich sie ihr an, aber sie lehnte ab, dann nahm sie die andere Nachbarin und versprach, dafür den Zaun gegenüber dem Haus, im Hof, richten zu lassen. Ihr Sohn hat es versprochen, aber er macht es nicht, nämlich den Zaun richten. Wenn ich zu Hause bin, muß ich jemand finden, der ihn richtet, und der Nachbarin vorschlagen, für die Kiste zu zahlen. Mit der dritten Nachbarin, die sich meinen Schuppen aneignete, rede ich auch nicht. Wenn sie ein Gespräch beginnt, antworte ich, aber von selber beginne ich keine Gespräche. Wegen meiner Pension muß ich auf die Hauptpost fahren, obwohl der Briefträger nebenan wohnt, kann er mir die Pension nicht auszahlen. Bei schlechtem Wetter muß ich Lena bitten, mit mir zu gehen. Einmal im Monat, aber sie macht es ungern. Man muß sie sehr bitten. Ich muß auch Gena bitten, daß er mir die Wäsche zu der Frau bringt, die für mich wäscht, sie wohnt beim Bahnhof, man muß hinfahren. Ich bin immer mit Riva hingefahren, aber jetzt kann sie nicht mit mir fahren. Ich wasche auch selber, aber die große Wäsche gebe ich weg. Am 8.3. habe ich Gäste eingeladen, wir waren zu zehnt, alles Verwandte: Gena mit seiner Familie, 4 Personen, die drei von uns, Riva und Lena mit ihrer Tochter. Sie kamen um 1 Uhr und gingen um 4 Uhr nachmittags, es war eine schöne Jause, und abends ein Treffen mit Rina Zelenaja.

13.3.83
Ich setze meine Notizen fort. Das Leben fließt normal dahin, ohne besondere Ereignisse. Dank Riva bin ich von Fürsorge und Aufmerksamkeit umgeben. Vom Sohn habe ich einen Brief bekommen. Im April wird er im Puschkin-Museum eine Einzelausstellung haben. Wie ihn das inspiriert. Die Zeiten ändern sich. Seine Arbeiten erregen Aufmerksamkeit. Er hatte eine Ausstellung im Künstlerverband. Wie gut, daß ihn seine Arbeit befriedigt, daß er groß herausgebracht wird, das ist doch die Hauptsache für einen Künstler. Materiell bringt ihm das gar nichts, aber moralisch ist er befriedigt, daß er anerkannt und ausgestellt wird. Schade, daß er wenig darüber schreibt, seine Briefe sind so nett zu lesen. Er versprach, im Frühjahr zu kommen. Ich möchte ihn bei Riva empfangen. Bei mir kann ich ihn nicht aufnehmen, dazu habe ich nicht mehr die Kraft. Von jeder Bewegung gerate ich außer Atem. Am Morgen bis 11 Uhr kann ich mich noch bewegen, aber dann bekomme ich so unwahrscheinliches Kreuzweh, daß ich mich hinlegen muß. Nach einer zweistündigen Ruhepause kann ich mich wieder bewegen. Trotzdem mache ich nach Möglichkeit etwas im Haus. Ich wasche ab, kehre zusammen und wische Staub. Zu mehr bin ich nicht fähig. Auch schreiben fällt mir schwer. Trotzdem schreibe ich. Die linke Hand tut weh und zittert unaufhörlich, gut, daß die rechte noch normal ist. Bei uns ist alles beim alten. Der Kleine geht zweimal die Woche in den Schachzirkel. Er ist ein sehr nervöses Kind. Aber am Schachbrett ist er ruhig, kann mit jedem spielen bis zum Schlafengehen, also bis 9 Uhr. Wie wird er das Sitzen in der Schule aushalten? Dieses Jahr geht er in die Schule. Ich schrieb meiner Bekannten, sie solle ihre Memoiren verfassen. Sie hat ein schweres Leben gehabt. Sie wurde verhaftet, saß 8 Jahre und war Repressionen ausgesetzt. Meine Freunde sind gestorben, mit denen ich mich viele Jahre bei einer Tasse Tee getroffen habe. Regina Pavlowna, Irina Andrejewna. Unseren Kreis gibt es jetzt nicht mehr. Unsere Garde geht unwiderruflich ab. Bald komme auch ich an die Reihe. So muß es sein. Aber ich bin mit meinem Leben zufrieden. Nach meiner schweren Vergangenheit habe ich jetzt Ruhe und Glück erlangt. Wahr ist, daß ich auf eine Einzimmereigentumswohnung warte, um die sich mein Sohn so bemüht hat, man wird sehen, wie es kommt. Meine Wohnung ist eingerichtet, und dort herrscht völlige Ruhe. Im Juni muß ich in meine Wohnung gehen und sie renovieren lassen. Ob Riva über den Sommer zu mir kommen kann? Sie ist noch so schwach, ich werde allein bleiben müssen. Man wird sehen.

27.4.83
Endlich ist die Renovierung fertig. Ein entfernter Verwandter hat das ganz ausgezeichnet gemacht. Rivas verstorbene Schwägerin hatte eine Schwiegertochter, deren Vater. Er verlangte 150 Rubel, ich gab ihm noch 10 Rubel drauf. Jetzt kommt meine Arbeit dran, in den Truhen, im Schrank aufräumen, das Gartenhaus aufräumen. Das betrifft ihn nicht. Das muß ich selber machen, aber mir fehlt die Kraft. Heute habe ich damit angefangen und bin kaum nach Hause gekommen vor Müdigkeit. Ich denke, ich werde den Mai über noch hier bleiben, dann allerdings muß ich in meine Wohnung gehen. Meine Kräfte sind völlig am Ende. Das Gehen fällt mir sehr schwer. Mit Mühe setze ich einen Fuß vor den anderen. Der Rücken und das Kreuz tut mir weh. Die Wohnung sollte schon verkauft werden, ich kann sie nicht beaufsichtigen.
Auch um die Ernährung muß ich mich kümmern, ich bin aber nicht imstande, mir zu kochen. Riva wird kaum in den

Sommermonaten zu mir kommen können. Sie fühlt sich auch schlecht — das Herz, und jetzt auch die Zähne. Man muß in die Stadt fahren, bei uns ist kein Arzt. Was wird mit der Eigentumswohnung. Ende dieses Monats wird die Rate fällig. Und dann fangen sie erst zu bauen an. Ob ich die Fertigstellung des Baues erlebe, und dann müssen wir mit Gena zusammenziehen. Ob meine Zeit reicht für das alles? Die Jahre, die ich noch zu leben habe, sind doch gezählt. Meine Kräfte lassen nach.

5.5.1983
Ich bekam eine Verständigung vom Exekutivkomitee. Man muß die Dokumente erneuern, die 1982 abgegeben wurden. Der Akt für das Jahr 1983 muß überprüft werden, eine Bestätigung der Hausverwaltung und des Inventarbüros wird verlangt. Ein Vertreter des Exekutivkomitees kam mit mir nach Hause und stellte den Akt zusammen, eine Polizeibeamtin unterschrieb die Bestätigung, der Zuständige wird die Bestätigung über den vorhandenen Wohnraum am 11.5. ausstellen. Offenbar sind alle Formalitäten erledigt und man kann auf die Nachricht über die Einzahlung der ersten Rate warten. Mein Sohn hat mir schon 2000 Rubel geschickt. Wie hoch die erste Rate sein wird, weiß man noch nicht. Gehobene Stimmung. Ich warte auf das Zimmer, auf das Zusammenziehen.

12.5. Heute hat mich mein Sohn angerufen und mir eine Freude gemacht. Galja hat um 5 Uhr in der Früh ein Töchterchen geboren. Gewicht 3600 Gramm, alles in Ordnung, Mutter und Tochter fühlen sich gut. Jetzt bin ich schon Urgroßmutter, wozu mich mein Sohn beglückwünschte. Noch ein Ereignis, aber weniger wichtig. Ich habe mir endlich einen Sommermantel gekauft, den ich mir schon so lange gewünscht habe. Riva ging zufällig in unser Kaufhaus, und dort war ein Mantel Größe 48. Er kostet 100 Rubel 80 Kopeken. Sie hat auch das Geld besorgt. Wie aufmerksam sie zu mir ist. Mein Sohn versprach, 200 Rubel zu schicken. Für den Mantel gab ich 101 Rubel aus, für die Geburtstagskinder 5 x 5 = 25 Rubel, für das Essen 16 x 2 = 32 + 5 = 37 - 10 - 27 R. = 153 Rubel. Riva gab ich 30 Rubel zum Geburtstag von der Pension. Bleiben 46 Rubel zum leben.

6.6. Ich ziehe in meine Wohnung. Man muß noch aufräumen und die Möbel umstellen. Kommt Riva mit mir und für wie lange? Ich ziehe ja für 4 Monate dorthin. Hier herrscht schon eine feste Ordnung. In der Früh gehe ich 1 bis 1 1/2 Stunden spazieren. Dann das Frühstück. Abwasch und dann schon um 11 Uhr bin ich erledigt. Der Rücken und das Kreuz tun mir weh. Bis 1 Uhr mittag lege ich mich nieder. Dann mache ich irgend etwas, lese. Um 5 Uhr ist Mittagessen. Wieder Abwasch. Ich lese die Zeitung, schaue fern. Alles geht glatt, wie am Schnürchen. Jetzt ändert sich alles. Die Ordnung wird zerstört. Ich hänge sehr an einem festen Tagesablauf, ich will nichts ändern, aber es muß sein. Das Haus ist zwar renoviert, aber man muß noch Ordnung machen. Ob ich bis 1. Juni fertig werde? Die Sachen sind an verschiedenen Orten. Einmal muß ich alles an einen Ort bringen. Die Einzelausstellung meines Sohnes ist auf Juni verschoben worden. Er ist ein glücklicher Großvater. Dieses Jahr am 30.9. wird er 50 Jahre. Wie fürsorglich und aufmerksam er zu mir ist. Am 3.5. schickte er mir ein Päckchen mit Orangen und Buchweizengrütze. Er versprach noch, Butter zu schicken. Wie wird sich Galja mit der Kleinen erholen. Vika und Irina werden zu ihr kommen, aber sie wohnen weit von ihr. Sie hat einen guten Mann. Hauptsächlich wird er helfen. Mögen sie glücklich sein und möge der Nachwuchs gesund und kräftig aufwachsen.

1.6. Heute übersiedle ich zu mir nach Hause. In der Nacht habe ich nicht geschlafen, nur nachgedacht. Am 30.5. war die erste Mitgliederversammlung der Wohnungskooperative. Beim nächsten Treffen wird mitgeteilt, wie hoch die Rate ist und wo man einzahlen muß. Angeblich soll der Bau in einem Jahr fertig sein, aber daran glaubt niemand. Es wird ein 4-stöckiges Haus, ein Ziegelbau, für Kleinfamilien. Insgesamt 90 Wohnungen. 78 Einzimmerwohnungen, 12 m² und 14 m². 12 Zweizimmerwohnungen. Nicht weit von Riva, wo die nächste Haltestelle von Nr. 17 ist. Jetzt warte ich, ich denke daran, Riva eine Schenkung zu machen, soll sie selber verkaufen für wieviel sie will. Schon der Gedanke, mich mit dem Verkauf zu befassen, erschreckt mich. Soll sie oder Gena das erledigen. Ich fühle mich nicht besonders. Ob ich die neue Wohnung noch erlebe? Ich habe Angst davor, allein zu Hause zu sein. Wir sind es gewohnt, mit Besuch zu leben. Die Jungen kommen und gehen. Sie erzählen alles. Ich denke, einmal in der Woche zum Baden hinzufahren. Am Samstag. Riva wird nicht bei mir sein. Vielleicht kommt sie auf ein paar Tage und fährt wieder. Es fällt ihr schwer bei mir. Kein Komfort.

фамилией, а моя роспись совсем другая. Придется переделывать обязательство. В числах 15.УП будет объявлено куда вносить деньги 2000 руб. Всего стоимость комнаты 5000 Руб. Комнаты маленькие в зависимости от количества людей. Будут 12-14-16 кв. метров. Мне конечно достанется 12 метров. Вся обстановка не поместится. Я думаю когда дождусь комнаты подарить Риве мою квартиру, согласовав с сыном.

Пусть за сколько хочет продает. А получив комнату, обещают к сентябрю 1984 года соединиться или с Генси или с Ривой Гена обещают 3х комнатную квартиру, если он получит ее, тогда Риве их четырех комнатную. Но когда это будет. Самочувствие неважное. Трудно ходить. Болит спина и поясница. Отдыхаю с 11 до 1 ч. дня. Тогда более трудное предстоит, как стирка, уборка. Мне трудно, но все же я у себя. Вспомню как у Ривы зимой я не у дел. Хочется жить самостоятельно. Ведь я привыкла жить одна со своим хозяйством. На сколько меня хватит. Только бы не быть в тягость никому. Обслуживать себя. Пока я сама себя обслуживаю. Правда стирку сдаю. Полы приходит женщина мыть. Жить бы да радоваться. Но нет этой радости. Живу в тревоге, как будет дальше со здоровьем. Никуда не хожу. Риса приезжает в субботу и в воскресенье, мы еде к ней. Купаюсь у нее, ночую, а в понедельник еду к себе. Она привозит мне привозит обед, который мне хватает на 4-5 дней. Плачу из того же расчета 2 руб. в день. Погоды стоят жаркие. Курортников полно и у обоих соседей тоже. Я никого не пускаю, уже с прошлого года. Сын возражает, да и я больше не могу видеть посторонних у себя в доме. Спасибо сыну, что посылает мне деньги, т.к. пенсии мне не хватает. А 52 руб., сделала ремонт квартиры стоит 176 руб. Купила летнее пальто за 100 руб.

I.УШ - Наконец все закончилось с кооперативом. 19.УП- было последнее собрание. Дно отношение для пересылки взноса на расчетный счет в банк и 2 .УП я разделила на 2 книжки мои деньги. На одну 2000 руб и на другую 1000. 29.УI я заполнила обязательство. Деньги 2000 руб списали в банк. Таким образом с кооперативом все закончено осталось только ждать квартиры, а дождусь ли и еще осталось оформить завещание на сына на 2000 р. Если не дождусь комнаты, хотя бы вернули сыну деньги. Обещал Валерий зайти за мной, чтобы пойти к нотариусу. Я сама никуда не хочу. Нет устойчивости в ногах. Трудно входить и выходить из автобуса. Вчера 31.УП за мной зашел Гена. Вышли в 5 ч. пришли в 9 ч. Поехали купаться к Риве. Устала ужасно. Еле поела. Спина и поясница меня одолевают. Да и рука сильно дрожит. Вот подожду пока разъедутся курортники пойду к невропатологу. Рука беспокоит. Теперь я мою полы сама. Женщина 2 раза помыла и больше не захотела. Стираю я и сама, но крупные вещи. Сдаю. Обещал сын приехать в августе. У Ривы гости - 5 человек из Ростова и Киева. Все ради Миши. Риса простужена. Ей так трудно с чужими людьми. Они уедут 13. УШ.

16.X-84 г.
Дороги мои дети, Гита Моисеевна и Антошенька!
Как поживаете? Здоровье всех вас? У меня все попрежнему со здоровьем. Перемен нет. Рука дрожит. Ноги также. Если нужно отправиться к нотариусу берут такси и кто нибудь меня сопровождает. Наконец завершилась великая эпопея по кооперативной квартире. 13.X- дали ордер и я осмотрела свое будущее жилище. Была ужасная погода, мел все время дождь. Не асфальтированая дорога к дому утопала в грязи. Тут же выдавали ордера. Больше я к дому не подходила. Всем заправляет Рива. Она ходит каждый день, ловит мастеров, Подключили воду, свет, поставили двухкомфорную плиту газовую. Когда подключат газ не известно. Начали циклевать пол в жилой площади. Несколько дней будут приходить мастера, обобьют дверь для утепления. В воскресенье Валерий и Люся помыли окна в комнате и кухне. Все в миниатюре. но думаю что поместится вся моя обстановка за исключением письменного стола. Нужно тщательно предварительно замерить, чтобы поместить все нажитое имущество. Нужно еще со мной поехать в старый домик чтобы уложить все в мешки, за исключением стола, шкафов и стульев. Думаю, что не поместится все на одной машине. С проданой моей квартиры пока подали но заседание Исполкома. Это будет 1.XI, а

30.6. Lange habe ich nicht in mein Tagebuch geschrieben. Am 27.6. war die zweite Versammlung der Kooperative « Sieg », nichts Wesentliches wurde gesagt, aber die Verpflichtungserklärungen wurden ausgefüllt. Aus Dummheit habe ich mit vollem Namen unterschrieben, dabei ist meine Unterschrift ganz anders. Man muß es umändern. Ungefähr am 10.7. wird verlautbart, wo die 2000 Rubel einzuzahlen sind. Der Gesamtpreis des Zimmers beträgt 5000 Rubel. Die Größe des Zimmers hängt von der Anzahl der Personen ab. Es gibt 12-14-16 m². Ich werde natürlich 12 m² bekommen. Ich denke, wenn ich das Zimmer erlebe, werde ich Riva meine Wohnung schenken, nach Übereinkunft mit meinem Sohn. Soll sie die Wohnung verkaufen für wieviel sie will. Wenn ich das Zimmer habe, ist ausgemacht, daß wir im September 1984 entweder mit Gena oder mit Riva zusammenziehen. Gena wurde eine 3-Zimmerwohnung versprochen, wenn er sie bekommt, dann hat Riva eine 4-Zimmerwohnung. Aber wann wird das sein. Ich fühle mich nicht besonders. Das Gehen fällt mir schwer. Der Rücken und das Kreuz tun mir weh. Von 11 — 1 ruhe ich mich aus. Dann kommt das Schwierige, wie Wäsche waschen und aufräumen. Es fällt mir schwer, aber wenigstens bin ich zu Hause. Ich erinnere mich, wie ich im Winter bei Riva nicht zurechtkomme. Man möchte selbständig sein. Ich bin ja gewohnt, allein zu wirtschaften. Wie lange wird es noch gehen? Nur niemand zur Last fallen. Für sich selber sorgen. Jetzt sorge ich noch selber für mich. Nur die Wäsche gebe ich außer Haus. Eine Frau kommt aufwaschen. Ich könnte mich an meinem Leben freuen. Aber das geht nicht. Mich regt auf, wie es mit meiner Gesundheit weitergeht. Ich gehe nirgendwo hin. Riva kommt am Samstag oder am Sonntag und wir fahren zu ihr. Ich bade bei ihr, übernachte, und am Montag fahre ich wieder zu mir. Sie bringt mir Essen, das mir für 4-5 Tage reicht. Ich zahle ihr dafür 2 Rubel pro Tag. Das Wetter ist heiß. Alles ist voll von Sommerfrischlern, auch bei beiden Nachbarn. Ich vermiete schon seit letztem Jahr nicht mehr. Mein Sohn ist dagegen, und ich mag auch keine Fremden mehr bei mir sehen. Meinem Sohn sei gedankt, daß er mir Geld schickt, denn die Pension reicht mir nicht. 52 Rubel, die Wohnung habe ich renovieren lassen, kostet 176 Rubel. Einen Sommermantel um 100 Rubel habe ich gekauft.

1.8. Endlich ist mit der Kooperative alles erledigt. Am 19.7. war die letzte Versammlung. Das Dokument zur Überweisung der Rate auf das Bankkonto ist ausgefertigt, und am 2.7. teilte ich mein Geld auf 2 Sparbücher auf. Auf einem sind 2000 Rubel, auf dem zweiten 1000. Am 29.6. habe ich die Verpflichtungserklärung unterzeichnet. 2000 Rubel wurden der Bank überwiesen. So ist mit der Kooperative alles erledigt, jetzt warte ich nur noch auf die Wohnung, ob ich das erlebe, dann bleibt noch das Testament zugunsten meines Sohnes, für 2000 Rubel. Valerij versprach, vorbeizukommen, um zum Notar zu gehen. Ich selber gehe nirgendwo hin. Keine Kraft in den Beinen. Das Ein- und Aussteigen aus dem Bus ist schwer. Gestern, am 31.7., hat mich Gena abgeholt. Um 5 Uhr sind wir gegangen, um 9 Uhr zurückgekommen. Wir waren bei Riva baden. Ich war furchtbar müde. Ich konnte kaum essen. Das Rückenweh macht mich fertig. Auch die Hand zittert stark. Wenn die Sommerfrischler weg sind, gehe ich zum Neurologen. Die Hand beunruhigt mich. Jetzt wasche ich den Fußboden selber. Zweimal hat die Frau aufgewaschen, dann wollte sie nicht mehr. Die Wäsche wasche ich selber, die große gebe ich außer Haus. Mein Sohn hat versprochen, im August zu kommen. Riva hat Gäste — 5 Personen aus Rostov und Kiev. Alle wegen Mischa. Riva ist erkältet. Mit fremden Leuten zu sein, fällt ihr so schwer. Sie fahren am 13.8. ab.

16.10.84
Meine lieben Kinder, Gida Moissejewna und Antoschenka! Wie geht es Euch? Seid Ihr alle gesund? Meine Gesundheit ist wie gehabt. Keine Änderungen. Die Hand zittert. Die Beine auch. Wenn ich zum Notar muß, nehme ich ein Taxi und jemand begleitet mich. Endlich hat die großartige Epopöe mit der Eigentumswohnung ihren Abschluß gefunden. Am 13.10. kam die Order und ich besichtigte meine zukünftige Wohnung. Es war ein schreckliches Wetter, die ganze Zeit hat es geregnet. Der nicht asphaltierte Weg zum Haus war ein Schlammloch. Gleich dort wurde die Order ausgegeben. Näher ans Haus bin ich nicht gegangen. Riva organisiert alles. Sie geht jeden Tag hin und kümmert sich, daß die Handwerker kommen. Wasser und Strom sind angeschlossen, ein zweiflammiger Gasherd aufgestellt. Wann das Gas angeschlossen wird, weiß man noch nicht. Mit dem Bodenverlegen im Wohnraum wurde begonnen. Einige Tage lang werden die Handwerker kommen, die Tür wird gepolstert wegen der Wärme. Am Sonntag haben Valerij und Ljusja die Fenster im Zimmer und in der Küche geputzt. Es ist alles in Miniatur, aber ich denke, ich bringe alle meine Sachen unter, bis auf den Schreibtisch. Man muß vorher alles genauestens

прийти за ответом 5.XI. У меня все безжалостно снесли. В операции участвовали Валерий, Гена и Миша. Снесли обе беседки и злополучный сарай. Но разрешить продажу пока нельзя, т.к. у соседей есть беседка и они будто тоже подлежат сносу. Но архитектор обнадежил, что продажу разрешат. Всем этим заворачивает Люся. Ей приходится отпрашиваться с работы. После исполкома нужны подписи у нотариуса соседей, что они не возражают к продаже моей квартиры. Покупатель ждет, но аванс он не дал, не зная или их пропишут. Муж, жена и школьник сын. Все в проекте. Рива бегает по моим делам, боже чтобы не простыла. Каждый день дождь и похолодание. Настроение суматошное. Идет ремонт. Все разбросано, не на месте. Вот приедешь, сынок сам увидишь. Сделали шкаф в коридоре, но не закончили, а комнаты начали. Сначала туалет и ванную обкладывают плиткой. Позвони когда приедешь.

    Будьте все здоровы, счастливы.

Любящая мама

ausmessen, damit ich mein ganzes Hab und Gut unterbringe. Man muß mit mir in das alte Häuschen fahren, um alles in Säcke zu tun, mit Ausnahme des Tisches, der Schränke und Stühle. Ich glaube nicht, daß alles in eine Fuhre paßt. Über den Verkauf meiner Wohnung wird auf der nächsten Sitzung des Exekutivkomitees entschieden. Das wird am 1.11. sein, den Bescheid bekomme ich am 5.11. Bei mir wurde schon alles erbarmungslos abgetragen. An der Operation beteiligten sich Valerij, Gena und Mischa. Beide Gartenhäuschen wurden abgetragen, ebenso der unglückselige Schuppen. Aber über den Verkauf kann vorläufig nicht entschieden werden, weil die Nachbarn ein Gartenhäuschen haben, und der Abriß sie offenbar auch betrifft. Aber der Architekt meinte, man könne hoffen, der Verkauf werde erlaubt. Mit all dem ist Ljusja befaßt. Sie muß sich von der Arbeit freinehmen. Nach dem Exekutivkomitee müssen die Nachbarn beim Notar unterschreiben, daß sie gegen den Verkauf meiner Wohnung nichts einzuwenden haben. Der Käufer wartet, aber Vorschuß hat er keinen gezahlt, da er nicht weiß, ob sie die Anmeldung bekommen. Mann, Frau und schulpflichtiger Sohn. Alle sind an dem Projekt beteiligt. Riva ist in meinen Angelegenheiten unterwegs, wenn sie sich nur nicht verkühlt. Es regnet jeden Tag und kalt ist es auch. Ich fühle mich ganz wirr. In der Wohnung sind Handwerker. Alles ist in Unordnung, nichts am Platz. Wenn du kommst, mein Sohn, wirst du es selber sehen. Im Vorzimmer ist ein Einbaukasten gemacht worden, aber fertig ist er noch nicht, die Zimmer sind begonnen. Erst wird die Toilette und das Bad gekachelt. Ruf an, wann du kommst.
Bleibt alle gesund und glücklich.
Eure liebende Mutter.

Album Photos Photo Album Album der Fotografien Фотоальбом

1.

2.

1.
1920. Marioupol. Promotion d'école du travail (ancien gymnase de filles de Marioupol). Au centre B. Y. Solodoukhina.
Mariupol, 1920. A group of graduates from the labor school (formerly Mariupol Women's Gymnasium). In the center B. Yu. Solodukhina.
1920 Mariupol. Gruppenbild der Absolventinnen der Arbeiterschule (früher: Mariupoler Mädchengymnasium). In der Mitte: B. Ju. Soloduchina
1920 Мариуполь. Группа выпускников трудовой школы (б. Мариупольская женская гимназия). В центре: Б.Ю.Солодухина

2.
Août 1935. Marioupol. Assis: première à droite Riva Youlievna Blékher avec son fils, B. Y. Solodoukhina avec son fils. Debout: à droite Y. G. Blékher.
August 1935, Mariupol. Sitting: first from the right — Riva Yulevna Blekher and son, B. Yu. Solodukhina and son; standing: from the right — Yu. G. Blekher.
August 1935, Mariupol. Sitzend, von rechts, Riva Juljevna Blecher mit Sohn, B. Ju. Soloduchina mit Sohn; stehend: rechts Ju. G. Blecher.
Август 1935 г. Г.Мариуполь. Сидят: первая справа Рива Юльевна Блехер с сыном, Б.Ю.Солодухина с сыном; стоят: справа Ю.Г.Блехер.

3.
1922. Photo d'identité.
1922. A photo for an ID card.
1922, Paßbild.
1922 г. Фото для пропуска

4.

5.

6.

4. Dniépropétrovsk, rue Bojkaïa. 1934.
   Dnepropetrovsk, Bojkaya Street, 1934.
   Dnepropetrovsk, Bojkaja Straße. 1934.
   Г.Днепропетровск, ул. Бойкая. 1934 г.

5. Dniépropétrovsk. Parc Chevtchenko. 1938.
   Dnepropetrovsk, Shevchenko Park, 1938.
   Dnepropetrovsk. Schevtschenko Park. 1938.
   Г.Днепропетровск. Парк им. Шевченко. 1938 г.

6. 1936. Marioupol.
   1936, Mariupol.
   1936, Mariupol.
   1936 г. Мариуполь.

Album photos Photo Album Album der Fotografien Фотоальбом
238

8.

7.

9.

7.
Moscou, Ecole des Beaux-Arts. 2 novembre 1947.
Moscow, Secondary Art School. November 2, 1947.
Moskau, Moskauer künstlerische Mittelschule. 2. November 1947.
Г.Москва, средняя художественная школа. 2 ноября 1947 г.

10.

8.
Berdiansk. En souvenir du séjour du 31/1/1958 au 9/1/59 (achat de maison).
Berdyansk. A memento of our stay from 1/31/1958 through 11/9/1959 inclusively (purchasing a little house).
Berdjansk. Zur Erinnerung an den Aufenthalt vom 31.1.1958 bis zum 9.2.1959 (Kauf des Häuschens).
Г.Бердянск. В память пребывания с 31/I-1958 по 9/II-59 включительно (покупка домика).

9.
Y. G. Blékher retouche une photo.
Yu. G. Blekher retouching a photograph.
Ju. G. Blecher retuschiert ein Foto.
Ю.Г.Блехер ретуширует фотографию.

10.
Berdiansk. Dimanche sur plage. Photo Y. Blékher.
Berdyansk. A day off on the beach. Photo by Yu. Blekher.
Berdjansk. Am Strand an einem Feiertag. Foto Ju. Blecher
Г.Бердянск. На пляже в выходной день. Фото Ю.Блехер

11.

11.
Berdiansk, 7 rue des Partisans rouges. Première à droite : maison de
B. Y. Solodoukhina.
Berdyansk, 7 Red Partisans Street. First from the right : B. Yu. Solodukhina's house.
Berdjansk, Straße der roten Partisanen, Haus Nr.7. Erstes Haus von rechts : das Haus von B. Ju. Soloduchina.
Г.Бердянск, ул. Красных Партизан, д.7. Первый справа: дом Б.Ю.Солодухиной.

12.
Berdiansk, 7 rue des Partisans rouges. Cabane construite par Y.G. Blékher.
Berdyansk, 7 Red Partisans Street. A gazebo in the courtyard built by Yu.G. Blekher.
Berdjansk, Straße der roten Partisanen 7, Gartenhaus im Hof, gebaut von Ju. Blecher.
Г.Бердянск, ул. Красных Партизан, 7. Беседка во дворе, которую построил Ю.Г.Блехер.

13.
Berdiansk, rue des Partisans rouges, 7. B. Y. Solodoukhina dans la cour de sa maison.
Berdyansk, Red Partisans Street. B. Yu. Solodukhina in her yard.
Berdjansk, Straße der roten Partisanen. B. Ju. Soloduchina im Hof des Hauses.
Г.Бердянск, ул. Красных Партизан. Б.Ю.Солодухина во дворе дома.

14.

15.

НАШЕЙ БЕРТЕ в день рождения

    Мудрец сказал: "Жизнь наша сон,
    Минутный дар судьбы превратной."
    Не спорю, прав быть может он,
    Так пусть-же будет сон приятный!

Вот снова год прошел, как миг, как сновиденье,
И снова шлют друзья, свои Вам поздравленья.
Жалет-ли нам промчавшиеся годы,
И солнечные дни, и бури непогоды?
Или надеяться на лучшие мгновенья,
И прошлое забыть, навек, без сожаленья?
В сегодняшний Ваш день, в день Ваших имянин,
Я дам Вам, наша Берта, такой совет один:
"В прошедшем лучшее не надо забывать,
А в будущем, добра и счастья ожидать".
И вместе с Вашими друзьями и родными,
Бокал заздравный дружески подымем.
Живите счастливо! Живите много лет!
Пусть радостью горит неугасимый свет,
Пусть освещает он, Ваш путь звездою ясной,
Что-б жизнь Вам была и светлой, и прекрасной.
Ваш труд общественный, пусть будет Вам порукой,
За Ваш успех в борьбе, с мещанством и со скукой.
Прожить Вам много лет, без страха, без волнений,
Найти в своем труде и смысл и вдохновенье.
И всюду и везде, в минуты жизни трудные,
Отбросить мысли мрачные, тяжелые и нудные —
Не считать свои старания напрасными,
И радостно смотреть на мир глазами ясными.

В будущем году, в день Вашего рождения
Этим пожеланьям будет продолжение,
А на сегодня — хватит,
Что-б лишних слов не тратить,
И не читать стихи до самого утра —
В честь имянинницы —
                УРА! УРА! УРА!

29/XI 1965 г.
                Б. Блехер

16.

14.
Berdiansk. 21/7/1963. A gauche R. Y. Blékher, au centre B. Y. Solodoukhina.
Berdyansk.VII/21/1963. R. Yu. Blekher (on the left), B. Yu. Solodukhina (in the center).
Berdjansk, 21.7.1963. Links R. Ju. Blecher, in der Mitte B. Ju. Soloduchina.
Бердянск, 21/VII 1963. Слева Р.Ю.Блехер, в центре Б.Ю.Солодухина.

15.
Berdiansk. 29/11/1965. « A notre Berthe, le jour de son anniversaire. » Vœux de la famille Blékher. Poème de Y. G. Blékher.
Berdyansk, XI/29/1965. "To our Berta on her birthday." Birthday wishes from the Blekher family. Verses by Yu. G. Blekher.
Berdjansk, 29.11.1965. » Unserer Berta zum Geburtstag... « Glückwunsch von der Familie Blecher. Verse von Ju. G. Blecher.
Г.Бердянск, 29/XI-1965. «Нашей Берте в день рождения...» Поздравление от семьи Блехер. Стихи Ю.Г.Блехера.

16.
R. Y. Blékher, B. Y. Solodoukhina, B. B. Kabakova, 23, rue des Fédérés, Berdiansk. Devant la maison de R. Y. Blékher.
R. Yu. Blekher, B. Yu. Solodukhina, B. B. Kabakova. Berdyansk, 23 Communars Street. Next to R. Yu. Blekher's house.
R. Ju. Blecher, B. Ju. Soloduchina, B. B. Kabakova. Berdjansk, Kommunardenstraße 23. Neben dem Haus von R. Ju. Blecher.
Р.Ю.Блехер, Б.Ю.Солодухина, Б.Б.Кабакова. Бердянск, ул.Коммунаров, 23. Возле дома Р.Ю.Блехер.

17.

17.
Berdiansk. 24/9/1963. Chorale de vétérans du travail auprès du club Kirov.
Troisième à gauche dans le premier rang B. Y. Solodoukhina.
Berdyansk, IX/24/1963. Amateur choir of the Veterans of Labor at the Kirov Club.
B. Yu. Solodukhina is in the first row, third from the left.
Berdjansk, 24.9.1963. Chor der Veteranen der Arbeit beim Kirov-Klub. In der
1. Reihe dritte von links B. Ju. Soloduchina.
Бердянск. 24/IX-1963. Хор самодеятельности ветеранов труда при клубе
им.Кирова. В первом ряду третья слева Б.Ю.Солодухина.

18.
Berdiansk 1965. B. Y. Solodoukhina se produit sur la scène du club Kirov.
Berdyansk, 1965. B. Yu. Solodukhina on stage at the Kirov Club.
Berdjansk, 1965. B. Ju. Soloduchina tritt im Kirov-Klub auf.
Г.Бердянск. 1965 г. Б.Ю.Солодухина выступает на сцене клуба им.Кирова.

19.

20.

20.

19.
Moscou 1982. Visite à Kolomenskoïe.
Moscow, 1982. Excursion to Kolomenskoe.
Moskau, 1982. Ausflug nach Kolomenskoje.
Москва, 1982 г. Экскурсия в с.Коломенское.

20.
B. Y. Solodoukhina et R. Y. Blékher. Kolomenskoïe, 1982.
B. Yu. Solodukhina and R. Yu. Blekher, Village of Kolomenskoe, 1982.
B. Ju. Soloduchina und R. Ju. Blecher. Kolomenskoje, 1982.
Б.Ю.Солодухина и Р.Ю.Блехер. Село Коломенское, 1982 г.

21.
Moscou, 1982. Kolomenskoïe.
Moscow, 1982. Village of Kolomenskoe.
Moskau, 1982. Kolomenskoje.
Москва, 1982 г. Село Коломенское.

22.

22.
Berdiansk, printemps 1987.
Berdyansk, Spring 1987.
Berdjansk, Frühjahr 1987.
Г.Бердянск, весна 1987 г.

Installations Installations Installationen Инсталляции

En relisant pour la énième fois les *Mémoires*, je me rends compte que le panorama de la vie de ma mère ne se présente pas dans ma tête dans son intégralité mais à travers des éléments éclatés. Comme si un rayon dans la nuit de la mémoire parcourait des souvenirs, en faisant momentanément jour sur un événement, un détail avant que celui-ci ne s'éteigne et ne sombre à nouveau dans le noir. Cette image du rayon égaré et tatonnant dans le noir qui arrache à la nuit un tel objet ou un autre est à l'origine de l'installation *Mère et fils*, où *L'Album de ma mère* occupe la place centrale. Voici la brève description de l'installation construite au Musée juif à New York.
Derrière la porte entrouverte, le spectateur voit un espace sombre dont les dimensions il est incapable de définir. Il n'aperçoit que la faible lumière d'une ampoule suspendue sous le plafond. A côté de la porte, sur une étagère accrochée au mur, il y a quelques torches électriques; équipé de cette lumière, le spectateur entre dans l'univers des ténèbres. Le faisceau de la torche fait apparaître un nombre infini de détritus: de vieilles boîtes d'allumettes, des bouts de papier, des fils électriques, des flacons vides et d'autres broutilles munies d'étiquettes avec des textes. Chaque texte est une phrase du fils adressée à sa mère, bribes de paroles quotidiennes: des demandes de toute sorte, des accrochages au sujet des repas, des vêtements mal boutonnés, des discussions d'affaires courantes, de la famille. Souvent ces phrases sont prononcées avec une irritation incompréhensible. Ces bribes sont suspendues dans tout l'espace de la salle noire au niveau de l'œil du spectateur, qui est noyé dans cet océan de paroles. Au fur et à mesure qu'il avance, il découvre que sur le périmètre de la salle, à hauteur d'homme, sont fixées les planches encadrées de *L'Album de ma mère*. Le texte de *L'Album*, biographie de la mère, englobe, entoure l'« univers des paroles » du fils.
Malgré le fait que le spectateur ne voit que les éléments mis en lumière par sa torche, il devient témoin du dialogue entre mère et fils.
Quelques mots sur l'ambiance générale de cette installation. Le spectateur armé de la torche est plus qu'un sujet examinant les objets qui l'entourent, il fait partie de l'installation — aux yeux d'autres spectateurs qui y pénètrent avec leurs torches. La salle se remplit de lumières fuyantes et l'ensemble fait penser à une quête du mystérieux dans les ténèbres, ce qui se marie bien avec l'ambiance de tristesse et d'abandon qui, en fait, constitue notre passé.

Rereading the text *Memoirs* for the umpteenth time, I catch myself thinking that what appears in my imagination is not an integral picture of my mother's life, but sort of separate fragments of it. It's as though some sort of ray, running around in the darkness of memory from one recollection to another, suddenly illuminates some event, some detail and at the very next moment all of this is extinguished and once again submerged in darkness.
This image of a ray, wandering around aimlessly and sweeping the darkness, plucking first one and then another object from the darkness, served as the main installation of *Mother and Son* in which *My Mother's Album* occupies the central place.
Here is a brief description of this installation which was built in the Jewish Museum in New York.
Through a half-opened door the viewer sees a dark, unilluminated space the size of which he is unable to determine. Only a weak light from a bulb hanging from the ceiling is visible in the very depth. There are a few flashlights standing on a shelf attached to the wall near the door. Having armed himself with this light, the viewer enters into the dark world. And an infinite quantity of small items of "garbage" are illuminated under the ray of the flashlight: old matchboxes, scraps of paper, cords, empty perfume bottles, and other such nonsense with little labels containing texts attached to each of them. Each of these texts are the son's utterances addressed to the mother, the scraps of everyday phrases, of things which are usually said to her during the course of the day — all kinds of requests, arguments over food, over unbuttoned clothing, conversations about what's going on, about relatives — often incomprehensible agitation can be heard in them.
These "scraps" are hanging throughout the entire space of the dark room at the viewer's eye level, he is submerged in this sea of words. But moving into the depth with the flashlight, he discovers that the entire room along its perimeter is

surrounded by framed pages from *My Mother's Album*, also hanging at eye-level. The album's text, my mother's biography, surrounds the son's entire "world of words" the former encloses the latter inside itself. And despite the fact that the viewer can see only fragments, only what has fallen under the ray of his flashlight, he becomes a witness to a unique dialogue between the two of them.

And now a few words about the installation itself as a whole. The viewer with the flashlight inside the installation is not only a "subject", examining what surrounds him, but he himself becomes a part of this installation for other viewers who are entering into it with the same kinds of flashlights in their hands. The room is filled with lights running in all directions, and all of this together is like searchings for something mysterious in the darkness, which combines very well with the atmosphere of sadness and abandonment which, in essence, fills our past.

Während ich den Text der *Aufzeichnungen* zum soundsovielten Mal lese, ertappe ich mich dabei, daß vor mir nicht ein vollständiges Lebensbild meiner Mutter ersteht, sondern so etwas wie einzelne Fragmente davon. Als würde ein Lichtstrahl, der im Dunkel der Erinnerung von einem Bruchstück zum nächsten huscht, unvermutet ein Ereignis, ein Detail beleuchten, damit im folgenden Augenblick all das erlischt und wieder in Finsternis versinkt. Dieses Bild des Lichtsstrahls, der zufällig in der Dunkelheit herumirrt und herumstöbert, da einen, dort einen anderen Gegenstand aus dem Dunkel herausreißt, bildet die Grundlage der Installation *Mutter und Sohn*, in der das *Album meiner Mutter* die zentrale Stellung einnimmt.

Hier eine kurze Beschreibung dieser Installation.

Durch die halboffene Tür sieht der Besucher einen dunklen nichtbeleuchteten Raum, dessen Ausmaße er nicht feststellen kann. Nur tief drinnen ist das schwache Licht einer Lampe sichtbar, die von der Decke hängt. Neben der Tür liegen auf einem kleinen Wandbrett einige Taschenlampen, und ausgerüstet mit diesem Licht betritt der Besucher die dunkle Welt. Und dieser Lichtstrahl der Taschenlampe beleuchtet eine unendliche Menge kleiner » Abfall « — Gegenstände — alte Zündholzschachteln, Papierfetzchen, Drähte, leere Fläschchen und ähnlichen Unsinn, an die jeweils ein Täfelchen mit Text befestigt ist. Jeder dieser Texte ist ein Ausspruch des Sohnes, gerichtet an die Mutter, Bruchstücke von Alltagsphrasen, das, was man ihr gewöhnlich sagt im Laufe eines Tages: alle möglichen Bitten, » Streitereien « wegen dem Essen, wegen nicht zugeknöpfter Kleidung, Gespräche über Sachen, die erledigt werden müssen, Gespräche über die Verwandten — oft wird darin eine Gereiztheit spürbar.

Diese » Bruchstücke « hängen überall im dunklen Zimmer verteilt, sie hängen in Augenhöhe des Besuchers, er ist in dieses Meer von Worten vertieft. Aber während er sich mit der Taschenlampe in die Tiefe bewegt, entdeckt er, daß der gesamte Raum in Besucherhöhe von Blättern des *Albums meiner Mutter* umgeben ist. Der Text des Albums, die Biographie der Mutter, umgibt die ganze » Welt von Worten « des Sohnes, schließt ihn in sich ein.

Und ungeachtet der Tatsache, daß der Besucher nur die Bruchstücke sieht, auf welche der Strahl der Taschenlampe fällt, wird er zum Zeugen eines Dialog zwischen den beiden. Einige Worte über die Ausstellung als solche. Der Besucher mit der Taschenlampe ist darin nicht nur das » Subjekt «, welches das betrachtet, was ihn umgibt, sondern er wird selber Teil dieser Installation — für die anderen Besucher, welche mit ebensolchen Lämpchen in ihr herumgehen. Das Zimmer füllt sich mit Lichtern in alle Richtungen, und alles zusammen erinnert an die Suche nach etwas Geheimnisvollem in der Dunkelheit, was sich sehr gut verbindet mit der Atmosphäre von Trauer und Verlassenheit, die unsere Vergangenheit recht eigentlich erfüllt.

Перечитывая в который уже раз текст «Записок», ловлю себя на том, что передо мной, в моем воображении встает не цельная картина жизни моей матери, а как бы отдельные фрагменты ее. Как-будто какой-то луч, перебегая во мраке памяти с одного воспоминания на другое, высвечивает внезапно какое-то событие, подробность, чтобы в следующее мгновение все это погасло и погрузилось вновь во мглу.

Installations Installations Installationen Инсталляции

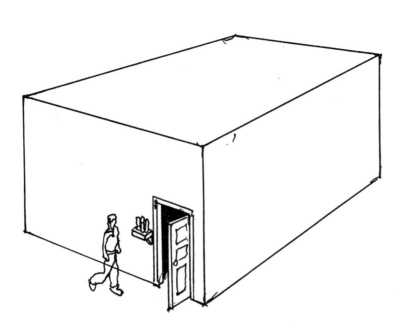
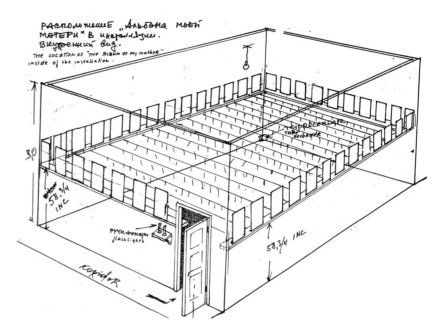

Этот образ луча, случайно забредшего и шарящего в темноте, вырывающего из мрака то один, то другой предмет, послужил основой инсталляции «Мать и сын», в которой «Альбом моей матери» занимает главное место. Вот краткое описание этой инсталляции, построенной в Еврейском музее Нью-Йорка.

Сквозь полуоткрытую дверь зритель видит темное неосвещенное пространство, размер которого он никак не может установить. Виден только в самой глубине слабый свет висящей под потолком лампочки. Возле двери, на приделанной к стене полке, стоят несколько ручных фонариков; вооружившись этим светом, зритель входит внутрь темного мира. И, под лучом фонарика, вспыхивает, высвечивается бесконечное количество небольших «мусорных» предметов — старых спичечных коробков, обрывков бумаги, проволочек, пустых флакончиков и прочей чепухи с привязанными к каждому из них табличками с текстами. Каждый из этих текстов — высказывание сына, обращенное к матери, обрывок одной из бытовых фраз, то, что обычно говорится ей в течение дня — всевозможные просьбы, споры из-за еды, из-за незастегнутой одежды, разговоры о делах, о родственниках — часто в них слышно непонятное раздражение.

Эти «обрывки» висят во всем пространстве темной комнаты на уровне глаз зрителя, он погружен в это море слов. Но продвигаясь с фонариком в глубину, он обнаруживает, что вся комната по своему периметру, тоже на высоте человеческого роста, окружена листами «Альбома моей матери», помещенными в рамы. Текст альбома, биография матери, окружает весь «мир слов» сына, заключает его в себя. И несмотря на то, что зритель может видеть только фрагменты, то, что попало в луч его фонарика, он становится свидетелем своеобразного диалога между обоими.

Несколько слов об атмосфере самой инсталляции в целом. Зритель с фонариком в ней не только «субъект», разглядывающий то, что его окружает, но и сам становится частью этой инсталляции — для других зрителей, которые входят внутрь ее с такими же фонариками в руках. Комната наполняется бегающими во все стороны огнями, и все вместе напоминает поиски чего-то таинственного во мраке, что очень хорошо соединяется с атмосферой печали и покинутости, чем, в сущности, и наполнено наше прошлое.

Installations Installations Installationen Инсталляции 253

Installation *Mère et fils*. Musée juif, New York, 1993

Installation *Mother and Son*. Jüdisch Museum, New York, 1993

Installation *Mutter und Sohn*. Jewish Museum, New York, 1993

Инсталляция «Мать и сын». Еврейский музей, Нью-Йорк, 1993

Quand je pense au monde dans lequel ma mère a vécu sa vie, de par son expression métaphorique, je vois un couloir, long et sombre, en forme de labyrinthe qui s'enroule, où derrière chaque tournant, chaque coude, au lieu d'une sortie lumineuse, on ne découvre que les mêmes murs gris, poussiéreux, qu'on a mal recouverts de peinture, à peine éclairés par des ampoules de 40 watts.
En 1990, en m'inspirant de ses mémoires j'ai construit chez Ronald Feldman, à New York, l'installation qui a ce titre : *Couloir. L'Album de ma mère.*
Voici la description de cette installation.
L'installation se présente comme un couloir étroit, au plafond bas, mal éclairé, construit en forme de labyrinthe ou plus précisément de spirale qui d'abord s'enroule puis se déroule. L'ensemble rappelle le couloir d'un appartement communautaire, sale et laissé à l'abandon : le plafond fissuré est soutenu par des planches, d'où descendent des ampoules encrassées qui ne répandent presque plus de lumière, le sol n'a pas été balayé depuis longtemps. Comme dans tout appartement communautaire, on trouve ici un grand nombre de portes. A chaque tournant du couloir on découvre une nouvelle porte, certaines sont condamnées, d'autres entrouvertes, laissant une voie de passage étroite. Le haut du couloir et le plafond sont peints en gris, le bas, comme partout dans les « lieux communautaires », en un affreux rouge marron. Tout le long du couloir qui doit mesurer dans les cinquante mètres, sur un des murs, sont accrochées des photos, des textes et des coupures de cartes postales collés sur le papier peint et encadrés.
Les photos sont des vues de Berdiansk, petite ville au bord de la mer d'Azov, prises avec beaucoup d'amour par Yu. Blekher, photographe professionnel, durant trente ans.
Les coupures de cartes postales sont des vues fragmentées de nos villes ; quant au texte de cette grande série — environ soixante-quinze feuilles —, ce sont les mémoires de ma mère.
Tout, l'accrochage monotone, l'abandon du couloir, le pauvre éclairage, l'ennui de la ville provinciale et le récit d'une vie tragique raconté avec des mots simples mais bouleversants, tout cela vise un spectateur solitaire, se retrouvant seul à seul avec lui-même dans ce couloir.
A cet état de solitude concentrée contribue une voix qui chante en sourdine des romances russes, juste pour soi-même, qui chante souvent faux en s'arrêtant parfois. C'est au centre de l'installation que cette voix résonne le mieux. A mesure que l'on avance dans l'installation, la voix s'amplifie et lorsque le spectateur en franchit le milieu, elle faiblit pour se taire définitivement à la sortie.

When I think about that world in which my mother's life passed, about the condensed image of it, what arises in my imagination is a long and semi-dark corridor which is twisted like a labyrinth, where behind each new turn, behind each bend, there is not a bright exit glimmering in the distance, but just the same grubby floor, the same gray, dusty, poorly painted walls illuminated by weak, 40-watt light bulbs.
I built the installation called : *Corridor. My Mother's Album* in the Ronald Feldman Gallery in New York in 1990. Here is a description of this installation.
The installation is a narrow, poorly lit corridor built in the form of a labyrinth, or more precisely, at first a winding spiral followed by an unwinding spiral. All of this taken together reminds one of a neglected corridor in a communal apartment that hasn't been cleaned up for a long time : the ceiling is cracked in many places and is supported by wooded boards, the floor hasn't been swept for a long time, soot-covered light bulbs that barely emit any light hang from the ceiling. And as in any communal apartment, there are many doors. A new door is revealed behind every turn of the corridor ; some of them are tightly shut, others are slightly open so that you could go through them with some difficulty. The upper part of the corridor and the ceiling are painted gray, the lower part, as in ordinary "communal" places, is covered with an unpleasant red-brown paint. Photographs, texts, and cut-outs from postcards are hanging in frames and pasted on wallpaper along one side of the entire length of this corridor, approximately 50 m.
The photographs were taken by Yu. G. Blekher, a professional photographer, and they depict views of the city of Berdyansk, a small city on the shore of the Azovsk Sea which he lovingly photographed during the course of almost 30 years.
The cut-outs from postcards are fragments of views of our cities, and the text of this large series — around 75 pages — is the text of the my mother's memoirs. All of this taken

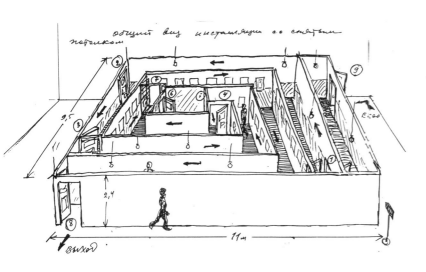
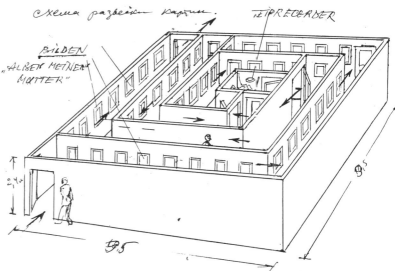

together: monotonous arrangement of the ehxibition, the neglected state of the corridor, the weak light, the photographs of a boring, provincial city and the tragic story of a life told in simple words that turn one's soul inside out — all of this is intended for a solitary viewer who has remained in the corridor alone, only with himself.
Corresponding to this state of concentrated loneliness is a voice quietly singing Russian romances in a way that is called "under one's breath", "for oneself", singing out of tune and at times stopping.
This voice resounds strongest in the center of the installation. As the viewer moves through the labyrinth from the beginning the voice gets louder and louder, and when the viewer passes the middle of the labyrinth it becomes weaker and it disappears altogether when the viewer exits to the outside.

Wenn ich an die Welt denke, in der das Leben meiner Mutter ablief, über seine Verdichtung als Metapher, ersteht in meiner Vorstellung das Bild eines langen, halbdunklen Korridors, der sich windet wie ein Labyrinth, wo hinter jeder Ecke, hinter jeder Biegung, sich kein heller Ausgang auftut, der in der Ferne leuchtet, sondern immer dieselben grauen, staubigen, ungestrichenen Wände, beleuchtet von einer schwachen 40 Watt Lampe. Im Jahr 1990 habe ich zum Thema dieser Aufzeichnungen eine Installation errichtet, welche sich so nennt: *Korridor. Album meiner Mutter*. Das ist die Beschreibung dieser Installation.
Die Installation stellt einen engen, niedrigen, schlecht beleuchteten Korridor dar, der als Labyrinth angelegt ist, oder genauer als Spirale, die sich zuerst einrollt und dann wieder entrollt. Zusammengenommen erinnert all das an den verwahrlosten, lang nicht aufgeräumten Korridor einer Gemeinschaftswohnung: die Decke ist an vielen Stellen gesprungen und wird mit Holzbrettern abgestützt, der Fußboden ist seit langem nicht gekehrt, von der Decke hängen verräucherte Glühbirnen, die kaum Licht spenden. Und wie in jedem Gemeinschaftskorridor gibt es auch hier eine Menge Türen. Hinter jeder Biegung zeigt sich eine neue Tür; einige sind fest zugesperrt, andere sind einen Spalt offen, durch den man sich gerade noch durchzwängen kann. Der obere Teil des Korridors und die Decke sind grau gestrichen, der untere ist — wie an »Gemeinschafts« — Orten üblich, in einer unangenehmen rotbraunen Farbe gestrichen. Den ganzen Korridor entlang, vielleicht ungefähr 50 m, hängen an einer Seite gerahmte, auf Papiertapeten geklebte Fotografien, Texte und Postkartenausschnitte.
Die Fotografien stammen von Ju. Blecher, einem professionellen Fotografen, und stellen Ansichten von Berdjansk dar, einer kleinen Stadt am Ufer des Asow'schen Meeres, welche er liebevoll im Lauf von fast 30 Jahren aufgenommen hat.
Die Ausschnitte aus Postkarten sind Fragmente von Ansichten unserer Städte, und der Text dieser ganzen großen Serie, ungefähr 75 Blatt, sind die Erinnerungen meiner Mutter. Alles zusammen: die monotone Hängung, der vernachlässigte Korridor, das schwache Licht, die Fotografien, die Langeweile eines Provinzstädtchens und die tragische Lebensgeschichte, erzählt in einfachen, herzergreifenden Worten — all das rechnet mit einem einsamen Betrachter, der in diesem Korridor mit sich selbst allein ist.
Diesem Zustand konzentrierter Einsamkeit entspricht eine Stimme, die leise russische Romanzen singt, sie singt und summt vor sich hin, manchmal falsch, manchmal abbrechend. Am stärksten klingt diese Stimme im Zentrum der Installation. Während sich der Betrachter durch das Labyrinth hindurchbewegt, wird sie zuerst, der Mitte zu, immer stärker, dann, beim Ausgang der Installation, erlischt sie ganz.

Когда я думаю о том мире, в котором прошла жизнь моей матери, о сгущенном образе его, в воображении встает длинный и полутемный коридор, скрученный наподобие лабиринта, где за каждым новым поворотом, за каждым его коленом не светлый выход, брезжущий вдалеке, а все тот же затертый пол, все те же серые пыльные, плохо покрашенные стены, освещенные слабыми сорокасвечевыми лампочками.
В 1990 году в галерее Фельдмана в Нью-Йорке я построил инсталляцию, которая так и называлась:

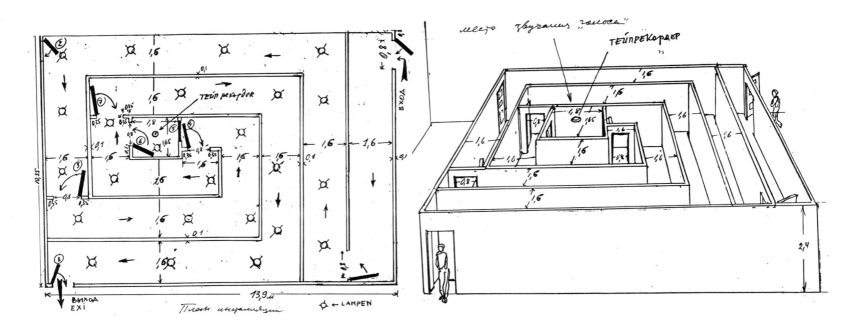

«Коридор. Альбом моей матери».
Вот описание этой инсталляции.

Инсталляция представляет собой узкий, низкий, плохо освещенный коридор, построенный в виде лабиринта, а точнее, сначала скручивающейся, а затем раскручивающейся спирали. Все вместе это напоминает запущенный, давно не убиравшийся коридор коммунальной квартиры: потолок во многих местах треснул и подпирается деревянными досками, пол давно не подметался, с потолка свисают закопченные, почти не дающие свет лампочки. И как в любом коммунальном коридоре, здесь множество дверей. За каждым поворотом обнаруживается новая дверь; некоторые из них наглухо заперты, другие слегка полуоткрыты, так чтобы сквозь них можно было с трудом пройти. Верх коридора и потолок покрашен серой краской, низ — как и в обычных «коммунальных» местах — неприятной красно-коричневой краской. Во всю длину этого коридора, где-то около 50 м, с одной его стороны, висят в рамах наклеенные на бумажные обои фотографии, тексты и вырезки из почтовых открыток.

Фотографии сделаны Ю.Блехером, профессиональным фотографом, и изображают виды Бердянска, маленького города на берегу Азовского моря, который он любовно снимал на протяжении почти 30 лет.

Вырезки из почтовых карточек — фрагменты видов наших городов, а текст всей этой большой серии — около 75 листов — текст воспоминаний моей матери. Все вместе: монотонная развеска, заброшенность коридора, слабый свет, фотографии, скука провинциального городка и трагическая история жизни, рассказанная простыми, переворачивающими душу словами, — все это рассчитано на одинокого зрителя, оказывающегося в этом коридоре наедине с собой. Этому состоянию сосредоточенного одиночества соответствует голос, который негромко поет русские романсы, что называется «себе под нос», «для себя», фальшивя и временами останавливаясь. Сильнее всего этот голос звучит в центре инсталляции. По мере движения по лабиринту, он звучит все слышнее, а когда зритель проходит середину лабиринта, он слабеет и у выхода из инсталляции совсем исчезает.

Installation *Couloir. L'Album de ma mère*
Ronald Feldman Fine Arts, New York, 1988

Installation *Corridor. My Mother's Album*
Ronald Feldman Fine Arts, New York, 1988

Installation *Korridor. Album meiner Mutter*
Ronald Feldman Fine Arts, New York, 1988

Инсталляция «Коридор. Альбом моей матери»,
Галерея Роналда Фелдмана, Нью-Йорк, 1988

Installations Installations Installationen Инсталляции

Installations Installations Installationen Инсталляции 260

EXPOSITIONS DE *L'ALBUM DE MA MÈRE*

L'Album de ma mère existe en deux versions. La première, créée à Moscou, en 1987, est reproduite dans cet ouvrage.

Expositions de la première version (*Mère et fils*) :

1. Riverside Studio, Londres, 1989 (dans l'installation *Ten characters*)
2. Orchard Gallery, Londonderry, 1990 (dans l'installation *Ten characters*)
3. Museo d'arte Contemporanea, Prato, 1990 (dans l'installation *The underground golden River*)
4. Jewish museum, New York, 1993 (dans l'installation *Mother and Son*)
5. Nykytaiteen museolla, Helsinki, 1994 (dans l'installation *Mother and Son*)
6. Museet för nutidskonst, Oslo, 1994 (dans l'installation *Mother and Son*)
7. Museum für Gegenwartskunst, Bâle, 1995 (dans l'installation *Mother and Son*)

Expositions de la seconde version (*Couloir*) :

1. Ronald Feldman Fine Arts, New York, 1990
2. Sezon Museum of Modern Art, Nagano, 1991
3. Louisiana Museum of Modern Art, Humlebaek, 1993
4. Bayerische Staatsgemäldesammlungen, Munich, 1993
5. Le Magasin, Grenoble, 1994

ВЫСТАВКИ «АЛЬБОМА МОЕЙ МАТЕРИ»

«Альбом моей матери» существует в двух вариантах. Первый был сделан в Москве, в 1987 году, и напечатан в этом издании.

Выставки первого варианта («Мать и сын»)

1. Риверсайд Студио, Лондон, 1988 (в составе инсталляции «10 персонажей»)
2. Оршард Галери, Лондондерри, 1990 (в составе инсталляции «10 персонажей»)
3. Музей современного искусства, Прато, 1990 (в составе инсталляции «Золотая подземная река»)
4. Еврейский музей, Нью-Йорк, 1993 (в составе инсталляции «Мать и сын»)
5. Музей современного искусства, Хельсинки, 1994 (в составе инсталляции «Мать и сын»)
6. Музей современного искусства, Осло, 1994 (в составе инсталляции «Мать и сын»)
7. Музей современного искусства, Базель, 1995 (в составе инсталляции «Мать и сын»)

Выставки второго варианта («Коридор»)

1. Галерея Роналда Фелдмана, Нью-Йорк, 1990
2. Сезон музей современного искусства, Нагано, 1991
3. Луизиана, музей современного искусства, Хумлебэк, 1993
4. Баварская художестяениая галерея, Мюнхен, 1993
5. Ле Магазэн, Гренобль, 1994

ILYA KABAKOV

Biographie
1933
Né à Dniépropétrovsk (URSS)
1951
Ecole secondaire des Beaux-arts, Moscou
1957
Institut des Beaux-Arts V. A. Sourikov, Moscou
Vit et travaille à Moscou, New-York et Paris

Commandes
1991
Ville d'Orly, monument *Normandie-Nemen*
1992
De Nederlandse Opera *Life with an Idiot* (Décors et costumes)

Expositions personnelles
1985
Galerie Dina Vierny, Paris (catalogue)
Kunsthalle, Berne, *Am Rande*, ensuite au Centre de la Vieille Charité, Marseille (1986), Kunstverein für die Rheinland und Westfalen, Düsseldorf (1986), CNAP, Paris (1987) (catalogue)
Museum Bochum — avec V. Yankilevsky, E. Steinberg (catalogue)

1986
Schlössli Götzental, Dierikon, *Konzert für eine Fliege*

1987
Museum für Gegenwartskunst, Bâle — avec I. Tchouïkov

1988
Portikus, Francfort, *10 Personen* (catalogue)
Kunstverein, Graz, *Vor dem Abendessen* (catalogue)
Neue Galerie, Schlössli Götzental, Dierikon
Ronald Feldman Fine Arts, New York, *10 Characters* (catalogue)
Kunstverein, Bonn — avec E. Boulatov

1989
Galerie de France, Paris, *Que sont ces petits hommes?* (catalogue), ensuite à l'Institute of Contemporary Art, Philadelphie, *Who Are These Little Men?*
DAAD-galerie, Berlin-Ouest, *Ausstellung Eines Buches* (catalogue)
De Appel, Amsterdam, *Witte schilderijen en witte mensjes*
Kunsthalle, Zürich, *Die Kommunalwohnung — Das Schiff* (catalogue)
Institute of Contemporary Art, Londres, *The Untalented Artist and Other Characters* (catalogue)
Riverside Studio, Londres, *Ten Characters* (catalogue)
Université de Sarrebruck, *Zwei Alben*
The Genia Schreiber Art Galerie, University of Tel Aviv, *The Beautiful Sixties* — avec M. Grobman

1990
Neue Galerie - Sammlung Ludwig, Aix-en-Chapelle, *Das Schiff*
Kasseler Kunstverein, Cassel, *7 Ausstellungen eines Bildes* (catalogue)
Hirschhorn Museum and Sculpture Garden, Washington, *Ten Characters* (catalogue)
Fred Hoffman Gallery, Santa Monica, *The Rope of life & Other Installations* (catalogue)
Ronald Feldman Fine Arts, New York, *He lost his Mind, Undressed, Run Away Naked* (catalogue)

1991
Ateliers Municipaux d'Artistes, Marseille, *52 entretiens dans la cuisine communautaire*, ensuite à La Criée, Rennes (1992) (catalogue)
The Power Plant, Toronto
Peter Pakesch Galerie, Vienne, *Die Zielscheiben* (catalogue)
Wewerka & Weiss Galerie, Berlin, *Meine Heimat (Die Fliege)* (catalogue)
Dresdner Bank, Francfort, *Ripped off Landscape*
FIAC, Paris, Galerie Dina Vierny, *La cuisine communautaire*

1992
Ludwig Museum, Cologne, *Unaufgehängtes Bild*
Kanaal Art Foundation, Courtrai, *Illustration as a way of survive* (catalogue), ensuite au Centre of Contemporary Arts, Glasgow (1993), Ikon Gallery, Birmingham (1993) — avec Y. Sooster
Deweer Gallery, Otegem, *In memory of Pleasant Recollections* (catalogue)
Galleria Sprovieri, Rome (catalogue)
Ronald Feldman Fine Arts, New York, *Incident at the museum or Water music* (catalogue)
Galerie Dina Vierny, Paris, *Dans la cuisine communautaire. Nouveaux documents* (catalogue)
Krannert Art museum and Kinkead Pavilion of Illinois at Urbana-Champain, Urbana
Kölnischer Kunstverein, Cologne, *Das Leben der Fliegen* (catalogue)

1993
Kunsthalle, Hambourg, *NOMA* (catalogue)
Chinnati Foundation, Marfa, Texas, *Deserted School*
Musée Maillol, Paris, *Cuisine communautaire*
Kunstverein, Salzburg, *Das Boot meines Lebens*
Museum of Contemporary Art, Chicago, *Incident at the Museum or Water Music* (catalogue)
Château d'Oiron, *Concert pour les Mouches*
Städelschule, Francfort, *Das leere Museum*
Stedelijk Museum, Amsterdam, *Het Grote Archief* (catalogue)

1994
Nykytaiteen museolla, Helsinki, *Operation Room (Mother and Son)*, ensuite au Museet för nutidskonst, Oslo (catalogue)
Galerie Barbara Weiss, Berlin, *The artist's despair*
Hessisches Landesmuseum, Darmstadt, *Zwischenfall im Museum oder Wassermusik*

Le Magasin, Grenoble, *Le Bateau de ma Vie, La Rivière souterraine dorée, L'Album de ma Mère*
Jablonka Galerie, Cologne, *In the apartment of Nicolai Victorovich*

Expositions collectives (sélection)

1965
Castello Spagnolo, L'Aquilla, « Alternative Attuale 2 »

1967
Galleria Il Segno, Rome, « Quindici Giovani Pittori Moscoviti »

1970
Galerie Gmurzynska, Cologne, « Die Russische Avantgarde in Moskau heute »

1973
Galerie Dina Vierny, Paris, « Avant-garde russe » (catalogue)

1976
Musée d'art russe en exil, Montgeron

1977
Venise, Biennale, « La nuova arte sovietica »

1979
Bochum Museum, « 20 Jahre unabhängige Kunst aus der Sowietunionen »
Malaïa Grouzinskaïa, 28, Moscou, « Tzvet, forma, prostranstvo »

1984
Musée de Tartu, Estonie, « Photograph and Art »

1986
Kunstverein Düsseldorf, « Die Wahlverwandtschaften, Steirischer Herbst' 86 »

1987
FIAC, Paris, Galerie de France

1988
Kunstmuseum, Berne, « Ich Lebe, Ich Sehe: Künstler der Achtziger Jahre in Moskau » (catalogue)
Venise Biennale, « Aperto », *Before Supper*
ARCO 88, Madrid

1989
S.E.Massachusetts University, N. Darmouth, « Post Utopia: Paintings and Installations by Soviet Conceptualists: Bulatov, Kabakov, Komar & Melamid » (catalogue)
MNAM, Centre Georges Pompidou, Paris, « Les Magiciens de la Terre », *L'Homme qui s'est envolé dans l'espace* (catalogue)
Wiener Secession, Vienne, « Wittgenstein: Das Spiel des Unsagbaren », ensuite au Palais des Beaux-Arts, Bruxelles (1990) (catalogue)
Exit Art, New York, « The Green Show », ensuite à The Dunlop Art Gallery, Regina (1990), The Mendel Art Gallery, Saskatoon (1991) (catalogue)

1990
The New Museum, New York, « Rhetorical Image », *Medical Screens* (catalogue)
Seoul Art Festival, *Works on Hanji Paper* (catalogue)
Columbus Museum of Art, Columbus, « The Quest for Self Expression: Painting in Moscow and Leningrad 1965-1990 », ensuite à la Weatherspoon Art Gallery University of North Carolina, Greensboro (1991), Arkansas Art Center, Little Rock (1991) (catalogue)
Stedelijk Museum, Amsterdam, « In de USSR en erbuiten », *The Rope of Life and other Installations* (catalogue)
Orchard Gallery, Londonderry, « Four Cities Project », *Fly with the Wings* (catalogue)
DAAD-galerie, Berlin, « Die Endlichkeit der Freiheit », *Zwei Erinnerungen an die Angst* (catalogue)
Alpha Cubic Gallery, Tokyo, « Soviet Contemporary Art 1990 » (catalogue)
Tacoma Art Museum, Tacoma, « Between Spring and Summer: Soviet Conceptual Art in the Era of Late Communism », *The Album of my Mother,* ensuite à l'Institute of Contemporary Art (1991), Moines Art Center, Des Moines (1991) (catalogue)
Aldrich Museum of Contemporary Art, Ridgefield, « Adaption & Negation of Socialist Realism » (catalogue)
The Biennale of Sydney, « The Ready Made Boomerang », *Three Russian Paintings* (catalogue)
Museo d'arte Contemporanea, Prato, « Artisti Russi Contemporanei », *The Underground Golden River* (catalogue)

1991
Stedelijk Museum, Amsterdam, « Wanderlieder », *Before Supper* (catalogue)
Art Fair, Montreal
Große Orangerie—Schloß Charlottenburg, Berlin, « Schwerelos » (catalogue)
Carnegie Museum of Art, Pittsburgh, « 1991 Carnegie International », *We are leaving here forever* (catalogue)
MoMA, New York, « Dislocations », *The Bridge* (catalogue)
ICA, Philadelphie, « Devil on the Stairs: Looking Back on the Eighties » (catalogue)
Newport Harbor Art Museum, Newport Beach (catalogue)
Kunsthalle, Düsseldorf, « Sowietische Kunst um 1990 », *Der Rote Waggon* (catalogue)
Israel Museum, Jerusalem, « Soviet Art around 1990 », *Why « Red Wagon » didn't come to Israel* (catalogue)
Rooseum, Center for Contemporary Art, Malmö, « TRANS/Mission », *Mental Institution or Institute of Creative Research* (catalogue)
Kunstverein, Hanovre, « Kunst, Europa: Sowjetunion », *Fliege mit Flügeln* (catalogue)
Centraal Museum, Utrecht, « Words without Thoughts Never to Heaven Go/Night Lines » *Who's are those Wings?* (catalogue)
Bibelgesellschaft, Francfort, « Bilder zur Bible heute », ensuite Evangelistische Akademie, Iserlon
University of Hawaii, Art Gallery, Honolulu, « Perspectives of Conceptualism », ensuite à The Clocktower, New York, North Carolina Museum of Art, Raleigh
Sezon Museum of Modern Art, Nagano, « Art on Edge », *Communal Kitchen* (catalogue)

1992
Akademie der bildenden Künste, Vienne, « Uber Malerei — Begegnung mit der Geschichte », *Vor dem Dialog* (catalogue)
Cassel, « Documenta IX », *Toilet* (catalogue)
Newport Harbor Art Museum, Newport Beach, « Devil on the Stairs », *The Man who flew into Painting* (catalogue)
Groninger Museum, Groningue, « EX USSR », *Communal Kitchen* (catalogue)
Seville, Expo'92, *The Blue Dish*
County Museum of Art, Los Angeles, « Parallel visions: Modern Artists and Outsider Art »
Villa Campolieto, Ercolano, « A Mosca. A Mosca », ensuite à la Galeria Comunale d'Arte Moderna, Bologne (catalogue)
Tzentralnyï dom khoudojnika, Moscou « Sovetskoe iskusstvo okolo 1990 goda », *Why « The Red Wagon » didn't come to Moscow* (catalogue)

1993
Kunsthalle, Cologne, « Russische Avantgarde im 20. Jahrhundert: Von Malewitsch bis Kabakov » (catalogue)
Lyon, Deuxième Biennale d'art contemporain, (« Et tous ils changent le monde »), *Sortie de secours* (catalogue)
Taejon Expo, « Recycling through Art », *Rope of life* (catalogue)
Venise, XLV Biennale, *Il Padiglione Rosso* (catalogue)
Jewish Museum, New York, « Time, Place, Memory », *Mother and Son* (catalogue)
Musée de la Poste, Paris, « Adresse provisoire pour l'art contemporain russe », *Cube blanc* (catalogue)
Domaine de Kerguehennec, « De la main à la tête, l'objet théorique », *The End of Empire or the Experiments of visual Poetry*, ensuite au Museum van hedendaagse kunst, Gand (catalogue)
Museum van hedendaagse kunst, Gand, « Rendez(-)vous », *Unfinished installation* (catalogue)
Le Magasin, Grenoble, *Le Bateau*
Louisiana Museum of Modern Art, Humlebaek, « At the Edge of Chaos: New images of the World », *My Mother's Album II. (Labyrinth)*, ensuite aux Bayerische Staatsgemäldesammlungen, Munich (catalogue)
PS1, New York, « The Art of Social Realism »

1994
La Caixa Fondacion, Madrid, « 8 ideas of Space », *For Sale*
MAK, Vienne, « Tyrannei das Schönen », *Der Rote Waggon*
Kunst- und Ausstellungshalle der Bundesrepublik Deutschland, Bonn, « Europa-Europa », *The Man who never threw anything away*
National Gallery of Australia, Canberra, Biennale of Contemporary Art, (« Virtual Reality »)

Publications
Das Fenster/OKHO. Berne, Benteli, 1985.
Boris Groys (entretiens avec), *Die Kunst des Fliehens*. Munich, Vienne, Carl Hanser, 1991
Das Leben der Fliegen/Life of Flies. Stuttgart, Cantz, 1991.
Yuri Kuper (entretiens avec), *52 entretiens dans la cuisine communautaire*. Marseille, Rennes, 1991.
Dans la cuisine communautaire: Nouveaux documents et matériaux. Paris, Galerie Dina Vierny, 1993.
NOMA, Stuttgart, Cantz, 1993.
5 Albums. Helsinki, Oslo, 1994.

Conception: Ilya Kabakov
Coordination: Emilia Kabakov
Mise en page: Cultura, Wetteren
Impression: Artprint, Helsinki

Traductions:
Galina Kabakova (russe — français)
Cynthia Martin (russe — anglais)
Liesl Ujvary (russe — allemand)

L'éditeur tient à remercier Elena Balzamo, Marie Louise Bonaque, Marc Dachy, Maarit Rajala pour leur contribution à la réalisation de cet ouvrage

© 1995 Ilya Kabakov & Flies France, Paris

Cet ouvrage a été achevé d'imprimer en février 1995
Dépôt légal mars 1995
ISBN: 2-910272-00-1